DEPP V HEARD

THE UNREAL STORY

NICK WALLIS

Published May 2023
ISBN 978-1-7391349-4-5

*The book contains potentially offensive language and descriptions
of violence and sexual abuse.*

Bath Publishing Limited
27 Charmouth Road
Bath
BA1 3LJ
Tel: 01225 577810
email: info@bathpublishing.co.uk
www.bathpublishing.co.uk

Bath Publishing is a company registered in England: 5209173
Registered Office: As above

To everyone I met in America.

Thanks for having me.

CONTENTS

PREFACE

Talking and writing about what may or may not have happened between Johnny Depp and Amber Heard across the course of their four-and-a-half year relationship is fraught with difficulties. Multiple, competing, intertwining narratives offered up by interested and disinterested parties point to contradictory conclusions. Hard evidence is thin on the ground.

I have spent hundreds of hours reviewing sworn testimony and statements, reading court transcripts, watching videos, listening to recordings and scrolling through endless tweets, texts and emails. At the conclusion of one multimillion pound trial in 2020, the allegation Johnny Depp was a wife-beater was ruled 'substantially true'. At the conclusion of another, held in 2022, a jury found Amber Heard had lied about her allegations of abuse.

In this book I have tried to build a picture of who Johnny Depp and Amber Heard are, why they matter and how their relationship became so toxic. I've worked through the details of each alleged incident of violence to see whose story stands up, and I've picked out some of the key moments in both trials, either because they inform a wider truth, or because they felt significant at the time. I've also attempted to give you a flavour of what it was like reporting everything first hand, trying to make sense of the overwhelming volumes of information flooding out of each trial and the raging passions of the online armies who invested so much of themselves in the proceedings and the outcome.

My basic working methods involved examining primary and secondary source documents and assessing their credibility before inserting them into the narrative. Credibility is a subjective measure, and weighing the credibility of a source can be complex. Contemporaneous documentary evidence is the best, though it needs context. Court transcripts are an undisputed and accurate record of the recollections of primary witnesses. Unfortunately those recollections could be cloudy, mistaken or deliberately misleading.

I have tried to include as much as I think you need to know about the story without being overwhelmed by pointless detail. I have also tried to do this dispassionately, without being dull. This book distils the several million words which have been written and spoken about this case into a few hundred pages. Not everything is going to make the cut.

Unless an event is generally agreed to have happened in a manner which is largely unchallenged, I flag it as alleged, reported, apparent and so forth. In doing this, the qualifiers can stack up. To improve narrative flow, there are occasions where I have not described every single action within a contested event as alleged, if I feel I have made it clear that the entire event is denied or not accepted as true by one or more parties. Please be assured I am acutely aware just how strongly many people feel about the events depicted in this book. I am not claiming anything definitely happened, unless I was there to witness it myself.

I was in court on most days of Depp v NGN[1] in the UK and Depp v Heard in the US, but I don't know Johnny Depp or Amber Heard. I wasn't in the Diamond Head compound in Australia in 2015, I wasn't on the Boston to LA plane flight in 2014 and I've never been to Johnny Depp's private island in the Bahamas. I wasn't there when the alleged acts of violence are said to have occurred.

In putting together this book I've spoken to a number of people close to the story, many of whom do not wish to be acknowledged, let alone quoted. Whilst they have all been helpful, none of them have any better idea of the truth of what really happened than I do. That is bound up in the competing narratives of the protagonists, the contemporaneous documentary evidence, and the recollections of the witnesses. I want to state for the record I am not here to be partisan. I want to let the facts – such as they are – speak for themselves.

---

[1]   NGN stands for News Group Newspapers, the Rupert Murdoch-owned parent company of The Sun newspaper.

READER NOTES

Johnny Depp's residences

Aside from his European homes, Depp owns an island in the Bahamas and a number of properties on Sweetzer Avenue in Los Angeles. During the period he was in a relationship with Amber Heard, Depp also owned all five penthouses at the Eastern Columbia Building (ECB) in downtown LA. These penthouses shared an outdoor pool and had three internal levels: main, mezzanine and upper.

Amber's friend Raquel 'Rocky' Pennington lived for a time in Penthouse 1 with her boyfriend Josh Drew. Depp's childhood friend Isaac Baruch lived in Penthouse 2. Depp and Heard's main home together was in Penthouse 3 and Whitney Heard, Amber's younger sister, lived for a time in Penthouse 4. Penthouse 5 was mainly used for storage. A guard shack with access to the main corridor was situated adjacent to Penthouse 5. PH1 and PH2 are self-contained, but PH3, PH4 and PH5 are connected on their upper levels by adjoining doors, which means (if you have the right key), you can move from PH5, through PH4, to PH3 without going into the main level corridor.

To make this easier to understand there is a floorplan of the main level of the ECB penthouses at the beginning of *The Phone Incident* chapter.

Footnotes and sources

Copious academic footnotes can really disrupt a reading experience so I have tried to limit my footnotes to narrative asides. If you want to read my book for research purposes and/or check on each specific stated fact, please buy the ebook edition of *Depp v Heard: the unreal story* which links quotes and sections of text (where possible) to the relevant online source. There's a general note on sources at the back of the book.

Legal terms and lawyers

I try to explain many of the important legal terms as we go along, but it might be useful to flag the following up front: libel is the act of publishing something defamatory. Both The Sun's article about Johnny Depp in the UK and the Washington Post article by Amber Heard were alleged to be defamatory. In the UK we tend to call these cases libel actions, in the US they tend to be called defamation actions. They are essentially the same thing. By the same token, barristers, solicitors and attorneys are all types of lawyer. Generally speaking, barristers and solicitors are UK-based, with solicitors working behind the scenes and barristers examining witnesses in UK courts. Attorneys in the US work behind the scenes *and* examine witnesses in US courts depending on their respective skillsets.

Names and pronouns

Whitney Heard gave evidence using her married name, Whitney Henriquez. In this book I have referred to most people, once introduced, by their surnames. Without any disrespect intended, and purely to reduce any potential confusion when writing about her or Amber, I have called Whitney Heard/Henriquez mainly by her first name.

Nurse Erin Boerum, an addictions and mental health nurse, also changed her surname over the period covered by this book, giving evidence in 2022 under her married name, Falati. Again, without any disrespect intended, I have mainly referred to Nurse Erin by her maiden name – Boerum.

Amber's former friend, iO Tillett-Wright, shifted genders during the course of this story. He currently presents as male. To reduce potential confusion and again without wishing to cause any offense, I have generally applied masculine pronouns to his name throughout this book.

A warning

Depp v Heard: the unreal story contains a lot of swearing, plus multiple descriptions of graphic violence and sexual abuse. If you think this might upset you, please do not read any further.

Johnny Depp and Amber Heard at the 72nd Venice Film Festival,
5 September 2015.

'Television probably contaminates everything it touches with unreality, and the nature of an historic event alters in some way when it is broadcast on television because television distorts (if not trivialises and demeans) the way we perceive things.'
Javier Cercas, The Anatomy of a Moment

'You're not paid back for the bad you do nor the good you do. It all comes out uneven at the end.'
Philip K Dick, Flow My Tears, the Policeman Said

KISS IN A SHOWER

In 2008, the movie star Johnny Depp secured enough funding to produce an adaptation of *The Rum Diary*, a lost novel written by his great friend, Hunter S Thompson.

Depp took the lead role and began casting the other parts. Amber Heard, a young, beautiful actor auditioned for Chenault, the female lead. Chenault was a siren, described by Thompson in his book as 'all hips and thighs and nipples and long-haired charm.'

The 45-year old Depp coaxed Bruce Robinson out of retirement to write and direct the movie. Robinson believed Chenault represented a 'dream' – the ultimate object of desire, but always out of reach. He met Heard and was impressed, later describing her as 'Doris Day and Marilyn Monroe rolled into one.' But Robinson wasn't sure about her acting ability. He asked Depp to read with her. Depp demurred.

'I said, "Bruce, if you've auditioned her five times, you've seen the best and the worst... I think it's a far better idea that we just meet so that I can see how she behaves, see how she reacts".'

Heard was summoned to Depp's production offices in Los Angeles for a chat. She found the experience disorientating. Heard 'wasn't a fan' of Depp's work but she 'knew who he was... one of the most famous people in the world, so it was already a weird thing to go and get called into his office... I'm a no-name actor. I was 22.'

Depp says on meeting Heard, he 'took one look at her and I thought, "Yeah, that's the Chenault that Hunter wants. That's the one... she could definitely kill me".'

The pair hit it off. 'We liked a lot of the same stuff,' said Heard. 'Obscure writers... interesting books and pieces of poetry I hadn't heard anyone else reference or know or like.'

This, for Heard, was even stranger 'because he's twice my age and he's a world famous actor and here we are getting along about obscure books and weird old blues... I thought it was unusual and remarkable.'

After the meeting, Depp gave her a call. 'My phone rings,' said Heard, 'and I hear this deep voice on the other line and he said "you're it kid... Hunter wrote this part, and you're the dream. You're it, kid".'

Heard began filming her scenes for *The Rum Diary* in March 2009 in Puerto Rico. 'It was a very colorful shoot in general. I could not have asked for a better scenario... occasionally Johnny would talk to me and then he started to be really kind to me.'

The film required Depp and Heard to kiss in a shower.

'It didn't feel like a normal scene,' said Heard. 'It felt more real. There are certain things you do in the job to be professional... you don't use your tongue if you can avoid it and there are certain things you do to just, to maintain a certain line, and it just felt like those lines were blurred... he really kissed me.'

Recalling that same moment, Depp said: 'I felt like something I shouldn't be feeling.'

At the time, Depp was in a relationship. He had been with the French model and actor Vanessa Paradis for more than a decade. She was the mother of his two children, Lily-Rose and Jack. Heard was living with the artist Tasya van Ree. Their relationship had developed to the extent that Heard was using van Ree's surname.

During filming, Heard visited Depp's trailer. She had bought him a bottle of wine. 'I set it down and at some point I'm going... back to set and he kicked his foot up in the air and lifted the back of my bathrobe up... I just kind of giggled and batted it away playfully.' Depp then apparently pushed Heard down in a 'playful and flirtatious' manner onto what she described as a 'bed/sofa' in the trailer 'and he said: "Yum." And he kind of lifted up his eyebrows.'

Heard said that throughout the shoot she felt a 'chemistry' which went 'beyond the pale' of her job, but nothing significant happened. Both actors were spoken for.

In October 2011 Depp and Heard began a press tour to promote the release of *The Rum Diary*. Depp has indicated his relationship with Vanessa Paradis had broken down by this stage. Likewise, Heard has intimated that by that date she and Tasya van Ree were in the process of going their separate ways[1].

One evening, during the press tour, Depp invited Heard to his hotel room. He told her Bruce Robinson was going to be there. Robinson, if he was invited, didn't show. Heard and Depp drank red wine and Heard said 'the reconnection was almost instant... it felt like there was an electricity to the room... we talked, finished some wine and... as I went to leave, he grabbed both sides of my face – similar to what he did in Puerto Rico when we were filming that scene – and kissed me.'

Heard 'kissed him back.' Asked what happened next, Heard replied: 'We fell in love.'

---

[1] Depp only formally announced his split from Vanessa Paradis in June 2012. The same month, the Daily Mail newspaper reported Heard and van Ree's split.

A fateful romance had begun. 'This man knew me,' said Heard, 'and saw me in a way no one else had. I felt he understood me. I felt he understood where I came from. I felt like that when I was around Johnny I felt like the most beautiful person in the world... he made me feel like a million dollars.'

It was nice while it lasted.

THE UK TRIAL

Navigating the summer of 2020 was an unsettling experience for anyone living in the UK. We had come out of the first coronavirus lockdown, and life was supposed to be getting back to normal, but COVID was still killing people, and the world was weeks away from any vaccine being announced, let alone rolled out.

My main source of freelance income – TV news reporting – had all but dried up. The few dates I had left were booked for Channel 5 News. I was grateful for the work. For weeks, every story they sent me to cover was about coronavirus. I found myself traversing the country meeting and filming (but not getting too close to) people who were essentially trying to work out a way to survive.

By the time July came round the initial wave of horror was over, and the severest restrictions had been relaxed. On the evening of 6 July 2020 I was called by the 5 News planning editor who told me I would not be making a COVID piece the next day, but would instead be attending the High Court in London to cover Johnny Depp's libel case against The Sun or, more specifically, the Sun newspaper's parent company, NGN.

In April 2018, Dan Wootton, the Sun's 'Executive Editor' had written a column attacking JK Rowling, published with a headline asking how the *Harry Potter* author could be happy casting Johnny Depp, a 'wife-beater' (the Sun's term), in her new *Fantastic Beasts* film[1].

Wootton wrote: 'Overwhelming evidence was filed to show Johnny Depp engaged in domestic violence against his wife Amber Heard. She was granted a restraining order after alleging Depp assaulted her following a drunken argument and submitted photographs to the court showing her bruised face. Heard – backed up by numerous friends on the record – recounted a detailed history of domestic abuse incidents, some of which had led to her fearing for her life.'

Depp took umbrage at being called a wife-beater, and issued legal proceedings against Wootton and NGN in June 2018.

I had no idea the trial was happening. We were only three months past being told we could not leave our own homes unless it was

---

[1]   The article's headline was quickly changed to remove the term 'wife-beater'. The article, with the amended headline, remains online.

absolutely necessary. The whole world was a mess. But now the news desk was sending me to cover a celebrity libel trial at the High Court, brought by an American movie star. This would be unusual at the best of times. During an apparent apocalypse, it seemed almost preposterous.

'He's not going to actually *be* there, is he?' I asked.

'We think so,' replied my ever-knowledgeable editor. 'He's definitely in the country.'

I read into the story, and the next morning travelled up to London on an empty train. As soon as I saw the photographers lined up along the temporary crush barriers outside the Royal Courts of Justice, I realized Depp was almost certainly going to be there. Paps don't go where the story isn't. But they did look incongruous – as if they'd been teleported from the center of a buzzy celebrity premiere to an almost wholly deserted central London.

Inside the normally bustling Royal Courts of Justice Great Hall, it was eerily quiet. To aid social distancing, five separate courts had been set aside for Depp v NGN. The main Court 13 was for the judge, the protagonists and the important lawyers. An overspill court was handed to less important lawyers. Two (initially under-populated) courts were given to spectators and one court in the completely separate West Green Wing was reserved for the perennial dirt on the legal system's shoe – reporters.

To be fair, Court 38 was spacious, air-conditioned and comfortable. Plug sockets, rare as hen's teeth in the nineteenth-century main courts, were plentiful and easy to access. I took a seat among twenty or so fellow hacks, and decided I would have a pop at live-tweeting the trial.

Accredited journalists and legal commentators are allowed to live-tweet court proceedings in the UK without first asking the permission of the presiding judge. I figured a court case featuring Johnny Depp might be of interest to the twittersphere, and I was sure Channel 5 wouldn't mind me offering a blow-by-blow commentary, especially as I could point any new and existing followers towards the evening news programme and my end-of-day TV report.

I asked my colleagues, by now all seated in Court 38, if Johnny Depp had definitely turned up. There were murmurs of affirmation. One reporter produced his phone and showed me a freshly-published paparazzi shot of the star making his way up the steps of the main entrance to the Royal Courts of Justice. Depp was wearing shades and a bandana face mask. He looked cool. I plugged in my laptop, booted up TweetDeck and established a connection to the outside world with my mobile phone. I told my followers where I was and why, adding that

Johnny Depp was not only already in court, but due to give evidence that day.

Before proceedings began, a smartly-dressed woman appeared at my shoulder. She smiled and told me she was from the company handling Amber Heard's PR. The woman gave me her business card and asked me to get touch if I needed anything. I had never experienced something like this in a courtroom before, so I tweeted it.

A closed-circuit TV relay was Court 38's only connection to Court 13. The camera positions were not ideal and the sound quality was poor. We were going to have to make the best of it. As the judge – Mr Justice Nicol – entered Court 13, the occupants of Court 38 were commanded to rise by the usher[2] tasked with keeping an eye on us. We sheepishly complied, sitting back down as we saw the judge make himself comfortable.

Nicol made a few housekeeping remarks and then we were off. As I began to describe the barristers' opening arguments, something unexpected happened. My Twitter following *exploded*. Given Depp v NGN involved an authentic Hollywood superstar, I knew there would be some interest in what was going on, but I was not anticipating this kind of response.

What I also hadn't twigged was that – due to the pandemic – no US journalists had been allowed into the UK to cover the case. As is usual in Britain, the trial was not being televised. It seemed that few of my colleagues in Court 38 had any interest in posting Twitter updates – they were busy collecting copy for their own publications. I was the only hack in the room – and therefore the world – producing real time trial updates on social media. As my mentions started spinning like fruit machine reels, I plugged away, trying to give a flavour of what it was like to be sitting in this surreal environment, reporting what I soon realized was going to be a gripping case.

After I'd put my evening news piece together, I asked the 5 News planning desk if they needed me to cover day two of the trial. My services were not required, so I asked my new followers on Twitter if they would like me to continue reporting Depp v NGN for them. Yes, came the unequivocal response. As I had no work booked, I thought I'd give it a go.

---

[2] Ushers perform a similar role to Deputy Sheriffs in the US judicial system, but they wear cloaks, exhibit the air of harassed librarians and don't carry guns. They prepare the courtroom, greet people entering court and call defendants and witnesses to the stand.

There was a small problem. I wasn't sure if I would be able to get back into court for day two. One journalist who wasn't on the designated list had been turfed out by the ushers, so as not to compromise the strictly enforced social distancing rules. I emailed a request to the High Court press office asking if I could attend Depp v NGN as an independent freelancer, but I did not receive a response.

The best three words of advice to any budding reporter are: Get. There. Early. Arriving well before something is scheduled to begin gives you the opportunity to ingratiate yourself with people who may end up helping you. With this in mind, I pitched up in good time on day two, got through front entrance security, made my way to the West Green Wing and spent a few minutes outside Court 38 chatting to my fellow early-doors reporters.

Half an hour before proceedings began, a hurried-looking usher, black robes flapping behind him, came to unlock the courtroom door. As he was leaving, one of the journalists asked if it was alright to go in. There were only four of us. In the usher's eyes we looked kosher, and possibly familiar from the previous day. Rather than check us off his list, he nodded and silently held the door open for us, before rushing off again.

I strolled in, sat down and established a data connection. Using the available downtime to repurpose an online tip jar (set up to fund my coverage of a previous court case), I told my Twitter followers I had a place in court. I posted a link to the tip jar and suggested that if anyone wanted to make a small contribution towards my travel and lunch costs for the day I would be grateful.

And off we went. I tweeted everything that was happening that day and for the next two weeks, funded by donations from people all over the world, desperate for information about what was being said in court.

CAPTAIN JACK SPARROW

Until 2016 I guess *most* people would probably consider Johnny Depp to be a credible actor with a reasonable number of decent films under his belt. Committed fans might think him a special talent who has made a large number of brilliant films. A subsection of those fans could feel an even stronger connection with Depp. It's possible you're reading this because Depp's fine looks and talent once moved you profoundly. Or made you horny. Or both[1].

Whatever you think of the pre-2016 Johnny Depp, it is impossible to begin to understand why so many people invested in the raging battles around his relationship with Amber Heard until you accept that he is more than a famous screen actor. To large numbers of people alive today, Johnny Depp is a bona fide cultural icon, and as such he has crept into the mechanism through which millions of people define their identities and find meaning.

He achieved this by giving us Captain Jack Sparrow.

There have been plenty of enduring cinematic characters. In a subjective list, based on length of service, worldwide fame and ubiquity, I would go for James Bond, Spider-Man, Superman, Batman, Darth Vader and possibly Sherlock Holmes. Top of Empire magazine's list is Indiana Jones. The only female to make their top 20 is Ellen Ripley from the *Alien* franchise. Unless you begin to include animated characters, there are precious few others. In the real world, there are certain artists and sports stars who become global icons in their own right – think of Muhammad Ali, Madonna, Pelé, John Lennon or Beyoncé – but I am struggling to think of anyone else this century who has achieved worldwide cultural ubiquity whilst *embodying* a fictional alter-ego. Especially a fictional alter-ego which also happens to be an established cross-cultural archetype.

In creating Sparrow, Depp tapped into something which existed as a fully-formed concept in our minds since pre-school – the swashbuckling, sea-faring PIRATE! – and gave it a staggeringly successful makeover. Not only that, he invested significant elements of his own character and interests into Sparrow. This, in turn, amplified and elevated our own understanding of Johnny Depp's public persona. No one (I hope) thinks Johnny Depp is Jack Sparrow or that Jack Sparrow is

---

[1] If you have bought this book without any idea of who Johnny Depp is, all I can say is... thank you.

Johnny Depp, but all of the things which make Sparrow cinematically unique – his looks, his manner, his sense of humor, his appeal to men and women of all ages – were informed by the personality, life and career of the already much-loved Johnny Depp. Due to the absence of any personal history or defining acting roles which are starkly at odds with Sparrow's character, Depp and his creation have built a home within our collective unconscious.

To try to understand how this happened, let's go back to the beginning.

John C Depp II was born on 9 June 1963 in Owensboro, Kentucky, son of John Christopher Depp, a civil engineer, and Betty Sue Wells, a waitress. He was the youngest of four children. During the early days of the Depp v Heard trial in the US, Depp was asked about the complex relationship he had with his mother.

'She was quite violent and she was quite cruel,' he told the court. 'There was physical abuse certainly, which could be in the form of an ashtray being flung at you... or you'd get beat with a high-heeled shoe or a telephone or whatever was handy.'

Depp testified that John Depp Senior wasn't shy of using violence himself. On the stand, Depp described being told by his dad to 'take the dog for a walk... or take out the garbage, something menial.' The teenage Depp refused. His father gave him 'a quick shot' to the face and Depp was knocked down. 'It rattled my head,' said Depp, 'with birds and stuff.' His father's (alleged) actions had an immediate effect on Depp's noncompliant attitude. Depp told the court he became 'excited to take care of' the chore.

This kind of spontaneous paternal violence, as described by Depp, appears to have been an exception to the norm. Although Depp testified that his father dished out regular beltings to his son at the behest of Betty Sue, Depp describes him as 'kind', 'quiet', 'a good man' and a 'gentleman.' Depp's mother was the tyrant, directing barrel-loads of psychological and physical abuse at her children. Betty Sue also attacked her husband, but Depp told the court he refused to respond in kind:

'He swallowed it. He took it. There was never one moment, never a moment when my father lost control and attacked my mother, or hit my mother, or even said a bad thing to my mother.'

It was an unstable home environment, compounded by Betty Sue's refusal to stay put. 'Her feet were on fire,' remembered Depp. 'She had to move, so we moved constantly.' Depp repeatedly found himself the new kid at school – tough for anyone, not least a shy fourth child. To cope with the trauma, Depp turned to drugs. He'd noticed how his mum became more placid when she ordered him to fetch her nerve pills. He stole some, and they numbed his pain.

When Depp was 15, his father walked out. The family were, by this stage, living in South Florida. Depp drove to see his dad at work, still not sure of the situation. He started with a joke.

'I said, "Listen, it seems as though somebody stole all your clothes out of the closet".'

According to Depp, his father replied: 'Yeah... I'm done. I can't do it anymore. I can't live it anymore. You're the man. You're the man now.'

Depp did not take well to this. Betty Sue, unable to cope with the stigma of being left by her husband, sank into depression. She tried to take her own life. Depp found her one afternoon in their living room, moving in 'a slow motion crawl [with] drool coming out of her mouth.' She survived by having her stomach pumped. After this, Depp watched his former 'firecracker' mother progressively withdraw into herself. He heaped the blame for the family's predicament on his father, who he described as 'cowardly'.

Depp decided he needed to get out. He had already left school to try and make it as a musician. In 1983 he moved with his band to Los Angeles.

Although Depp's career ascent once he got to Hollywood has the whiff of magic about it, the early days don't sound like fun. Depp's band, The Kids, were moving in the right circles, but they couldn't get a record deal, and weren't making much money. Depp began working in telesales. Before moving to LA, he started a relationship with Lori Anne Allison, the sister of one of his bandmates. Lori Anne was five years Depp's senior. He proposed and they wed, but as the band disintegrated, so did the marriage. Nonetheless, they continued to hang out. When Lori Anne began dating a promising actor called Nicolas Cage, Depp became his drinking buddy.

Cage soon suggested his new friend give acting a try. Depp was introduced to Cage's agent and at the age of 20 was cast in *A Nightmare on Elm Street* – a well-executed slasher pic which took a surprising $25m at the box office. With this calling card and an acting course at the Loft Studio under his belt, Depp was able to secure a minor part in the Oscar-winning Oliver Stone movie, *Platoon*.

'Oliver scared the shit out of me!' Depp told Interview magazine. 'I read for him and he said, "OK, I need you for 10 weeks in the jungle." It was a great experience.'

On returning from the jungle, Depp joined a new band, but the rock star dreams were parked when another acting job came up. Depp was cast as an undercover cop in the teen TV drama, *21 Jump Street*.

A lucrative career began. *21 Jump Street* reportedly paid him $45,000 per episode. As the show's success grew, Depp was plastered on magazine covers across the US. But by season four, Depp was deeply uncomfortable. Desperate to escape what he saw as a conformist straitjacket, Depp took the lead role in a John Waters film called *Cry-Baby*, which sent up his heart-throb status. Then, at the age of 26, he was cast by Tim Burton in the role of *Edward Scissorhands*, the film which made him an international movie star.

From that moment, Depp had the clout to pick his film roles and live the life he wanted to lead. He was not the best actor in the world, but he had a fan base, name recognition, stunning looks, screen charisma, and a counter-cultural sensibility which only added to his appeal.

Although the nineties were Depp's for the taking, he made some patchy choices. *What's Eating Gilbert Grape*, *Ed Wood* and *Donnie Brasco* are fine films, but there were plenty of average turns in average movies and nothing to suggest that Depp's career was fulfilling its potential. But Depp was cool. He became friends with Marlon Brando and Hunter S Thompson. He dated Winona Ryder and Kate Moss. He had tattoos, trashed hotel rooms and liked a drink or two.

Most movie actors of his generation would have killed to be in Depp's position, and it's entirely possible that as he drifted from the nineties into the 2000s, Depp would have continued to make good, or at least profitable films. There was a growing maturity. Fatherhood – through his relationship with Vanessa Paradis – and a relocation to Paris suggested a man at ease with himself.

At the turn of the century, Depp's career was on an upswing. Another Tim Burton collaboration, *Sleepy Hollow*, had done decent business, and he remained in demand as a leading man. Then the script for *Pirates of the Caribbean* came his way.

Captain Jack Sparrow was not created for Johnny Depp – he found the character on the page formulaic – but it had potential. Depp decided he wanted the part, and got to work. The creative stepping-off point was the cartoons he watched with his young daughter, Lily-Rose. In court in 2022, Depp described his inspiration:

'Wile E. Coyote gets a boulder dropped on his head and he's completely crushed,' said Depp, 'and they cut to the next scene and he's just got a little bandage.'

It became an idea: 'I started thinking about the parameters that were available to cartoon characters.'

On being cast in the role by Disney, Depp's thoughts began to crystallise: 'I tried to incorporate these kind of ideas into the character... so that I could try to push those parameters and control the suspension of disbelief.'

This meant, in Depp's mind, putting Sparrow's 'actions, words [and] movements' in a place where he could be 'ludicrous' and yet somehow completely believable:

'Cartoon characters can get away with things we can't. Captain Jack Sparrow can do things that I could never do. He could say things that I could never say.'

Disney was not convinced, but Depp persevered. He continued to develop the character. Keith Richards' gypsy look and outlaw persona were obvious influences. Sparrow's swaying and dopey expressions were again, cartoon-like, but Depp gave them a premise: 'I figured that this is a guy who has been on the sea for the majority of his life. Quite possibly his brains may have been scrambled a bit by the sun.'

Stillness is an essential quality in film and TV acting. With Sparrow, Depp threw decades of received wisdom out of the window. 'I thought that he'd been on the sea for so long that he had his sea legs, but when he got on land, he just didn't have his land legs, so he could never quite stand still.'

Depp describes himself as being 'on a pretty good mission' when trying to persuade the 'somewhat upset' studio execs how Sparrow could work. 'I believed in the character wholeheartedly,' he said, and felt that 'if it panned out,' he and Disney would be looking at a creation 'who would be accepted by five year olds and forty-five year olds and sixty-five year olds and eighty-five year olds, in the same way that Bugs Bunny is.'

The resistance Depp faced in getting his version of Jack Sparrow onto the screen has become the stuff of Hollywood legend, largely stoked by Depp himself. In one interview he claimed Disney's then CEO Michael Eisner saw the daily rushes during production and declared Depp was 'ruining the movie'. It's not known exactly how much pressure Depp came under, but he recalls being forced to issue a trust-me-or-fire-me ultimatum to his employers. Eventually Disney backed down, and Depp was left to make his semi-permanent mark on popular culture.

With the arrival of Captain Jack Sparrow, the hackneyed Hollywood notion of the noble outlaw (think Robin Hood, Zorro or Batman), seemed terribly old-fashioned. Depp's Sparrow re-worked the inherent contradictions of the hero outsider into an amiable, morally wayward chancer who always seemed to luck out. He was no dark, conflicted anti-hero, but someone it was possible to both root for and laugh at. Sparrow was by turns pathetic, hopeful, *funny*, and occasionally touched by genius.

And he connected. When *Pirates of the Caribbean: The Curse of the Black Pearl* was released, audiences loved it. Legendary critic Roger Ebert described the actor's performance in *Pirates* as 'original in its every atom', drawn from 'deep wells of nuttiness' in which Depp appeared to be ignoring every standard heroic convention and instead, playing the part as if he were 'channeling a drunken drag queen.' Ebert rhapsodised:

'There has never been a pirate, or for that matter a human being, like this in any other movie... his behavior shows a lifetime of rehearsal. He is a peacock in full display.'

At the height of his powers, Johnny Depp had managed to successfully reinvent and personify an archetype which, thanks to Disney's global reach, resonated with millions of people around the world. *Pirates of the Caribbean: The Curse of the Black Pearl* made more than half a billion dollars. Depp, already world-famous, was catapulted into an entirely new stratosphere.

WATCH ME

Amber Heard was born on 22 April 1986. Sixteen months later, her sister Whitney came along. The girls grew up in a small town called Manor, twelve miles north of Austin, Texas. Their mother, Paige, worked in telecommunications for the state of Texas. Their father, David, sounds like a caricature. He ran a small construction company, painted houses and broke horses for a living. He liked to hunt, shoot and fish. Amber testified he was also an abuser:

'My father was violent to my mother, growing up,' she told the High Court in 2020. 'He is an addict and an alcoholic, and he was very violent, but I love him very much.'

David Heard did not seem much bothered Amber was, in her own words, 'a girly girl'. He took her hunting and used her as 'a crash test dummy' when it came to the horses.

'I would help him,' she said. 'When you train a horse... it's a wild animal, it doesn't necessarily like to be ridden.'

Heard said her father was intent on 'raising someone who could keep up with him.' She learned not to show fear: 'be tough and calm.'

It wasn't just (the now deceased) Paige who allegedly suffered at David Heard's hands. Years later in court, a clinical psychologist told the jury Amber's 'history is having been violated by her father physically.'

Amber Heard was a scholarship kid, winning places at various Catholic schools on the wealthier side of town. She worked for charities, at first because it was part of the compulsory volunteering at her school, and then because 'it meant I wasn't at home, and it was important to me not to spend time at home.' She worked with deaf children, and taught herself sign language.

Perhaps unsurprisingly, Heard wanted to get out of Texas as soon as she was able:

'I just always pushed myself to be able to accelerate the process. I wanted to get out of school as fast as I could, and I wanted to do more things with my life.'

On leaving school at sixteen Heard began work at a modelling agency, raising enough money to get her head-shots – professional photos used as calling cards in the entertainment industry. Heard flew to meet with agents in New York. The city enthralled her but ultimately, the prospect of being a model held no interest. 'I hated it,' she told The Independent.

The following year, Heard's 'very best friend', an older boy called Logan, was killed in a car crash. The teenagers had met whilst working as lifeguards at a local pool. Logan was well liked and close to the Heard family. His death had a profound effect. Heard quietly renounced her Catholic upbringing and embraced atheism.

For an ambitious, beautiful teenager with a grinding work ethic, Heard's thoughts shifted towards Hollywood. In 2012, David Heard told the Daily Mail his daughter had wanted to be an actor 'since she was 12-years old.'

After landing a part in *Friday Night Lights* – a film set and shot in Texas – the 17-year old Heard signed with an agent. In 2003, she moved permanently to Los Angeles.

On arriving in LA, Heard said she 'hustled from one audition to another... just working my butt off.' She attended up to ten castings or meetings a day.

'I put myself out there,' she told jurors in 2022. 'I didn't have a car, because those are expensive. So, I took the bus around LA. It was before smartphones. I had a Thomas Guide in my bag and a change of tank tops... and would change clothes if I needed to in the back of the bus I was taking.'

The hustle paid off. Heard was cast in *North Country*, *Zombieland*, Judd Apatow's *Pineapple Express*, and as the lead in *All The Boys Love Mandy Lane*. Her performances weren't exactly heralded, but she was seen as one to watch.

In 2008, Heard began a relationship with the artist Tasya van Ree. The following year, she was arrested for allegedly assaulting van Ree at Seattle airport. The charges were dropped. In 2016 van Ree described the arrest as 'homophobic'. This was disputed on a Facebook post by the arresting officer – a lesbian – who wrote: 'I am so not homophobic or mysoginistic! [*sic*] The arrest was made because an assault occurred (I witnessed it).'

Heard came out as bisexual in 2010 whilst seeing van Ree. She made the announcement during a red carpet interview at an event hosted by GLAAD – the Gay and Lesbian Alliance Against Defamation. She told her interviewer:

'I'm with who I'm with, I love who I love... I think that the injustice of people staying in the closet is more than I can bear with a clear conscience and I couldn't sleep at night if I was a part of that problem, if I was part of the lies... GLAAD is one of the many reasons that I, as a 24-year old, can come out.'

Many years later, at an event organized by The Economist, Heard reflected on her decision to speak publicly about her sexuality.

'I just answered honestly. I could tell by the look on this person's face it was a big deal. My poor publicist. Then I realized the gravity of what I had done and why so many people – studio execs, directors, advisors, agents – did not want this... before my name. I became attached to a label.'

Heard said Hollywood found this problematic. 'As a leading lady, there's a certain amount of wish-fulfilment you need to sell,' Heard told The Economist. 'I was asked, "How is anyone going to invest in you romantically if they think you're unavailable?"'

Her response?

'Watch me.'

MULTIPLE ALLEGED ASSAULTS

On her Domestic Violence Restraining Order request form, submitted to Los Angeles Municipal Court in May 2016, Amber Heard alleged she 'endured excessive emotional, verbal and physical abuse' from Johnny Depp and that this happened 'during the entirety' of their relationship.

For the Depp v NGN trial in London in 2020, Heard alleged fourteen specific incidents of physical abuse. The first occasion was in March 2013, the last in May 2016[1]. Within those claims of violence, there were three allegations of sexual assault.

By the time we got to Virginia in 2022, Heard's chronology had changed back to the assertion she made on the DVRO request form – that the violence started much earlier than 2013. Heard explained the shift by suggesting she 'would have liked to believe that the period of time in which we fell in love and he was sober and he wasn't violent to me lasted for a lot longer than it did.'

Heard claimed to have forgotten that although he was sober for at least six months in 2012, Depp wasn't clean when the relationship began in October 2011, and that this period was 'really violent and chaotic.' In the US, Heard told the court she was 'embarrassed' to have got things so wrong, and said it was only in February 2022, in preparation for the Virginia trial, that she had properly gone through everything – her diaries, emails, doctors' and therapists' notes – and put together a proper timeline in what is known as an interrogatory. Unfortunately Heard's interrogatory has not been made public and my attempts to secure it have been stonewalled. Thankfully most incidents *have* been attached to specific agreed dates (even if what happened on each occasion is highly contested). They are listed in the timeline at the back of this book and stated at the top of each relevant chapter.

Incidentally, the three sexual violence allegations made by Heard against Depp were initially considered by the High Court in London in private. In the UK, anyone who makes a complaint that they have been sexually abused cannot be publicly identified as a victim of that alleged abuse without their written consent. Whilst journalists reporting the UK trial had guessed the judge was hearing evidence related to sexual assault (even before one witness blurted it out in open court[2]), we could

---

[1] These became known as the Tattoo Incident and the Phone Incident. Both have chapters to themselves later in the book.

[2] See the *Kate James Incoming* chapter.

not report it because to do so would likely identify Amber Heard as an alleged victim. This did not change until 2022 when it became apparent that Heard's claims of sexual abuse were going to be presented in open court to the US jury.

What follows is a close examination of the incidences of alleged violence (and dog-smuggling and bed-soiling and drug-taking) from the perspective of the people who were there, cross-referenced with information parsed from the available contemporaneous documentary evidence.

Lawyers for Amber Heard and NGN told respective courts on both sides of the Atlantic that if just one of Heard's allegations of assault is true, Johnny Depp is an abuser.

Let's take a long, hard look.

THE TATTOO INCIDENT

Los Angeles, 2011 or 2013

The tattoo incident is significant because Amber Heard alleges this is the first time Johnny Depp hit her. The setting was either Depp's house at Sweetzer Avenue (as described in Heard's own witness statement to the UK trial) or (less likely) Heard's rented home on Orange Avenue. Both are in Los Angeles. The suggestion it was Orange Avenue was made in court in London by NGN's barrister, Sasha Wass. She was not corrected. Although we don't have an exact location or date, it allegedly happened in LA and the weather, according to Heard, was 'cold... so it might have been winter.'

On the substance of the accusation, this is what Heard wrote in her witness statement to the UK court:

'We were talking about one of his tattoos, which he had had altered from Winona (his ex-partner) to say "Wino". I laughed at something he said... and he hit me with an open hand across my cheek.'

Heard described herself as 'stunned'. She wrote: 'I had never had a man other than my dad hit me. I was staring at him in shock... trying to decipher what was going on. I didn't know if it was some kind of joke.'

According to Heard, staring at Depp seemed to antagonize him. He allegedly hit her again, 'harder'.

Heard wrote: 'I thought to myself, "I can't believe this is happening to me, did he just hit me again?" I was still sitting next to him, looking at him. He was asking me, "are you fucking laughing, you think it's so funny bitch?" I didn't know what to say... I didn't know what to say and it was as if my silence provoked him further because he hit me again even harder. It felt like my eye popped out. Johnny wears a lot of rings, one on every finger. This third hit knocked me off balance and I fell to the floor.'

In the US trial in 2022 Heard was able to flesh her story out in more detail. She recalled that in the run-up to the alleged attack 'there was no fighting, no argument, nothing.' Depp was drinking, and whilst Heard hadn't seen him take any drugs, 'I think he was using cocaine because there was... a jar of cocaine on the table... an actual vintage jar.'

Heard took the jurors through the three 'slaps', the third of which knocked her onto the floor.

'It didn't physically hurt me,' she said. 'I was just sitting there on this... dirty carpet wondering how... I never noticed that the carpet was so filthy before... and I just didn't know what else to do. I didn't know what to say. I didn't know how to react.'

Heard said she realized something very bad had happened:

'I know you don't come back from that. You know, I'm not dumb. I know you can't hit a woman. You can't hit a man. You can't hit anyone.'

In court, Heard attempted to explain something which may sound familiar to every victim of abuse who has gone back to their abuser: 'I knew it was wrong. And I knew that I had to leave him. And that's what broke my heart. Because I didn't want to leave him. I thought if I got up out of that room, I would leave the best thing that ever happened to me.'

Heard picked herself up. She told the court: 'I remember looking at him in the eye and just looking at him, frankly, because I didn't know what else to do. And before I know it, he starts crying.'

This was an unexpected turn of events.

'I had never seen an adult man cry,' Heard told the court. 'I didn't even really see my dad cry at my grandma's funeral... And he's crying. Tears... just falling out of his eyes. He gets down on his knees and he grabs my hands and he's touching my hands and he's saying to me, "I will never do that again. I'm so sorry, baby. I put the fucker away, I thought I killed it, and it's done. I thought I put The Monster away, and I've done it before, it's done." But on his knees.'

Heard decided she would leave. 'I walked to the car. I didn't say anything. I made a point to not say, "Oh it's okay," or anything like that. I got up. I went to the car. I sat in my car, and I felt like I sat there forever.'

Heard described her confusion. 'I didn't want to turn the key, I just leaned my head up against the window. And I remember just seeing my breath on the windshield, on the glass of the window of the door, just seeing my breath and trying to will myself to have the strength to know what I should do in this moment. Because I was heartbroken. And I sat there for a long time, and I eventually turn the key and drove home.'

Johnny Depp says none of this happened. He has offered no alternative version of events. Questioned in court in April 2022, he simply said: 'Why would I take such great offense to someone making fun of a tattoo on my body? That allegation never made any sense to me whatsoever.'

WHAT'S THAT COMING OVER THE HILL?

The word 'monster' was mentioned in court 203 times over the course of the UK trial, offensively by NGN's lawyers and defensively by Depp. The idea appeared to be that when Johnny Depp took excessive amounts of drink or drugs he would not just be capable of monstrous behavior, but his normal personality would shut down and he would *turn into* The Monster – a sort of deranged alter-ego committing criminal acts which good ol' Johnny Depp would neither remember nor, when in his right mind, believe himself capable of.

On day one of the UK trial the court was shown a now infamous video, secretly recorded[1] by Amber Heard in the kitchen of one of Depp's properties on Sweetzer Avenue. Had she captured the first true footage of The Monster in the wild? The video starts with an image of Amber Heard's face as she starts the recording. She places the phone down as Depp tracks into shot, possibly drunk, definitely unhappy. He kicks some furniture and shouts 'Motherfucker', twice. Heard asks him what has happened. He ignores her, and approaches an eye-level kitchen cupboard. Something about it annoys him. He opens the cupboard doors violently, retrieves a glass and smashes the left hand door of the cupboard shut, breaking a piece of its wooden frame as he does so.

'Nothing happened this morning, you know that?' says Heard, trying again. Depp walks across the kitchen floor and disappears out of shot. We hear a glass smashing.

'Were you in here?' challenges Depp.

'No,' replies Heard.

'So then *nothing* happened to you this morning!' says Depp.

Heard moves the camera position.

'Yeah, you're right. I just woke up. And you were so sweet and nice,' she says.

Depp walks back across the kitchen to the same cupboard he has just broken and retrieves another glass.

'We were not even fighting this morning. All I did was say sorry,' volunteers Heard.

---

[1]   The exact date of the recording of this video has never been definitively established. Amber Heard's team believe it was filmed in February 2016. Johnny Depp thinks it was in 2013. It was leaked to celebrity news website TMZ in August 2016.

'Did something happen to *you*, this morning?!' slurs Depp. 'I don't think so!'

'No. That's the thing,' replies Heard.

She tries to obscure the camera with her body as Depp comes closer.

'You want to see crazy? I'll give you fucking crazy,' says Depp as he picks up a half-empty magnum bottle of red wine and starts to pour it into a goblet-style wine glass.

During the UK trial, Depp called the volume of liquid he poured into the glass goblet a 'mega-pint'. It was a knowingly ridiculous term, apparently conjured up in the moment to help NGN's barrister, Sasha Wass. Wass was cross-examining Depp at the time and struggling to describe or quantify the volume of the measure. The 'mega-pint' was thrown back at Depp two years later during the US proceedings, much to his amusement, when Amber Heard's trial attorney Ben Rottenborn suggested that the video showed Depp pouring himself a 'mega-pint' of wine. 'A mega-pint?!' Depp mugged, to laughter from the gallery. 'I poured myself a large glass of wine.'

The mega-pint has subsequently spawned several dozen mug and t-shirt designs (e.g. Make Mine A Mega Pint) all available for sale online.

Anyway – back to the video...

'Here's crazy. All your crazy,' says Depp as he slams the magnum down and contemplates the (mega-pint) glass. 'There's your crazy.'

'Have you drunk this whole thing this morning?' asks Heard, indicating the now four-fifths empty magnum.

Depp spots the phone. 'Oh you got this thing... you got this going?!'

'No I've just started it!' says Heard.

'Oh, really?' says Depp with the phone in his hand.

'Yes!' yelps Heard.

'*Really?!*' says Depp, smashing the phone down. 'Sneak that shit on me, motherfucker?'

'No I didn't,' says Heard. 'You were smashing shit.'

Depp says something indistinct ending in the word '... ass!' and storms off.

Heard appears to chuckle, off camera. The last thing we see is her face, as she calmly ends the recording.

NGN's barrister, Sasha Wass, suggested to Depp that in the video he was 'behaving, if you do not mind me saying, like a monster?'

Depp declined to agree. The Monster was useful for Team Heard (for convenience, I am including NGN and its lawyers under this umbrella term) because it helped explain their central thesis – that

Depp carried out his violent attacks on Amber Heard when he was off his face on drink and drugs. The sober Johnny Depp might tell a court (and genuinely believe) that he was not capable of hitting a woman, but according to Heard, his alter-ego – The Monster – certainly was. When the drink and drugs wore off, a sick and humbled Johnny Depp would re-emerge with little or no memory of what had happened.

Depp complained in court that The Monster was Heard's conceit, but texts sent by Depp himself belie that.

On 22 March 2012, early in his relationship with Heard, Depp sent an email to Elton John proclaiming a hundred days of sobriety. He told the singer, 'I would have been swallowed up by the monster, were it not for you. That is a simple fact.'

On 4 October 2014 the sobriety seemed to have gone awry, as Depp texted an unknown person to say, 'I am going to, quite gracefully, glide into a massage of my broken back and neck … I shall exit in one hour, a MONSTER!!! Shall we swallow an E each (or perhaps it's MDMA) at around 8pm and go to dinner with A few of my wee team at a wonderful Peruvian spot … ??? Let us enjoy this night my brother!!!'

The next year, Depp was back on the wagon. Responding to a message from his head of security about a brief period of serenity with Heard, Depp texted:

'Thank you, my dear Jerry!!! Very very kind mate!! All I had to do was send the monster away and lock him up!!! We've been happier than EVER!!! Love you brother JD.'

Even if Depp didn't invent The Monster, he seemed happy to perpetuate its concept, until he felt Heard was using it as a (verbal) stick to beat him with.

In London, Heard spelled this out, telling the court: 'I was not terrified of Johnny *as* Johnny. I loved him. I was terrified of The Monster. The Monster was almost a third party in this relationship, one that he identified early on and I came to know as the other half of my relationship. And it is that – The Monster – that I was terrified of.'

To me, repeated attempts to invoke The Monster's presence during the UK trial felt a bit silly, especially as no one was suggesting Depp really had a split personality or could become possessed by a separate entity. But the concept had strategic value to the defense team. They demonstrated it was Depp's own shorthand for a set of negative behaviors which he could not control or remember and which came to the fore under the influence of excess drink and drugs.

DISCO BLOODBATH

Los Angeles, March 2013

Although it's not clear as to whether the tattoo incident happened (or didn't happen) in March 2013, a lot else was going on that month. Evidence and testimony from both court cases suggest Johnny Depp's long crack at sobriety had fallen away. He was back on the booze and taking drugs. This led to, in Heard's words, 'one fight after another.'

In the UK trial initial evidence from Heard (partially corroborated by her sister Whitney) suggested that during March 2013 Depp had attempted to set fire to and/or deface one or more paintings. The sisters also claimed Depp had taken the cocaine-fuelled decision to hold a small dog out of the back window of a moving car. Heard also said that on 8 March, Depp hit her in the face 'with the back of his hand and drew blood, some of which ended up on the wall. He had silver rings on – he always wore rings – and I think those might have been what drew the blood.'

This became known as the 'Disco Bloodbath' incident, so-called because of a text exchange between the pair on 12 March 2013:

JD: Just thought you should know there exists a book titled "Disco Bloodbath". That's all...
AH: We need that book! Is it about last Friday night by any chance?
JD: How can you make me smile about such a hideous moment??? Yes it is... Funny bitch. I fucking love you, you cunt!!!

In the run-up to the UK trial, as more contemporaneous evidence came to light, it became apparent that the details around the alleged Disco Bloodbath, as described by Heard, could not have happened. In her seventh witness statement, signed just before the trial began, Heard attempted to make sense of it.

She wrote that rather than just one attack in March 2013, there were 'numerous incidents of violence' that month which 'coincided with Johnny's drug use.' Heard said she *was* a victim of assault on 8 March, but 'I now realize that the incident I had initially described as having taken place on 8 March 2013 took place on 22 March 2013.'

As we will see, for this timeline to work the second alleged assault would have to have taken place in the early hours of 22 March. But did it happen at all?

On the afternoon of that day, Depp was expected to be hosting Keith Richards and Tom Waits at Depp's house on Sweetzer Avenue, filming the second day of *Happy*, a documentary being made by Depp's production company Infinitum Nihil. Call time for the crew was midday.

After the first day of filming on 21 March, Depp had gone to Heard's apartment on Orange Avenue where, according to Heard, he started on a whiskey and cocaine bender. The couple got into an argument about a painting by Heard's former partner Tasya van Ree, which Heard kept on display. Depp allegedly demanded Heard remove the painting, and accused Heard of having an affair with van Ree.

The argument went on into the night. In her (partially disavowed) first witness statement for the UK trial, Heard says:

'I remember trying to walk away from him, just because I wanted to diffuse [sic] the situation, but this antagonized him. At various points he grabbed me hard, shook me and shoved me into a wall. I couldn't calm him down – he was so angry and just wouldn't let it go. He was drinking and doing cocaine. We barely slept.'

Sleep did come. Shortly after the midday call time on 22 March, Nathan Holmes, Depp's assistant, texted Heard with the message: 'On my way to get him.'

Heard replied at 12.37pm: 'Trying to wake him now.'

Heard evidently succeeded, but when Depp came to, Heard says he started where he left off – on the whiskey and cocaine.

There are various texts sent by Depp's assistants, agent, sister, Heard's sister and Heard herself all trying to work out how to get an uncooperative Depp from Heard's apartment to Sweetzer so they can get on with the second day of filming.

Eventually, Depp's assistant Stephen Deuters sent his boss a text to let him know they had begun shooting without him. Depp responded:

'GO GODDAMIT!!! I AM BUT A FLY ON THE WALL!!! Commence!!! There is nothing I can add to whatever magic is already there!!!GO!!!'

Whilst this was going on, Heard and Depp picked up their blazing row from the night before. Heard told the UK court:

'He wanted me to admit that I was having an affair with not only Tasya, my ex-partner, but also a gentleman I hardly knew in Shooter Jennings... He had just gotten it in his mind that I was, I had had all these... affairs, and he would not leave until I admitted it.'

During the argument, Heard says Depp attempted to set fire to the van Ree painting. Soon after, Whitney Heard arrived. In her witness statement to the UK court, Whitney says she noticed one side of her sister's face 'was super-red and she had what looked like a split lip.' It was, she says, 'suspicious', but the job in hand was to get Depp to the shoot, which did not sound easy.

Whitney wrote: 'I was trying to talk to him to figure out why he was upset. It was hard to make sense of what he was saying. He was very focused on how angry he was at her, but it was hard to get out of him why he was so mad... Eventually, I managed to get out of him that he had been upset about a painting on the wall by Amber's ex, Tasya van Ree.'

Whilst Whitney was trying to get some sense out of Depp, Nathan Holmes turned up at the property and sat outside in a car, waiting.

During the hours that followed, Heard sent a message to her mum, Paige, which said: 'Dealing with Johnny's spiral. It's terrible mom. I don't know what to do.'

Paige was obviously concerned for her daughter's wellbeing, suggesting she 'come home, go to a motel, anywhere that's safe until it passes... please leave.'

Later, Paige texted: 'you have to change something or what happened last time is inevitable.'

At 7.02pm Heard texted back: 'He's nuts mom. Violent and crazy. I am heartbroken that THIS is who I love.'

Eventually, Heard coaxed Depp into the car to get him from Orange to Sweetzer. On the way, a still intoxicated Depp is alleged to have held Heard's dog, Pistol, out of the window, causing some distress to the car's occupants, and possibly the dog.

By 7.15pm Depp had been delivered to Sweetzer and was filmed by the documentary crew. Paige remained concerned, and stayed in contact with her daughter. In response to another message from Paige, Heard texted to say:

'It's ok mom. He's not being violent with me. He's just... raging in general... the crazy mood swings and binges are really difficult for me to handle.'

Later that night, Heard texted her mum again, saying: 'My heart is broken. I'm ok physically. JD didn't hit me or anything last night. I told him that would be [it] if he did and it worked... But I'm scared by what I see and who I see now. It's Dr Jekyll and Mr Hyde – on a binge.'

Heard's evidence about being 'grabbed' and 'shoved' into a wall in the early hours of 22 March was not challenged in either the UK or US trial, but she *was* asked about being backhanded across the face hard enough to draw blood. During a particularly tortuous sequence of cross-examination in London, Heard shifted her position, claiming Depp 'backhanded' her on 8 March when she and Depp were arguing at Depp's suite of properties in downtown LA[1]. It was here that Depp allegedly 'cut the inside' of Heard's lip.

The confusion grew deeper when, in the UK court, Heard was shown a photo allegedly taken of her with Ian McLagan, a musician, on 23 March 2013. She claimed it was possible to see her 'bottom lip is swollen.' Depp's barrister then tried in vain to establish what Heard was saying about his client's alleged assault on 22 March which could have caused a swollen bottom lip, asking:

'Could you just say what it was physically that Mr Depp had done to you during the assault, physically? What action caused that mark?'

But the question went unanswered as NGN's barrister jumped in on a separate point and successfully managed to stop Depp's barrister from pursuing the issue. In his judgment, Mr Justice Nicol, the single judge presiding over Depp v NGN, decided the photo showed no obvious injury.

Waters are further muddied by Heard's texts, in which she specifically told her mother (twice) that Depp had not been violent. During re-examination by NGN's barrister in the UK, Heard explained she was not telling her mother the truth because she was worried Paige would tell Heard's father, and he would seek to confront Depp.

Parsing the details of this particular episode has been tricky, to say the least. Heard initially confused two alleged incidents. Once this had been established, she remained unclear on how events transpired across the course of March 2013. She was not helped by Whitney who corroborated the erroneous date of the alleged assault (when it was only a single alleged assault). Whitney also admitted in court that she had 'merged' her memory of Depp's alleged attempt to set fire to a van Ree painting with his successful attempt, in 2014, to deface a different van Ree painting. This was not a detail which had any bearing on whether or not Depp did assault her older sister, but it added to the noise surrounding what became known as the 'Painting' incident, making the truth of what happened all the more difficult to ascertain.

Even by the end of Heard's evidence in London it was still not precisely clear what was being alleged. Heard had described a visceral incident on 8 March 2013 during which she claimed Depp hit her with the rings on the back of his hand. This apparently made the inside of Heard's lip split against her teeth. The force with which Heard was hit

---

[1] Depp owned all five penthouses at the Eastern Columbia Building, known as the ECB.

caused blood to spatter on her t-shirt and the kitchen wall of Depp's downtown apartment.

Although she initially conflated the two events, by the end of the trial Heard separated the 'split lip' attack out from a different alleged assault which took place during the early hours of 22 March 2013. As part of this alleged attack Heard was 'grabbed' and 'shoved', and according to her sister Whitney, sustained an injury consistent with the alleged assault on 8 March – a split lip. Heard herself said she had a swollen lip in a photo which Depp's team contend was taken on 23 March, but even when asked to do so, she did not explain how it came about.

None of this means Heard was (or was not) assaulted on two (or more) occasions during March 2013. But it remained unclear what exactly was being alleged until we saw the written closing arguments from NGN at the end of the UK trial. These fell back onto Heard's original claim that Depp 'grabbed her, shook her and shoved her into a wall.' This was not explored in open court with either Johnny Depp or Amber Heard in the UK or US trials. In the UK, the judge decided it didn't need to be.

'Overall,' he ruled, 'I conclude that Mr Depp did assault Ms Heard.'

SECURING THE TRANSCRIPTS

London, July 2020

Live-tweeting makes it hard to publish everything said in court verbatim. Even if I could touch-type, the hang time between hitting send on a tweet and the tweet appearing means at least a couple of seconds go by when it is impossible to type anything. Dialogue is lost. You can therefore either tweet specific, but sporadic, direct quotes or you can tweet a summary of what is being said by paraphrasing it.

The legal requirement for any reporting from a UK court is that it must be 'contemporaneous, accurate and fair'. Live-tweeting is certainly contemporaneous, but the potential risks in tweeting inaccurately or unfairly are high. During Depp v NGN I decided I would only tweet verbatim if someone spoke very slowly and left long pauses after each sentence, which didn't happen very often. At all other times I focused on posting micro-summaries of each stage of proceedings, which I knew I might have to justify (possibly in court to a judge) as accurate and fair to all parties. Every morning I tried to remember to tweet a disclaimer stating that unless what I had published was in 'direct quotes' it was not a direct quote.

Although this real-time recording of events in court had value, I knew it was not hard information. Hard information was in the witness statements, the documents in the trial bundle[1] and the transcripts. During Depp v NGN, the wires agency PA Media had assigned two journalists – Sian Harrison and Sam Tobin – to cover proceedings from Court 38. The pair scored a significant victory during the trial when it became apparent Winona Ryder and Vanessa Paradis were not going to be called as witnesses. Both Ryder and Paradis had provided statements to the court, but no one beyond the parties knew what was in them. Depp's barrister said the decision not to call both witnesses was made because NGN had not and were not accusing Johnny Depp of violence against any woman other than Amber Heard. In his view Paradis and Ryder therefore had 'no need' to give evidence. It certainly saved them from being dragged into the drama.

---

[1] A trial bundle contains all the documents relevant to a case. It is not normally made available to the public, but when documents from the bundle are referred to in open court, they can be requested by journalists.

The withdrawal of these star witnesses meant their statements were in danger of remaining confidential – they are only usually given to journalists when a witness is sworn in. To secure their release, Sam schlepped his way from Court 38 in the West Green Wing to Court 13 in the Center Block of the main building to make his case in open court. As neither party's barrister had an objection, Mr Justice Nicol agreed the statements should be made available. On returning to Court 38, Sam was treated to a round of applause by the assembled hacks.

Thanks to Sam's efforts, we discovered that Winona Ryder and Vanessa Paradis had made strong statements of support for Johnny Depp. Ryder said Depp was, 'never, never violent towards me. He was never, never abusive at all towards me. He has never been violent or abusive towards anybody I have seen. I truly and honestly only know him as a really good man – an incredibly loving, extremely caring guy who was so very protective of me... I felt so very, very safe with him.'

Vanessa Paradis was equally pointed:

'I have known Johnny for more than 25 years,' she wrote. 'We've been partners for 14 years and we raised our two children together. Through all these years I've known Johnny to be a kind, attentive, generous, and non-violent person and father... I am aware of the allegations which Amber Heard has publicly accused Johnny of for more than 4 years now. This is nothing like the true Johnny I have known, and from my personal experience of many years, I can say he was never violent or abusive to me.'

Through Sam and Sian, I was able to pick up a lot of interesting evidence mentioned in court, but my attempts to secure transcripts failed. After three days of asking the parties politely, I took matters into my own hands.

Early on the morning of Friday 10 July I emailed both Depp and NGN's lawyers and told them I intended to make an application to the court to order the release of the transcripts. I forwarded the parties a copy of the application and sent it to the judge's clerk, letting her know I would be happy to address Mr Justice Nicol at the beginning of proceedings that day. I printed off several hard copies and took them up to London with me. On clearing security at the Royal Courts of Justice, instead of veering left towards the West Green Wing and Court 38, I hopped right into the gothic heart of the complex and parked myself on one of the mahogany benches outside Court 13. As the senior lawyers for both parties approached, I stood up, introduced myself and pressed copies of my application into their hands. Thankfully my email from that morning had reached the parties. The barristers on both sides appeared to be aware of what I was trying to do. They were cordial, but non-committal. I still had no idea if my email had reached the judge so I approached an usher and politely asked him to pass a hard copy of my application to Mr Justice Nicol whilst he was still in chambers.

The usher, who appeared to view my presence outside Court 13 as some kind of security risk, claimed fulfilling my request was impossible. He instead told me that once the court was in session he would pass my application to the judge's clerk who could hand it up to the judge when she saw fit. I explained this would be unsatisfactory. The usher eyed me suspiciously and, holding my application, disappeared into the court. A couple of minutes later, the smiling and helpful clerk came out to tell me she had passed everything on to the judge, so he would definitely see it before proceedings began. I relaxed and sat back down again.

As I waited on the bench, I became aware of a flurry of activity further down the corridor. I leaned forward and was treated to the sight of Johnny Depp strolling towards me, coffee cup in hand. He was flanked by at least four people – two security guards and a couple of flunkies. The group stopped in front of me, directly outside court. Depp handed the coffee cup to a member of his team. As he did so, a black-cloaked female usher opened the door to the court. Depp put his hand to his chest, bowed at the usher, and bobbed inside.

After this little vignette, I tried to find out if I might be able to sit or stand at the back of court so I could see how my request was being dealt with. The same usher who was reluctant to handle my application seemed to take special pleasure in informing me that social distancing restrictions meant Court 13 was full. As such he had no intention of allowing me in, unless the judge wanted me to speak. I had progressed from being a potential security risk to some kind of biohazard.

In the event, when the judge raised the application (in my absence) later that morning, neither party voiced an objection, which meant my request for the transcripts went through on the nod, without needing a court order.

A magic door had just opened. From then on I was given daily transcripts of proceedings. I posted them to my website as soon as I was able, allowing people around the world to read and download them as they wished. I felt this, in combination with the real-time tweets (which were soon getting around ten million page impressions a day), justified the donations being deposited in my tip jar.

HICKSVILLE

Joshua Tree, California, June 2013

In June 2013, Johnny Depp turned fifty. As part of the celebrations, Depp and Heard planned a party at a place called Hicksville Trailer Palace, near Joshua Tree, a hundred miles directly east of Los Angeles. Hicksville is a small but beautifully maintained vintage trailer park hotel complex out in the desert. In 2013 the maximum number of residents was 25. Depp's assistant Nathan Holmes booked the entire facility for the VIP party.

Morgan Night owned the trailer palace. As a surprise witness at the US trial, Night told the court Depp and Heard arrived on site mid-afternoon:

'Mr Depp got lost, so his security guard, who arrived early, asked me if I could go fetch them, because he had an old car that didn't really fare on the dirt roads out there, which are pretty horrible. So I went out and made sure that they got themselves and the car back to Hicksville safely.'

Night remembers Depp being 'super-excited about the place, really complimentary' adding that he 'seemed like he was in a really great mood.'

During the US trial, Whitney Heard described arriving with her then partner:

'We got there last,' she said. 'We were going around checking out the different Airstreams... each one of them had a different theme so it was kind of fun to see.' She went into Depp and Heard's trailer and saw 'cocaine on the table.'

Night said that while everyone got settled, he saw Depp chatting to one of the hotel 'innkeepers' – Jenna, a musician who lived nearby. Night joined them, and the trio began 'talking about books and music'. Heard saw them, came over and according to Night, 'kind of interjected. She seemed a little annoyed that Mr Depp wasn't spending time with her.'

With the place to themselves, the guests shared drugs as they sat around the campfire and watched the sun go down. Depp admits bringing alcohol and marijuana. He told the UK court Heard and her friends, Raquel 'Rocky' Pennington and a woman called Kelly Sue, were on MDMA and mushrooms. Depp denies taking MDMA or cocaine but admits eating three mushroom stems 'to no effect'. Heard admits eating a mushroom cap, and says Depp had taken a lot of cocaine. There were at least five people present who remained straight: Kristina Sexton, Heard's acting coach, Malcolm Connolly from Depp's security team, and the three members of hotel staff, including Morgan Night.

Whitney drank too much and retired to her trailer early. At some point Jenna got hold of a guitar. Jenna and Depp played a couple of songs around the park campfire, and the drugs began to take hold. Most of the party were sitting around chatting, stargazing and listening to music. The vibe was good, but Depp changed it. In her deposition to the US trial, Rocky Pennington said:

'Amber and Kelly Sue were sitting on a chair together hugging, and Johnny came up and said, "Get your hands off my woman." And it was surprising because it was... very benign, two friends, sitting on the same chair, hanging out. And it was also surprising because Johnny had been hanging out with everybody in a friendly way.'

Heard told the US court how events unfolded from her perspective. She told jurors she was sitting with Kelly Sue 'when the MDMA hit her.' Heard said Kelly Sue 'leaned into me and put her head on my shoulder and kind of grabbed my arm. I took it to be the effects of the drug.'

According to Heard, Depp did not like this. 'As soon as she did this... Johnny gets really activated, he gets really upset... She thought he was making a joke... But he was like, "Hey, man, what are you doing? What do you think you're doing?" And she giggled and leaned into me more. And I knew in my body just instantly that it wasn't a joke.'

Heard continued: 'She's still attached to my arm when he says it again to her, louder. He says, "Hey, man, you think you're touching my fucking girl? You think you're touching my fucking girl? That's my fucking girl." And he gets louder and louder. And she did this thing, half-understanding what was going on. I think she started to cry at this point, but she threw up her hands. And Johnny grabbed her wrist and kind of twisted it and pulled her into him and said, "Do you know how many pounds of pressure it takes to break a human wrist? Huh?" And he held her, and she just looked frozen. And she's crying and she was just denying understanding what was going on.'

Depp remembers things very differently. In 2020 he told the UK court: 'It was not around the campfire where I was playing the guitar. It was at nightfall when we were looking around the place. There was a pool table and there was a pool, and you could climb the ladder to get to it. As the girls were congregating, this Kelly Sue began to touch Ms Heard in ways that were beyond what one would accept as normal affection. They were quite sexual and they were quite aggressive and she was clearly very high... She was putting her hands on Amber and I thought it was an uncomfortable position to put her in.'

Depp decided to come to Heard's aid: 'I removed Miss Kelly Sue's hand from Ms Heard's body and I told her not to do that... first of all, that is my girl; second of all, it is rude and invasive.' Depp says Kelly Sue was 'quite glassy-eyed and she seemed pretty unsure of her surroundings. She seemed very unstable on her feet and I remember saying to her, "If you are going to take this drug, MDMA, you should know if you are able to handle it or not. Do not take it if you cannot handle it".'

Depp says the alleged threat he made to Kelly Sue, by suggesting he knew how many pounds of pressure might be required to break a human wrist, did not happen.

After the altercation, it seems Depp left the group and found Morgan Night. Night picked up the story for the benefit of jurors in the US:

'I was speaking with Mr Depp, just one on one, talking about Hicksville. And Ms Heard came over. She said, "I want to talk to you," and seemed really upset about something... she started yelling at him. And I didn't want to hear it, honestly. It was really triggering because I've been in an emotionally abusive relationship before.'

Night said he left them to it and went back to his quarters. In court, as soon as Night mentioned his own experience of abuse, Amber Heard's lawyer Elaine Bredehoft was on her feet. She strenuously objected to Night offering up anything to do with his personal history. That didn't stop him trying. Each time Night looked like he was going to correlate what he saw with what had happened to him, Bredehoft was on her feet with an objection. But Night was too quick. He was asked if Depp or Heard appeared 'intoxicated'. He told the court they both were. Of Heard he said:

'I think when she was angry at him, it seemed like she was intoxicated, but that's just based on my experience and my own personal trauma dealing with abuse.'

The Virginia judge, Penney Azcarate[1], immediately ordered that Night's mention of abuse should be struck from the record. Azcarate turned to the jurors and told them to disregard this element of Night's testimony, but it had already hit home.

On the face of it, Night didn't have much to say – he was with Depp when an upset Heard came over, took Depp off and started yelling at him. Night essentially saw a couple having a row. This happens all over

---

[1] Pronounced, joyously, Az-ka-RAH-tay.

the world in many millions of non-abusive relationships. The significance of the evidence is that Night found it 'triggering' and related it
to his own (unspecified and unexplored) experience of being abused.
Presenting as an abuse survivor gave his evidence authority, whatever
the judge's instruction.

Malcolm Connolly observed the same row Night says he witnessed.
Connolly told the US court he could 'see Johnny and Amber getting a
bit animated. And they were probably about maybe 25 feet from me. So
I approach... and I've been working with Johnny that long. I don't have
to really say anything. I only have to look at his face... He didn't need to
say a word... So I say in a low voice, "Guys, let's keep this private. Let's
start walking towards the caravan. Let's take this away from here." As
I'm walking ahead... I can hear bickering behind me. Johnny's kind of
talking, low tone, keeping a bit quiet. But Amber's getting a bit more
loud, a bit more narky.'

Connolly got them to their trailer and they went inside, alone.
Heard does not deny starting the argument, but she told the US court
that whilst they were rowing Depp accused Heard of 'lying' about the
real nature of her relationship with Kelly Sue, suggesting that she had
'invited' the woman's sexual advances. Heard says her denials caused
Depp to fly into a rage.

'He started smashing things,' she told the US court. 'He picked up
something on the table and threw it right into the glass cabinet. He hit,
with his hand, a wall sconce. He cleared the tabletop on the little fold-
down, like, kitchen/dining room area in this trailer. I mean, it's a trailer,
so there's only so much you can do. And he's screaming at me.'

Heard then testified for the first time in public about the evidence
which was presented in private during the UK trial:

'I went into the bathroom. And as I came out, he asked me where it
is and how long I've been hiding it. And I was like, "What are you talking about?" And he says, "You know what I'm fucking talking about,
you know what I'm fucking talking about. Be honest with me. Where
are you hiding it?"'

Heard says Depp began to pat her down, then ripped off her dress.
'And he's, like, grabbing my breasts, he's touching my thighs. He rips
my underwear off. And then he proceeds to do a cavity search.'

Depp was apparently looking for his cocaine. Heard told jurors:
'I was wondering how I, somebody who didn't do cocaine and was
against it... Why would I hide his drugs from him?... And he was telling
me, "We're doing... We're going to conduct a cavity search, shall we?"
Like, just shoved his fingers inside me. I just stood there staring at the

stupid light. I didn't know what to... You know, I didn't know what to do. I just stood there while he did that. He twisted his fingers around... I didn't say, like, "Stop or anything," I just...'

As Heard paused, she was taken in a different direction by her attorney. In her witness statement to the UK court, Heard described the trailer as 'trashed', remembering 'a lot of smashed glass.' Heard says Depp 'broke light fixtures and he broke the frosted glass front of a cabinet.'

Depp denies sexually assaulting Amber Heard but admits smashing the light fixture, which he told the UK court he did out of frustration: 'I was very upset at being yet again treated as the... turd in the punch bowl, and that was quite unpleasant. I did not feel that I deserved to be screamed at, demeaned, and treated like garbage for having done something that I felt was right and correct.'

NGN's barrister asked him if he had 'trashed' the trailer. Depp replied, 'No, I did not.'

The next day, Kristina Sexton, Heard's acting coach, came out of her trailer and joined those amongst the visiting party who were tidying up in preparation for their departure. Kelly Sue was among them. According to Sexton's witness statement to the UK proceedings, Depp's behavior was the sole subject of conversation:

'The entire group was discussing it,' she recalled 'and explaining what they had seen. I understood... mainly from Rocky – that Johnny had grabbed [Kelly Sue] and threatened her... saying something about breaking her wrist. She confirmed what had happened, saying "yeah, he grabbed my wrist and he hurt me". The impression I got was that the others in the group were shocked by his outburst.'

Sexton remembers one participant to the discussion describing Depp as 'jealous and angry' with another saying 'he lost his mind last night.' Sexton went to Depp and Heard's trailer. She said 'the trailer was trashed; it was a real mess. I remember seeing a lamp hanging off the wall.'

Sexton 'saw and overheard' Depp apologizing to Heard with the words: 'I'm really sorry babe; we can just pay for it and fix it.' Sexton also recalled hearing Depp say to Heard 'that he was sorry he lost control and sorry for what he had done.'

Whilst Sexton and Heard were in the trailer, Depp went outside to talk to security. Sexton says Heard told her that the night before Depp 'was throwing things at her.' Sexton says Heard 'pointed out the things he had thrown on the floor, and said Johnny had caused all this damage, pointing at the lamp hanging off the wall and broken stuff everywhere.'

A hungover Whitney also visited Depp and Heard's trailer that morning.

'It was like a bomb had gone off,' she said in her UK witness statement. 'The place was trashed, with furniture overturned, a lamp broken, and so on. Amber told me that Johnny had done it during a big fight and that he had also ripped off her dress.'

Morgan Night had by this stage been informed by his staff that one of his trailers had been damaged. Night told the US court he was 'extremely worried' about any breakages.

'All those trailers,' he said, 'were like my babies, and the one they were staying in was the only one that was mostly original and restored 1950s style... I was very concerned.'

On his arrival at Depp and Heard's trailer, Night observed 'there was a light sconce by the bathroom in the bedroom that had been broken off the wall and a couple of pieces were on the floor. And they were... basically just broken.'

Asked if anything else in the trailer was damaged, Night said: 'No, everything else looked fine. In fact... if there's anything, what we call, inconsiderate, or unusually large messes, we charge them extra... a $25 an hour cleaning fee. But they did not receive one of those, because everything outside of the light fixture looked fine.'

Night eventually found a vintage replacement light fixture on eBay for $62, which he billed, by agreement, to Nathan Holmes.

So what really happened? Rocky Pennington and Heard both allege seeing Depp assault Kelly Sue. Kristina Sexton heard of it the next day. Kelly Sue herself allegedly confirmed she was 'hurt'. Depp does not deny that he made unwanted physical contact with Kelly Sue.

Heard's evidence of assault in the UK trial was split into two. The non-sexual assault was an allegation that Depp ripped the front of Heard's dress, and in her words 'threw glasses' at her. The judge considered the 'cavity search' allegation in private.

In his ruling, the judge accepted that Depp had caused 'significant' damage to the trailer, largely due to Sexton's evidence. He did not have the benefit of hearing Morgan Night's testimony, which only came to light two years later.

Mr Justice Nicol also ruled that Depp *had* assaulted Amber Heard 'as she described' (ripping her dress and – she 'thinks' – throwing glasses at her). But when it came to the sexual assault – the 'cavity search' – Nicol wrote, 'I do not accept the further allegation made by Ms Heard in relation to this incident.' The confidential annex to the Depp v NGN judgment remains confidential, so we don't know why he chose to reject this particular assault.

We also don't know what effect Morgan Night's evidence had on the jury in Virginia, who rejected all of Heard's assault claims. Night has remained active on Twitter since his appearance at the US trial, describing Heard as a 'liar' and Depp as a 'spoiled alcoholic baby' and a 'perpetrator of emotional abuse'.

Heard maintains Night was never even there.

EVIDENCE AND MEMORY

In court, a judge or juror is required to accurately remember the possibly unreliable testimony they hear under oath, and apply the memory of what they heard (or think they heard) to the weighty decisions they are required to make. In the US, the jury in Depp v Heard listened to more than a hundred hours of witness testimony. They were allowed to take notes, but they weren't allowed access to transcripts. In coming to their conclusions, they were reliant on their own memories of the witness evidence.

In the UK, the judge was able to ask questions of the witnesses himself and, whilst preparing his judgment, was able to review the transcripts. In UK courts which sit without a jury, very little consideration is nowadays given to the 'demeanor' of a witness, because (rightly or wrongly) it is generally considered a poor guide as to whether or not they are telling the truth. A widely respected authority on this subject in the UK is Lord Justice Leggatt, who in 2018, wrote:

'Rather than attempting to assess whether testimony is truthful from the manner in which it is given, the only objective and reliable approach is to focus on the content of the testimony and to consider whether it is consistent with other evidence... and with known or probable facts[1].'

Yet a witness's 'performance' (a combination of what they say and the way they say it) under cross-examination certainly is a factor to be considered, especially in relation to existing documentary evidence. A regularly cited Court of Appeal ruling from the UK declares:

'The atmosphere of the courtroom cannot... be recreated by reference to documents (including transcripts of evidence).' A trial 'is not a dress rehearsal. It is the first and last night of the show.'

There is a tension, exacerbated by COVID and the growth of remote hearings, between the understandable human desire to see a witness giving evidence, and a growing body of scientific research, which suggests neither a judge nor a jury (nor any other competent human being) can smell a wrong-un, even if they think they can.

A 1994 study conducted by the University of Virginia concluded that people are bad lie detectors, and their ability to spot a lie does not improve with practice. To demonstrate this, the authors of the study

---

[1]   Though in the same breath Leggatt also states it is 'impossible, and perhaps undesirable, to ignore altogether the impression created by the demeanor of a witness giving evidence.'

conducted experiments involving students and federal law enforce-
ment officers 'who had worked for years at jobs that routinely involved
attempts to detect deceit.' They found the officers 'were no more accurate than the students at discriminating truths from lies – they only
thought they were.'

For those studying *this* case, it has been incredibly useful to hear
the direct testimony of both Johnny Depp and Amber Heard, extracted
on oath over several days in court on both sides of the Atlantic. There's
nothing like a first-hand account. The testimony of other primary witnesses has also been vital in building a multi-faceted picture of specific events. Yet relying on peoples' recollections of an event (even if
honestly held) can be problematic. Memory is an unreliable thing.

The first empirical study of memory, conducted in 1885, found it
took an hour for most human adults experiencing something to have
forgotten around 50% of what happened if they are not actively trying to remember it. This experiment was repeated more than a century
later with similar results.

What we remember is dependent on how much attention we are paying at the time, the levels of stress and/or externally introduced chem-
icals in our brains (including alcohol) and our own pre-programmed
biases. According to *The Neuroscience of Memory: Implications for the
Courtroom*, published by the American National Institute of Health in
2013, different people will remember different things about the same
event because each of us use 'our entire existing body of knowledge
and experiences to filter for what we perceive, attend to and use in
memory reconstruction.'

A confidently held, and expressed, recollection of an event may
therefore be false. According to the paper's authors, 'Jurors often place
great weight on how confident an eyewitness is regarding their memory of the event.'

But research into eyewitness testimony or the memory of traumatic
events has shown 'weak or even negative correlations between a person's confidence in the accuracy of a memory and the actual accuracy
of that memory.'

The natural assumption that 'confident, detailed memories are
always accurate and reliable is contrary to research.' In fact, 'the opposite is possible.' Although confidently held memories *can* be reliable,
they can also be unreliable. The same study notes that 'real memories
are not always highly confident and detailed.'

The unreliability of confidently held memories, adds the study, is especially prevalent 'in cases involving violence and high levels of stress.'

In 2009, the *Journal for Experimental Psychology* published a study conducted after the 9/11 terrorist attacks in America. If you are older than thirty you are likely to have your own very specific memory of what you were doing when you first heard about what was happening that awful day. For the study, more than three thousand Americans were asked about their recollection of the attacks between one and two weeks after they happened. They were asked again a year later, and then three years later. Recollections had changed in more than a third of the responses after one year and in 43% after three years.

Despite the drop in accuracy of the later memories, *confidence* in their accuracy remained high. *The Neuroscience of Memory* calls this 'an example of a negative relationship between memory confidence and accuracy.'

A further layer of unreliability is added by the way we remember the events we witness. Most people think memory works like a camera phone. We see or hear something, and provided we see or hear it clearly, it is recorded at the time by our brains and locked away with all the relevant metadata attached. Sadly, it doesn't work like that. This has implications not only for the memories described by witnesses in court, but for the memories of jurors watching and listening to the recollections of witnesses in court.

The Neuroscience of Memory explains that the chemical process of memory storage and retrieval is not only imperfect, the very process of retrieving a memory can *change* it:

'Reactivating a memory is thought to put that memory and the potentiated synapses in the memory into a labile[2] state, from which it must re-stabilize in order to persist. Without this process, known as "reconsolidation"... the information is lost. This reconsolidation process is thought to be functionally beneficial as it provides an animal with an opportunity to strengthen or weaken a memory or to update its contents. If the content of a memory is updated at the time of retrieval, memory distortion could occur of which the individual would presumably be entirely unaware.'

---

[2] Liable to change, easily altered.

To paraphrase, the very process of recalling a memory changes our recollection of it *and we are unlikely to be aware that memory has changed.*

It gets even more complicated if we have separate memories of the same event recorded at different times. This could be through witnessing an event first hand, and later watching a news report about it, or being told about it by someone else. *The Neuroscience of Memory* study found that: 'If two different memories exist of an event... or if there are two overlapping memories (e.g. the original memory of the event in question and memories of a subsequent event that shares several of the same components), attempting to retrieve the original event may very well inadvertently and unknowingly draw upon information from the second event.'

Eek. The issue of the unreliability of memory has been picked up by courts on both sides of the Atlantic. Writing in 2013, Lord Justice Leggatt said:

'I do not believe that the legal system has sufficiently absorbed the lessons of a century of psychological research into the nature of memory and the unreliability of eyewitness testimony. One of the most important lessons of such research is that in everyday life we are not aware of the extent to which our own and other people's memories are unreliable and believe our memories to be more faithful than they are. Two common (and related) errors are to suppose: (1) that the stronger and more vivid is our feeling or experience of recollection, the more likely the recollection is to be accurate; and (2) that the more confident another person is in their recollection, the more likely their recollection is to be accurate.'

Echoing *The Neuroscience of Memory* paper (published the same year), Leggatt wrote:

'External information can intrude into a witness's memory, as can his or her own thoughts and beliefs, and both can cause dramatic changes in recollection. Events can come to be recalled as memories which did not happen at all or which happened to someone else (referred to in the literature as a failure of source memory).'

He continued: 'Studies have also shown that memory is particularly vulnerable to interference and alteration when a person is presented with new information or suggestions about an event in circumstances where his or her memory of it is already weak due to the passage of time.'

Leggatt concluded that the very process of preparing a witness for a court battle can change the nature of their memories. He decided the best approach for a judge was 'to place little if any reliance at all on witnesses' recollections of what was said in meetings and conversations' and instead to focus on 'documentary evidence and known or probable facts. This does not mean that oral testimony serves no useful purpose – though its utility is often disproportionate to its length.'

A different judge, Lord Justice Males, wrote that documentary evidence is a court's best bet 'of getting at the truth, not only of what was going on, but also as to the motivation and state of mind of those concerned.' Contemporaneous documents, wrote Males, 'are generally regarded as far more reliable than oral evidence of witnesses, still less their demeanor.'

Males was making a ruling in a commercial case, but both his and Leggatt's comments are generally considered a good rule of thumb for all sides of civil and criminal law.

The inherent shakiness of memory, no matter how confidently it is asserted, nowadays means that, where possible, both judges and jurors are guided towards contemporaneous documentary evidence.

All this makes certain comments in the UK judgment against Johnny Depp look... odd. On at least two occasions, when Mr Justice Nicol was presented with contemporaneous audio evidence which contrasted starkly with what Amber Heard was saying in court, he preferred her testimony. Explaining why in his judgment, Nicol wrote that 'a witness giving evidence in court does so under an oath or affirmation to tell the truth, the whole truth and nothing but the truth,' whereas contemporaneous conversations may have 'had a purpose or purposes different from simply conveying truthful information.' Hmm.

In writing this chapter, I am not attempting to undermine the credibility of every witness's testimony or the cases they present, but I am trying to point out the limitations inherent to all evidence, and the limitations of juries and judges when it comes to interpreting evidence, unreliable or otherwise. No system is perfect, and when a system has flaws, it will lead to errors.

THE PLANE KICK

In May 2014, Amber Heard was with James Franco in New York filming *The Adderall Diaries*, a movie about misremembered abuse and murder. Adderall is the brand name of a legal amphetamine used in the US to treat ADHD and narcolepsy. It is regularly taken illicitly. Heard and Franco had known each other since working together in 2008 on the Seth Rogen movie, *Pineapple Express*.

Johnny Depp was not happy about Heard doing *The Adderall Diaries*. He was particularly surprised she would be keen to work with James Franco again after *Pineapple Express*. Heard had apparently reported to Depp that whilst working on that film she found Franco 'creepy' and 'rapey'. When Heard told Depp she would be filming a sex scene with Franco, he hit the roof. Heard told the US court:

'He was yelling at me about, "How could you?"... he kept saying, "How could you tell me this? How could you just tell me this?" And it was like I had told him I was having an affair or something.'

Heard says Depp eventually hung up on her, 'screaming'.

Depp was in Boston at the time, filming *Black Mass*, a movie about the mob boss, James 'Whitey' Bulger. Before the row, the couple had planned to charter a private jet which would take Heard from New York to Boston, pick up Depp and then fly them both back to Los Angeles for Lily-Rose's 15th birthday.

After the argument, Heard did not have any direct contact with Depp, but she spoke to his assistants and was assured the plan was still on. The following day Heard was informed the plane was on its way. She told the court she was 'nervous', but figured 'he sent the plane, so... he's not that mad at me. He's over it. We're moving on. He's sobered up.'

On 24 May, Heard took the chartered private flight from New York to Boston. She waited inside the aircraft for Depp and his entourage to join her. Eventually, Depp's SUV pulled up, but nothing happened. Heard told the US court the SUV sat on the tarmac, 'for a very long time. He knows I'm on the plane waiting for him. So I kind of started to anticipate that things weren't as I hoped.'

The waiting continued. In her witness statement to the UK trial, Heard said she knew the delay was due to Depp taking drugs:

'A long time went by – maybe an hour or more – and eventually Johnny got out. I saw immediately from his body language that he was stoned. I had been with him long enough to know what this was. He got on the plane and his eyes were black, he had clicked into another space.'

According to Heard, when Depp climbed aboard, he didn't say anything to her. He just stared.

Once Depp was in his seat, the plane taxied to the runway and took off. Depp and Heard were at the back of the cabin. One of Depp's assistants, Stephen Deuters, and his head of security, Jerry Judge, were sitting towards the front. Depp's favorite movie sound tech, Keenan Wyatt, was also on the plane, cadging a lift back to LA.

Heard says that at some point in the journey, Depp began to harangue her about the Franco sex scene, asking repeatedly if there's 'something' Heard had to tell him. Heard found it a grim experience:

'I already know that he's drunk. I already know he's using. He reeks of weed and alcohol. I mean, his breath smelled so bad, and I could anticipate that there was a no-win situation here. There was no me talking myself out of this or talking him down.'

Heard said she remained polite, but saw Depp was 'mad and drunk and high on drugs' and beginning to ramp up. She told the court:

'He went from, "Do you have something to tell me?" to "You want to tell me how much you liked it? Tell me, did he slip a tongue?" It got worse and worse.'

Depp apparently became more explicit. 'He was saying really disgusting things about my body,' Heard told the court. 'About how I liked it, how I responded. And then he started just straight up taunting me... He called me a go-getter. He called me a slut.'

In her witness statement to the UK court, Heard wrote, 'He kept referring to my "pussy", asking me if I was wet.'

By this stage, Heard said she was squirming with embarrassment, 'because he was speaking to me in front of people in this way, asking me if I liked it and if I was wet.'

Depp allegedly believed Heard's failure to look at him while he interrogated her was 'proof' that she was 'asking for it.'

Eventually, Heard felt she had taken enough. 'I remember getting up so slowly. I didn't want to aggravate him. I didn't want to give him any excuse to pounce on. I didn't want to upset him. I didn't want him to flip a switch and get worse.'

Heard moved towards the front of the plane. Depp apparently started 'throwing things' at her, 'ice cubes, utensils... talking about what an embarrassment I am.'

Then he came to sit next to her. She moved again. Heard said every time she moved seats, Depp came to sit closer to her. She tried to ignore

him, but then 'he slaps my face. And his friend [Wyatt?] is in our proximity. And it didn't hurt me. It didn't hurt my face. I just felt embarrassed that he'd do that to me in front of people. It was the first time
that anything like that had happened in front of somebody.'

Heard decided to move again. 'As I get up, he kind of kicks the swiv-
el chair into my hip... and he asked me, "What? What are you gonna do
about it?"'

Heard said she just stared at him, wanting 'to get through to him...
It felt like there was a blackness in his eyes. I wanted to look at him. I
wanted him to see me.'

Heard said she dropped her gaze and began to walk away from
Depp. At that point, he kicked her.

'My back is turned to him, and I feel this boot in my back. He just
kicked me in the back. I fell to the floor and caught myself on the floor
and I just felt like I was looking at the floor of the plane for what felt like
a long time. I thought to myself, "... did he just kick me?"'

Heard alleged that despite the violence, 'No one said anything. No
one did anything. It was like you could hear a pin drop on that plane.
You could feel the tension, but no one did anything. And I just remember feeling so embarrassed. I felt so embarrassed that he could kick me
to the ground in front of people, and more embarrassing I didn't know
what to do about it. I got up and I just... I walked to the front of the
plane. I sat down and I just looked out of the window.'

According to Heard, Depp's head of security Jerry Judge quietly
asked if she was okay. Later in the flight Heard composed herself and
decided to make an audio recording of Depp's behavior, figuring that
the next day he would have no knowledge of the state he was in. Various
clips of the recording were played a couple of times in the 2020 trial
and again in 2022. On both occasions we hear the roaring background
noise of a plane in flight and a man's voice howling. Depp agreed it was
him[1] making the noise. He sounds completely off his box.

In Depp's witness statement to the UK trial, he said: 'I remember
the flight from Boston to Los Angeles in detail.' Of the argument, he
said: 'I was drawing art sketches in my notebook, as I like to do when
traveling, when Ms Heard began to harangue me. I cannot remember
exactly what she was saying but it was the usual abusive stuff. Ms

---

[1]   Despite accepting it is his voice we hear howling on the tape, Depp refused to accept it was
recorded on the Boston/LA flight. This possibility was pursued by his legal team in the UK, but
by the time it got to the US, Depp's legal team did not contest that it was recorded on the flight
in question.

Heard progressed into a continuous verbal barrage with which I did not engage and instead continued sketching.'

As to whether or not he kicked Amber Heard, Depp wrote: 'When Ms Heard stood up at some stage during the flight, I stretched my leg out to tap her playfully on the bottom with my foot to non-verbally communicate something along the lines of "*hey, c'mon let's get past this*" in an attempt to make light of the argument and to try to defuse the situation, but I do not believe I was able to reach her. Ms Heard saw my attempt, however, and immediately took great offense at this act.'

When cross-examined in court, Depp contradicted his bold claim that he remembered the flight 'in detail', instead telling the court he was afraid he did 'not specifically remember' the incident. He added, 'I do not recall that I had been drinking. I do not recall that I had been taking cocaine.'

Depp confirmed that at the time he was addicted to Roxicodone (a prescribed opiate), and if Amber Heard thought he was the worse for wear, it was probably down to that. Heard could, Depp told the court, be quite 'judgmental'.

NGN's barrister, Sasha Wass, brought up Depp's jealousy of James Franco.

SW: James Franco was a subject that you felt quite strongly about, did you not, you have explained that to us already?
JD: I was. I suspected that Ms Heard was having an affair with Mr Franco.
SW: Right.
JD: And it has since been confirmed that she was.
SW: She was not having an affair with Mr Franco at this time, was she?
JD: I believe that she was.
SW: You believed that she was...
JD: I have been told that she was.

In court, Depp refused to accept he was 'screaming obscenities' at Heard on the plane, and refused to accept he would do so with his 'two assistants... my chief of security and two pilots and a stewardess' all in potential earshot.

Wass put it to him directly: 'When I say obscenities, you were talking about her getting fucked with James Franco, and you were talking about how she liked getting fucked on the set, and you were making vulgar references to her genitals?'

Depp replied: 'That is quite a stretch of her imagination.'

During the London trial, Stephen Deuters, one of Depp's assistants, was asked to give evidence about what he saw.

Deuters told the court Depp was neither drunk nor high, but quietly sketching away in his notebook, 'almost immovable, focused... very quiet.' Deuters put this down to opiate consumption. When Deuters was asked about Depp allegedly 'screaming obscenities', he said he could not recollect any screaming or obscenities.

Deuters was shown a text which Depp had sent to the actor Paul Bettany six days after the flight. In the text, Depp told Bettany:

'I'm going to properly stop the booze thing, darling. Drank all night before I picked Amber up to fly to LA this past Sunday... Ugly, mate... No food for days... Powders... Half a bottle of Whiskey, a thousand red bull and vodkas, pills, 2 bottles of Champers on plane and what do you get...??? An angry, aggro Injun in a fuckin' blackout, screaming obscenities and insulting any fuck who got near... I'm done. I am admittedly too fucked in the head to spray my rage at the one I love... For little reason, as well I'm too old to be that guy... But, pills are fine!!!.'

Wass asked Deuters: 'Does that accord with the recollection of this quiet man sketching on his notebook?'

Deuters replied that he supposed it did not. When it came to the alleged kick, Deuters again had a very different take to Amber Heard. In his witness statement to the UK court, Deuters wrote:

'At some point, Ms Heard stood up and when her left side was towards Mr Depp, Mr Depp made a playful attempt to tap her on the bottom with his shoe. From where I was sitting, I do not believe that Mr Depp made contact with Ms Heard.'

Deuters continued: 'Ms Heard took great offense at what was clearly a harmless gesture and increased her abuse of Mr Depp in an extremely unpleasant manner. By this time I had taken off my headphones and I could hear Ms Heard shouting at Mr Depp. I cannot recall the specifics of the abuse but I do remember her making out that the attempted tap was a significant issue.'

In court, Wass asked: 'Did you see any contact between Ms Heard's back and Mr Depp's foot?'

Deuters recalled seeing 'a raised foot or a raised leg', but declined to agree it had made contact with Heard at all.

Johnny Depp denies being verbally abusive, or slapping or kicking Heard. In fact, he told the court, it was Heard who was being abusive to him: 'berating me, screaming at me and whatnot.' Depp claimed it was Heard who began to get physical, and when she did, he 'grabbed a pillow' and retreated to the plane's bathroom to go to sleep.

When Depp was shown the text he sent to Paul Bettany, he (eventually) conceded it was 'very likely' that either before or during the flight he had taken 'pills, alcohol, cocaine, marijuana... Roxicodone as well.' He also agreed that on the flight he had some sort of 'blackout', but it wasn't a *total* blackout as he did have 'some memories' of the flight.

When pressed, Depp told the court: 'I might have said something ugly to her. I might have verbally insulted her or made some comment.' He also said: 'I may have done things that I have no memory of, but Mr Deuters was there, Mr Judge was there, who would never have let anything happen to Amber.'

Deuters' recollection of events is backed up by Keenan Wyatt, who gave evidence in Virginia. Wyatt says that from his seat he could see Depp and Heard very clearly, though this is contradicted by a sketch Stephen Deuters submitted in evidence to the UK court. It shows the full layout of the cabin with Wyatt sitting in a forward-facing seat.

Wyatt told the US court that over the course of the flight, Johnny *was* drinking, but he did not seem intoxicated and was not violent in any way towards Heard. According to Wyatt, when Depp's party got on the plane, Heard was 'giving Johnny the cold shoulder.' Wyatt says he approached Heard to remind her how much Johnny cared for her. Heard 'started yelling' at Wyatt, allegedly shouting 'How dare you talk to me? Get away from me.'

When the flight landed, Heard got off the plane first. She wrote in her witness statement that she 'went to a hotel[2] and called my friends.' Heard asked them to join her at the hotel, as part of her 'coping strategy'. Depp was taken to Sweetzer.

During his cross-examination in the UK, Stephen Deuters was shown a series of texts he sent to Amber Heard soon after she had disembarked.

'He's up,' Deuters texted from the plane. 'In the bathroom. Moving slowly. Will [let] you know when on route and how he is in the car... He's in some pain, as you might guess...'

Deuters was asked by Sasha Wass why Depp might be in pain. At first he speculated that Depp might be 'hungover' but then said Depp's opiate use would affect his stomach.

Wass asked for clarification, a little sarcastically: 'You thought he had tummy ache, did you?'

---

[2]   The hotel was the Chateau Marmont on Sunset Boulevard. For more about what happened here see the *Kate James Incoming* chapter.

Deuters could not say 'specifically'.

The court was taken to a later text update sent by Deuters to Heard: 'We're on our way to 80 [Sweetzer Avenue]... He's been sick. We're gonna get him straight to bed.'

'Tummy ache?' wondered Wass.

Deuters could not say.

'Do you think,' asked Wass, 'having seen what he said he had drunk and imbibed by way of controlled drugs, he might have just overdone it, and that is what made him ill?'

Deuters conceded it was a possibility.

Depp's contemporaneous admission to Paul Bettany that he was 'in a fuckin' blackout' is corroborated by a message from Deuters, who was with Depp overnight at Sweetzer and spoke to him the next day. Deuters subsequently texted Heard to tell her, 'He's much better. Clearer. He doesn't remember much, but we took him thru all that happened.'

Deuters told Heard: 'He's sorry. Very sorry. And just wants to get better... He's teary. He doesn't want to be a fuck-up any more – his words... He's gone back to sleep for a bit.'

A later text stated: 'He's incredibly apologetic and knows that he has done wrong. He wants to get better now. He's been very explicit about that this morning... Feel like we're at a critical juncture.'

Heard replied to Deuters: 'I'm sad he doesn't have a better way to really know the severity of his actions yesterday. Unfortunately for me, I remember in full detail everything that happened.'

Seconds later, Deuters responded: 'He was appalled. When I told him he kicked you, he cried... It was disgusting. And he knows it.'

The same day, Depp sent Heard a text. In it he said: 'Once again, I find myself in a place of shame and regret. Of course I am sorry. I really don't know why or what happened. But I will never do it again. I want to get better for you. And for me. I must. My illness somehow crept up and grabbed me. I can't do it again. I can't live like that again. And I know you can't either. I must get better. And I will. For us both. I love you. Again I am so sorry. So sorry.'

Both Depp and Deuters claim their texts were an attempt to 'placate' an unreasonable and angry Heard. Depp told the court: 'You have to condition yourself to use words that she finds pleasing as opposed to something that will set her off, so there is a great deal of placation that was always going on, a great deal of it. But also it could be that I could be apologizing for something that I said to her if things did get heated and we exchanged foul words.'

In his witness statement, Stephen Deuters suggested that using the words 'he kicked you' did not mean what they expressly stated, but were in fact part of an attempt to 'engage' with Heard 'on her own terms and simply apologize for what she was alleging had happened.'

Despite a huge legal fight, the texts between Amber Heard and Stephen Deuters were not allowed to be put into evidence in the US trial. The judge took the view they were inadmissible hearsay[3]. The texts *were* allowed into evidence by the judge in the UK. He concluded that on the Boston to LA plane flight, Depp had kicked Heard in the back.

---

[3]   In lay terms, hearsay is second hand information. In legal terms it is an oral or written statement of evidence made outside of court proceedings. If that statement is relied on 'to prove the truth of a matter' or a 'fact asserted', it can be fought over by legal teams who will seek to persuade a judge it should or shouldn't be allowed into evidence.

TWIST IN MY SOBRIETY

Although he has not formally admitted to being an alcoholic, Depp has a sobriety coach. During the early stages of his relationship with Amber Heard he was not drinking. Depp told the US court this was due to 'concern over the numbers, as they call it, about my liver.'

Alcohol, drunk to excess, causes liver problems. It also induces memory loss and blackouts.

When asked during the US trial if he drank whiskey in the mornings, Depp responded (to laughter): 'Isn't happy hour anytime?'

Depp is also a regular user of marijuana. He has, by his own admission, abused cocaine and MDMA and was, at one stage, addicted to prescription medicine. In May 2014, his addiction doctor, David Kipper, noted Depp had a 'long history of self-medicating behaviors involving multiple substances of abuse. These include alcohol, opiates, benzodiazepines and stimulants.' Kipper diagnosed Depp with 'Primary dopamine imbalance, ADHD, bipolar one' and 'depression' with additional 'insomnia' and 'chronic substance abuse disorder'. In August 2014, Kipper wrote that Depp 'romanticizes the entire drug culture, and has no accountability for his behaviors.'

Depp got addicted to Roxicodone after being treated for dental pain. He got off it using clonidine, Robaxin, Bentyl and anxiolytics. Kipper also treated him for benzodiazepine addiction, but Depp reacted badly to the treatment and was put back on the benzos. At various times Depp also took other prescription drugs including lithium, Seroquel, Adderall, Xanax, Ambien, Lexapro, Klonopin, Lamictal, Dexilant, Toradol, Augmentin and Glucophage. These drugs were not taken over the same period, and many do not have psychoactive effects, but it's quite a list. In the US trial, Depp's former business manager, Joel Mandel, told the court at one point Depp was spending 'thousands' of dollars a month on prescription drugs – though that sum would likely include the drugs being prescribed for Heard.

Of his psychoactive drug use (including alcohol), Depp admitted to the UK court 'there were blackouts, for sure, but in any blackout there are snippets of memory, and in recalling those memories, you see images that you saw and images that you went through, but you do not see the whole picture.'

Depp claimed these 'images' and 'snippets' were enough to remember his behavior had never been violent.

A psychologist Dr Kipper assigned to Amber Heard, Dr Connell Cowan, had a couples session with Heard and Depp together. Cowan described Depp as 'poorly controlled'. Cowan's notes were later mentioned in the US trial by an expert witness for Amber Heard called Dr Hughes[1]. Hughes told the court Cowan was 'concerned' about Depp's poor self-control 'because in those moments when he was not controlled... he could accidentally seriously hurt Ms Heard.'

In both courts, Depp attempted to be circumspect about the extent of his illegal drug and alcohol use, but the evidence for it was overwhelming. At the end of the UK trial Depp's own barrister, David Sherborne, turned his client's admissions into a virtue, praising Depp for being 'candid'. By contrast, said Sherborne, Amber Heard 'has deliberately sought to hide or play down her misuse of drink and illegal drugs. For example, suggesting not for the first time that the medical notes made of her reported history were wrong.'

Those medical notes were written by a nurse hired by Dr Kipper called Erin Boerum. Boerum summarizes: 'Client admits to history of anxiety, eating disorder, ADHD, bipolar disorder, co-dependence issues and occasional insomnia,' adding that Heard reports a 'history of substance abuse, including an addiction to cocaine and liquor. Client reports abstaining from cocaine for a couple of years but was unable to report exact dates.'

Heard said she had not reported this to Erin Boerum. Boerum, she believed, was recording incorrect information, probably fed to her by Dr Kipper. Heard told the UK court: 'I have never had an eating disorder. I have never been diagnosed with bipolar. I have never had a history of substance abuse or a problem with liquor, to be honest. I do report and have reported that I have a family history of that, as both my parents are alcoholics and addicts... The part she got right is I did have some anxiety and insomnia.'

The discrepancy was never satisfactorily resolved. Depp claimed that whilst he was trying to stay clean in the early days of their relationship, Heard 'continued to drink and take amphetamines, MDMA, magic mushrooms and other drugs' in front of him. It's true that in court, Heard seemed keen to divert attention away from her drug and alcohol use, but no one has suggested she got anywhere close to Depp's level of consumption. By his own admission, Depp has had to detox from drugs and/or alcohol on at least three occasions. Heard has not. Nonetheless, Depp's house manager, Kevin Murphy, calculated Heard was on two bottles of red wine a night, and her former personal

---

[1] For more on Dr Hughes, see the *Psych Out* chapter.

assistant, Kate James, said Heard drank 'vast quantities' of red wine on an almost nightly basis, often in front of Depp, when he was trying to stay sober.

Heard only admits to using mushrooms and MDMA on extremely limited occasions. She has denied using cocaine at any time during her relationship with Depp, but Depp told the UK court Heard prepared the drug for him 'many times' – describing how Heard would 'chop the cocaine with the razor blade into lines' then 'take the cocaine on her finger and rub it on her gums.'

In terms of prescription drugs, we know Heard has taken Ambien, Seroquel, Xanax, propranolol and Neurontin. Kate James testified to Heard's use of Accutane and Provigil throughout the time she worked for her, but Heard claims a lot of the drugs she was prescribed by Dr Kipper were part of Depp's idea to keep her compliant and anaesthetised. This might seem like paranoia, were it not for a revealing text Depp sent in July 2016 to Nurse Erin Boerum.

'I was the CLIENT, ultimately,' texted Depp. 'I was the one who asked for you to CALM HER DOWN AND KEEP HER UNDER CONTROL!!! Not because she was kicking DRUGS!!! It was to take her pressure away from me!!! Same reason that I hired her shrink... Who, by the way, only made her worse!!!'

It is impossible to say how loaded (if at all) any party was at any time during the events described in this book, but it is worth bearing in mind that both have used drugs which create altered mental states – Depp, by his own admission to an extreme degree – and both had ready access to legal and illegal drugs if they wanted them.

AUSTRALIA

There are three occasions in 2015 when things got completely out of control. Let's start with the big one – Australia.

In February 2015, Johnny Depp had a fair bit going on. During the first part of the month, he married Amber Heard, then he upped sticks to Australia's Gold Coast to film the fifth instalment of the *Pirates* franchise.

Before his wedding, those around Depp were urging him to get a pre-nuptial agreement sorted and signed in good time. This became a source of rancor, complicated by various miscommunications. Depp's team were understandably keen to ensure Depp could keep his wealth and assets out of Heard's reach if things turned sour. Depp himself seemed to vacillate between understanding the importance of a pre-nup to protect his children, and a slightly deranged idea (at least according to Heard) that the only way out of any forthcoming marriage was 'death'.

Shortly before the wedding, Heard was presented with a pre-nup, but it was never signed. Depp told the US court: 'There always seemed to be some reason' why Heard wouldn't put her signature on the paper, and when they did discuss it, 'it became an issue that would turn into a... springboard into unpleasantness.'

For her part, Heard told the UK court that she was perfectly happy to sign a pre-nup and discussed it with Depp's sister Christi Dembrowski (by then his personal manager) and a lawyer Heard hired. Heard said her lawyer worked on a draft of the pre-nup 'and sent it to Johnny's team through Christi,' whereupon it was 'left on Johnny's team's desk. No one did anything and someone forgot about it.'

When Depp's barrister expressed incredulity that Depp's team could just forget about the pre-nup, Heard clarified:

'I do not presume it was overlooked since a considerable amount of people in his life seem to be concerned about it, but I did hire the lawyer, we drafted it, we sent it, and I did everything I could to make sure that we would be able to get married.'

The pre-nup remained unsigned. Despite the ongoing volatility between the two and the considerable misgivings of those around Depp, the wedding went ahead with a private ceremony on 3 February at Depp's mother's house in West Hollywood. The couple then flew to the Bahamas for another ceremony and party on Depp's island. This event was notable for two things – the first being Heard's draft itinerary for the bridal group, which included the phrase: 'dance party and drugs and music'. The second was a recollection by Heard's friend, iO Tillett-Wright, who told lawyers for both parties that one of Depp's first statements as a married man was: 'Now I can punch her in the face and nobody can do anything about it.'

Nuptials over, it was time to fly to Australia to focus on *Pirates*. For the duration of the Gold Coast shoot, Depp would be staying in a secluded, ten-bedroom mansion on a 44-acre estate known as Diamond Head. His entourage – Nathan Holmes, Stephen Deuters, Dr Kipper, Nurse Debbie, Jerry Judge and Malcolm Connolly – were staying off-site, the latter a forty minute drive away in a town called Broadbeach. Diamond Head was, at the time, owned by the Australian motor-racing legend Mick Doohan[1]. It sits on a wide sweep of the Pimpana River with all the facilities you would expect from a luxury private compound – private security (remarkably absent from the events in this story), a tennis court, helipad, infinity pool, boat-ramp, go-kart track and a stand-alone covered pavilion with an outdoor bar and grill, dedicated to entertaining guests.

By the time he arrived in Australia, Depp had apparently been sober for a substantial period, telling those around him he had not had a drink for at least a year (something he later agreed in court couldn't be true[2]). Despite Depp's professed sobriety, Diamond Head was not a dry house. The bars had been stocked with thousands of pounds worth of wines and spirits, on the instruction of Depp's team.

Depp had been at Diamond Head about a month before his new wife flew out to join him. In the run up to Heard's visit, Depp had successfully been supplied with marijuana, but he was keen to source some cocaine and MDMA through his assistant, Nathan Holmes. During cross-examination in London in 2020, Depp said the cocaine was for him, but the MDMA was for Heard, who had asked him to find some for her in advance of her visit.

Depp was living the dream. He was rich, he was successful, he had just got married to one of the world's most beautiful women, he had assistants working to his every beck and call, and he had the lead role in one of the biggest movies on the planet.

---

[1] Doohan sold it in 2022 for a reported $40m.

[2] Because the Boston/LA plane flight had happened less than a year previously.

But Depp was not happy. Aside from his problems with Heard, there was what we might call a 'career trajectory issue'. The first *Pirates* film came out in 2003. Twelve years later he was making the fifth instalment of the same franchise. As one wag noted at the time, even Steve Guttenberg stopped at *Police Academy 4*. Things were looking a little shaky, and Depp knew it. On 6 March he sent a text to his sister Christi and Stephen Deuters railing at 'having whored for all these fucking wasted piece of shit nothing years on characters that I so ignorantly started to think of as my legacy.' Harking back to 2015 during the UK trial, he told the court that at the time he was 'unhappy' with his relationship, with his life and 'with the entire business of making films.'

It's not clear what Heard knew about Depp's mood on her arrival to Australia in March 2015, but she seems to have become aware of it pretty quickly. Her witness statement to the UK trial echoes the premise of a horror movie:

'I realized I was trapped... in a remote house, at least twenty minutes from help,' she wrote, 'isolated with a violent person suffering from manic depression, bipolar disorder and a pattern of repeated, drug-induced psychosis and violence.'

Heard memorably (but inaccurately, according to the UK judge) described what happened next as a 'three-day hostage situation.' Let's try to pick it apart.

Heard said she arrived at the property early on the morning of Friday 6 March and went up to the master bedroom to find Depp. She told the US court she was 'so excited to see him', but on finding him, she clocked he had become 'so skinny. He'd lost a ton of weight.' Heard says this signalled a problem. She knew 'something was up.'

Depp was required on set that day. Heard told the court: 'He kind of quickly kissed me and... we had some interaction. It was brief. He was leaving to go work.'

So far, so good.

That evening, Depp returned. The house chef had made dinner. During the UK trial, Heard said she 'wanted to connect' with Depp, but 'he just seemed to want to drink.'

Heard alleges that during dinner, Depp pulled out a bag of MDMA pills and suggested they both take some.

In her witness statement to the UK court, Heard said: 'I guess I had some sort of negative reaction to that. He said I was being "the moral police" and it was "not on the list" (of drugs we had agreed he was not supposed to take). I said something to him about losing weight. He said something to me about being "mouthy". He pushed me into the fridge and slapped me. He grabbed a bottle of wine or booze and took a swig from it in front of me and, at some point, he took a handful of ecstasy.' Heard later estimated Depp swallowed eight to ten pills.

Depp denies taking any drugs. Certainly not eight to ten ecstasy pills. During the US trial he said that if he had taken that much MDMA he'd be 'dead... probably rather quickly.'

Depp believes the source of their argument was primarily Heard's outrage at having to discuss a post-nuptial agreement with a lawyer hired by Depp who Heard described as 'rude and dismissive'. Heard was apparently convinced that the agreement she was being asked to sign was so unfair it could not have been sanctioned by Depp. Heard raised this with Depp's lawyer who allegedly sneered at Heard, telling her Depp knew 'everything' about it.

Depp believes Heard saw this as a conspiratorial affront. He told the US court:

'She kept saying, "I'm not even in your will. I'm not even in your will"... she could not let go of the [idea] that I was in on this post-nup agreement, and that I was trying to trick her into essentially getting nothing if something were to happen.'

Depp said that during their argument, Heard became 'irate' and 'possessed', calling him an 'ass-kisser to lawyers, or a pussy that didn't fight for her or stand up for her.' Depp says he tried to 'calm' Heard down, telling her he was 'not out to screw her over, or put her in a position that was uncomfortable.'

Unfortunately, this didn't work, and Depp told the court their argument 'escalated, and turned into madness, chaos, violence.'

Depp said that as the argument escalated he decided to remove himself from the situation 'as I normally would', but Heard wasn't having it. He claims it became relentless:

'The house that they had rented for me in Australia was quite a large place. It was a bit of a labyrinth... I think that I ended up locking myself in about at least nine bedrooms [and/or] bathrooms that day as she was banging on the doors, and screaming obscenities, and wanting to have a physical altercation.'

Depp remembers asking Heard to stop fighting 'multiple times... one of those times for at least 45 minutes when I was sitting on the floor, simply begging her to leave me alone. But she just wouldn't stop. The insults continued and she tried to hurt me as badly as she could, each time more and more.'

Heard maintains the argument had nothing to do with her feelings about a post-nup, and she was the one who was being harassed. Upset and angry at Depp's drinking and his decision to neck a load of MDMA pills, she 'stomped off to go to the upstairs bedroom.'

Heard says Depp pursued her. 'He got in front of me and wouldn't let me pass... I tried to push past him, but he pushed me to the ground. I fell like a rag doll.'

Heard got up from the floor, and here her recollections differ slightly. In the UK she said Depp challenged her to a fight and 'slapped me in the face.' In Virginia, she told jurors 'he shoves me up against the fridge. He has me by the throat... He started bashing me against the wall next to the fridge. And, at some point... I don't know if he had let go of my neck or loosened the grip, but I remember slapping him across the face, screaming at him.'

In both accounts Heard describes eventually getting away from Depp, going upstairs to a bedroom, where she locked the door and 'barricaded' herself in the room with furniture, eventually going to sleep.

It is possible, though not definite, that a cigarette burn to Depp's right cheek (evidenced in later hospital photographs) was sustained at some stage on this first evening. It may be it happened the following night. Depp claims Heard stubbed the cigarette out on his face. Heard claimed she watched him do it to himself in front of her.

The next day, Saturday 7 March, Heard says she came downstairs to find Depp fully clothed and awake. He told Heard he had not slept. Heard told the court she tried to get him to eat something.

Unfortunately, the couple soon picked up where they left off – arguing like hell. Depp's jealousy apparently resurfaced. Heard told the US court: 'He thought I was working with Billy Bob Thornton on the movie I just shot, but I had already worked with him a year earlier.'

The movie Heard had just finished was *The Danish Girl*, starring Eddie Redmayne. Heard said she reassured Depp that Redmayne was 'lovely, a gentleman.' According to Heard, Depp changed tack and brought up her delicate relationship with Christi.

'He was accusing me of being mean to his sister,' she said.

Heard recalled her efforts to deflect Depp's accusations: 'I tried to defend myself, explaining why [Christi] and I had kind of become cold to one another. I don't know how else to describe it because we never had any sort of direct interaction that was negative. We never had any sort of confrontation or anything. But I did my best to explain to him what I could answer to that accusation.'

Heard says she then watched Depp make a series of incoherent phone calls to America. She did not know who was on the other end of the line, but 'he's screaming at them. I got a sense that it was money, that he felt people had been stealing money from him and that the studio had been ripping him off, and that he was calling himself a whore, or he had been whored out.'

Heard says it was at *this* point she mentioned the post-nup, telling Depp that after communicating with Christi, Heard had hired a 'domestic relations attorney' called Michele Mulrooney to work on it. This apparently caused Depp to fly into another rage. He demanded Heard's phone, called Mulrooney and fired her, once more telling Heard the only way out of their relationship 'was death'.

Michele Mulrooney gave evidence via deposition at the Virginia trial, and remembered Depp's call well:

'He was very mean,' she said. 'He called me names.' Asked what names, Mulrooney replied slowly: 'My only exact recollection is that he called me a bitch.'

Mulrooney confirmed Depp then fired her 'on behalf of Amber.' Without prompting, Mulrooney also stated that Depp seemed to be 'under the influence.' When asked why she thought that, Mulrooney replied: 'He was slurring his words and his speech pattern was similar to my children's speech pattern when they were little.'

Mulrooney admitted to feeling 'rattled' by the call. 'I didn't want to be rude and hang up, but I told him I had to... after I realized what was happening.'

It didn't sound like a fun chat. 'It took me very off guard,' said Mulrooney. 'It really shook me up.'

Heard was in no doubt as to what was behind Depp's behavior: 'He needed to come down off the drugs... I had recognized that sort of delusion. I'd recognized that sort of unattached-to-reality rage... I knew already that he just needed to sleep it off, clean up, you know, sober up.'

That afternoon, Depp's staff (including his sobriety team, Dr Kipper and Nurse Debbie Lloyd) visited the compound. They discovered all was not well. At 3.12pm, Depp's assistant, Stephen Deuters, sent a text to Christi saying:

'Hi C. Not sure how much you are aware of right now, but I am at the house with Kipper and Debbie who are speaking with JD and Amber respectively, separately. Obviously, things have not been calmed over the last day or so – apparently he has been making calls to LA but I am not aware of the particulars there as well there has been fighting between the two here – so Kipper is now talking to JD, hoping to get thru to him, and explain to him that "this period" needs to end now before we get into real trouble.'

Within a few hours the situation appeared to be getting under con-trol. At 6.17pm Deuters sent another text to Christi telling her that 'conversations seem to be going well' and that Depp was 'agreeing to all that Kipper is requesting he do in order to turn himself around.' Deuters adds, 'of course, we've heard that before.'

Deuters, Lloyd and Kipper left the house. Depp and Heard were alone once more. Things were about to get several orders of magnitude worse.

THE BOTTLE RAPE

Before we embark on the specific details of the most violent period alleged in Johnny Depp and Amber Heard's relationship, it is important to stress that time and timings over the weekend of 6–8 March 2015 are both elastic and elliptical. By way of example Depp is, or was, certain that almost everything happened on the morning of Sunday 8 March. Heard is equally convinced that her recollection of the evening of Friday 6 March into the morning of Saturday 7 March, as described in the previous chapter, is accurate. Depp seems to have mentally compressed most events into the Sunday morning. The texts from Stephen Deuters and what we know about Heard's arrival at Diamond Head point to a violent row on the evening of Friday 6 March, followed by a further verbal argument on the Saturday morning, followed by the arrival of Kipper et al at some point on the Saturday afternoon and another huge row on Sunday morning.

A clue as to Depp's issues with recalling the exact sequence of events may be read into a text he sent his assistant Nathan Holmes at 9.17pm on the Saturday evening. 'May I be ecstatic again?' he asks. 'Helps...' There could be an innocent explanation to this request, or it could be that Depp was asking Holmes to re-supply him with ecstasy. Depp maintains he did not take cocaine or MDMA for the duration of Heard's visit. Heard is certain that Depp took eight to ten ecstasy tablets on the Friday evening and that on the second night 'he took even more.' She told the UK court she knows this is true because 'he did both in front of me.'

Let's start with Heard's account. On Saturday evening, once the couple had the house to themselves, Heard said she started prepping dinner, and then went back upstairs for an unspecified period of time. Whilst upstairs, she changed into her night-clothes. On her return, Heard says she found Depp at the kitchen bar drinking neat liquor out of two bottles. He was 'belligerent,' she said, and 'throwing things, screaming at me.' Heard says she was called names, including 'The Whore. The Slut. The Fat-Ass.'

Given the seriousness of the allegation Heard made about what happened in Australia, I have used as much as possible of her own words, as told under oath to the US court in Virginia.

First came the insults:

'He started to tell me that everyone had warned him about me and that he wished he had never married me, wished he had never met me, and no one liked me... and then, at some point, I shove him hard to get him off me, and he shoved me back and he said, "Do you want to go, little girl?"'

Again, time is elastic. Heard admits there are gaps in her own recollection, but after hearing Depp tell her no one liked her, Heard said the violence got worse. 'He throws me across the room. I land on a games table. It's like a ping pong table... he gets on top of me on the games table and he's just whacking me in the face, like repetitive.'

Heard told jurors Depp was swigging from a bottle, taunting her.

'He is telling me that I can't control him anymore, and that if I really wanted to try, take it... and he's holding out the bottle. I think, like, maybe the third time or so, I get a hold of it, I pick it up, and I slam it down on the ground, right in between us is a tile floor, a white tile floor. And I smashed the bottle on the floor. And that really set him off... I don't know if he backhanded me or hit me normally. I don't really recall. But I remember it sent me down to the ground. I remember by the time I picked myself off the floor, I stand up, he's got a bottle in his hand, and he threw it at me. It missed, thankfully, but I kind of pulled myself back into the bar area. I don't know how much time passed, but, at some point, he had a broken bottle up against my face, neck area, by my jaw line, and he told me he'd carve up my face... it was terrifying. It wasn't the first time he said that to me. He said that to me on the plane as well. But this time, he was holding a broken bottle to me.'

Heard says she again got herself out of immediate danger, but then Depp started picking bottles and cans from the bar and throwing them at her.

'They're coming at me one after the other... I remember feeling one of them go by my head really fast, I mean, a real velocity. I remember being terrified. I remember I couldn't move. I couldn't go anywhere.'

Depp eventually allegedly ran out of things to throw and moved toward Heard, who told the court, 'that's most likely when we got kind of in this struggle by the bar area, because I remember my feet slipping on the tile as he was slamming me from the wall to the countertops. At one point, he has me up against the wall and he's punching the wall. He had my nightgown and kind of ripped it off my chest. I remember at one point he's teasing me. He's taunting me that he has my breasts in his hands. My nightgown came completely off. It was ripped off me. So I was naked and I'm slipping around on this tile and trying to get my footing. I remember slipping on this tile. The glass is underneath me, and I remember just trying to get my footing. I felt really destabilised and vulnerable. I'm naked. He's flinging me around and at some point, I'm up against the wall and he's screaming at me that he fucking hates me, that I ruined his life... over and over. And he starts punching the wall next to my head, holding me by the neck.'

Heard got free. 'I kind of step back from him. And it's like his energy shifted to the phone. There was a wall-mounted phone on the wall next to where my head was. And he went from punching the wall to, like, realizing there was a phone there, and he picked up the phone and he's screaming. At the top of his lungs screaming: "I fucking hate you. I fucking hate you. You ruined my fucking life." And screaming at the top of his lungs. He picks up the phone and starts bashing the phone against the wall, against the wall where I was just being held.'

Heard says Depp then switched his attention back to her.

'At some point, he's on top of me... screaming the same thing, "I fucking hate you. You ruined my fucking life." I'm on the countertop. He had me by the neck, and it felt like he was on top of me, and I'm looking at his eyes, and I don't see him anymore. I don't see him anymore. It wasn't him. It was black. I've never been so scared in my life. It was black. I couldn't see him. And he was looking at me, and I was trying to get through to him. I was trying to say to him in some way that it was me. I was trying to get through to Johnny, but I couldn't see him. I couldn't see him at all. And my head was bashing against the back of the bar and I couldn't breathe. And I remember trying to get up, and I was slipping on the glass. My feet were slipping. My arms were slipping on the countertop, and I remember just trying to get up so I could breathe so I could tell him he was really hurting me. I didn't think he knew what he was doing. I don't know how... I couldn't breathe. I don't... I couldn't breathe. I couldn't get through to him. I couldn't get up. I couldn't get up.'

Then, according to Heard, Depp began to rape her with a bottle.

'I was bent over backwards on the bar, meaning my chest was up. I was staring at the blue light, and my chest... my back was on the countertop. And I thought he was punching me. I felt he was... I felt this pressure. I felt this pressure... I thought he was punching me. I just saw his arm. I could feel his arm moving. It looked like he was punching me, but I could just feel this pressure... on my pubic bone. And... I don't remember what I said. I just remember being really still, not wanting to move. I remember looking around the room. I remember looking at all the broken bottles, broken glass... not wanting to move, because I didn't know if it was broken. I didn't know if the bottle that he had inside of me was broken. I couldn't feel it. I didn't feel pain. I didn't feel anything. I just didn't want it... I looked around and I saw so much broken glass, but I didn't know if he would know if it was broken or not. And I just remember thinking, "Please, God, please, I hope it's not broken".'

Heard admitted to the court her memory of what happened next was patchy: 'I don't know how I got off the countertop. I just remember being in the bathroom. I remember retching. I remember the sound my voice was making. I remember I lost control of my bladder. I remember just retching. I remember there was blood on the floor. I got up at some point. I don't know how that night ended. I don't remember what happened. I don't remember. I have a memory of him begging me not to leave. I remember going outside the front door. I remember him coming out to the front area, but I don't remember if that was before or after this. I don't remember.'

Heard says as well as bleeding from the vagina, she sustained an injured nose, a split lip, a bruise across her jaw, cuts on her arms and 'sliced up' feet. She told the US court she eventually made it to bed and passed out with the assistance of a double dose of sleeping pills.

Heard's testimony was powerful. I was sitting outside the courtroom in Virginia while she described being raped, watching closely on the live YouTube feed. My concentration was broken as two Depp supporters burst out of court and collapsed onto a nearby bench. They sat for a bit, holding each others' arms, staring straight ahead and breathing hard. I partly knew one of them, and she saw me looking over.

'Just getting some air,' she explained. 'It's a little... *intense* in there.' I nodded. The pair were soon joined by another spectator. She joined the couple on the bench and puffed out her cheeks, taking deep breaths.

When Heard's session in the witness box ended for the day, the public gallery emptied. I watched everyone carefully. A voluble Brummie I had got to know called Sharon caught my eye. Over the heads of the departing spectators she announced: 'And the award for Best Razzie goes to...!'

Away from the main throng I bumped into a grizzled court professional who had been in court for Heard's testimony. He was almost white with shock. 'There's no way the jury are going to find for him after hearing that,' he told me. Later, outside the court building, Liz James, another Depp supporter, reflected on what she'd witnessed. James told me she found Heard 'somewhat convincing' adding 'if what she's saying is true... I've been a jerk to her, for... *ever*. And she didn't deserve that. She's been abused enough.'

WHAT HAPPENED TO JOHNNY'S FINGER?

Gold Coast, Australia, 7 and 8 March 2015

You will be unsurprised to hear that Johnny Depp's account of what happened in Australia differs considerably from Amber Heard's. Originally, he was certain the epic blow-up which led to him losing part of his finger happened between him getting up on the morning of Sunday 8 March ('which I recall was my day off') and security arriving at the house in the early afternoon. There had, according to him, been no bottle rape during the night.

In his witness statement to the UK trial, Depp says he wandered downstairs on the Sunday morning to find an unharmed Amber Heard watching TV, still angry about her conversation with Depp's lawyer. Depp claims he spent that morning 'trying to avoid Ms Heard in the house and retreating from her when we came into contact.' After 'hiding' in various bathrooms for what he described as 'hours' he gave up and began drinking, which is when the bottle-throwing, finger-smashing carnage began.

In the US trial, Depp emphasized to the court that by 8 March 2015 he had been sober 'for many, many months from alcohol and substances, aside from the marijuana.' This stance was undermined by a member of his personal security team, Malcolm Connolly, who during his evidence in Virginia, confirmed Depp had been drinking before Heard got anywhere near Australia. Either way, Depp's argument with Heard the previous evening had put him in a bad place. He described himself as 'a wreck... shaking. And I just didn't understand why all this was happening.'

Depp says to calm himself down, he went behind the bar counter, and picked out a bottle of vodka and a shot glass. He sat at the bar, poured himself 'two or three stiff shots of the vodka' and downed them.

At that moment Heard reappeared.

'And of course,' said Depp, she 'started screaming, "Oh, you're drinking again. The Monster," and all that.'

Depp says Heard grabbed the bottle of vodka 'and then just kind of stood back, and hurled it at me.' The bottle missed Depp by inches and smashed behind him.

Unable to pour himself another drink from that bottle, Depp told the court he again went behind the bar, picked up a larger bottle of vodka (known, because of its glass carrying hook, as a 'handle'), walked back round the counter to his bar stool, poured himself another shot, and drank it.

This set Heard off again, 'flinging insults left, right, and center.' According to Depp, Heard grabbed the bottle he'd just been drinking from, and from a distance of 'around eight feet' threw it at him.

In court, Depp described his exact position as the bottle came towards him. He was sitting on the stool with his right hand on top of the bar. Unable to react in time, the bottle smashed on Depp's right-hand middle finger, somehow slicing off the tip.

'I honestly didn't... I didn't feel the pain at first,' he told the court. 'I felt no pain whatsoever. What I felt was... heat. I felt heat, and I felt as if something were dripping down my hand. And then I looked down and realized that the tip of my finger had been severed. And I was looking directly at my bones sticking out, and the meaty portion of the inside of your finger. And it was... blood was just pouring out.'

A graphic photograph of Depp's severed finger was shown at both the US and UK trials. It can be found, uncensored, with a quick google search. It is a serious-looking injury, and not for the squeamish.

Depp told the court he felt as if he were suffering something akin to a 'nervous breakdown'. At this point in his narrative, Heard disappears.

Apparently left to his own devices, Depp began to write on the walls of the house using the blood dripping from his finger. He knew he wasn't thinking straight. 'Nothing made sense,' he told the court. 'I knew in my mind and in my heart, this is not life. This is not life. No one should have to go through this.'

When the blood coming from his finger began to run dry, Depp found some paint. He dipped his injured finger in the paint and continued to daub phrases around the house, including 'GOOD LUCK AND BE CAREFUL AT TOP,' 'SHE'S LOVES NAKED PHOTOS OF HERSELF. SO MODERN. SO HOT.' Another read: 'STARRING BILLY BOB EASY AMBER.'

Eventually, Depp says he went to 'hide in the bathroom' once more. From here, at exactly 11am, he texted Dr Kipper, telling him:

'She is as full of shit as a Christmas Goose!!! The constant insults, the demeaning, belittling, most heartbreaking spew that is only re-leased from a malicious, evil and vindictive cunt!!!! But, you know what... ?? FAR MORE hurtful than her venomous and degrading end-less "educational" ranting... ??? is her hideous and purposely hurtful tirades and her goddam shocking treatment of the man she was meant to love above all... Here's the real deal, mate... Her obsession with her-self...?? Is far more important... she is SO FUCKIN' AMBITIOUS!!!!

She's so desperate for success and fame... That's probably why I was acquired mate... !! Although she has HAMMERED me with what a sad old man, has been I am... I'm so very sad... I cut the top of my middle finger off... What should I do Except, of course, go to a hospital... I'm so very embarrassed for jumping into anything with her...'

What Depp didn't tell the US court was that immediately after texting Dr Kipper, he texted Nathan Holmes asking for 'more whitey stuff ASAP, brotherman... And the e business!!! Please... I'm in bad bad shape... Say NOTHING TO NOBODY !!!!'

Holmes obligingly responded: 'Okey-dokey.'

Heard says she had no role in Depp losing part of his finger. In the US trial, she described coming to in her bedroom after the violence of the night before. It was around midday on Sunday 8 March. According to her testimony, Heard ventured out onto the landing where she found 'mashed potatoes smeared all over the bedroom door[1].' Heard described 'being really confused at first as to what it was. It had little specks of green in it.' She assumed this was spinach.

Loud music was playing somewhere. Heard made her way towards the main living area. She noticed a brown staining on the walls. It was dried blood. A bird had flown into the house, which Heard felt added a 'surreal' touch. As she reached the open-plan living area Heard saw blue and brown paint had been smeared on the furnishings:

'It was on the walls, on the lampshades, pillowcases of the sofa, the sofa cushions,' she told the court. 'There was blood in the painting studio. My canvases have been covered with what looked like just brown, blue, green, red mess. It was just a mess.'

A painting belonging to the owners had a giant penis daubed on it.

Heard began moving towards the music, which was coming from the bar area. She found Depp in the study next to the bar. She described a disaster zone: 'It was just glass and blood... a broken window... The table was collapsed.'

Heard signalled to Depp that she was present. 'He just looked,' she said. 'He wasn't there anymore... It wasn't Johnny. He was standing at the office desk. He had his hand wrapped in rags... bandana rags. And I

---

[1] Later in her testimony, Heard described finding the raw steak she had left out for dinner the night before. 'It was cut up. And he had ripped my nightgown into pieces, into shreds, and wrapped the meat up, like wrapped the steak pieces up with my nightgown... I continued to find it throughout the rest of the time that I was in the house in Australia, just like pieces of it in the microwave, pieces of it in the produce drawer, in the closet drawer. I mean, just raw meat wrapped up in my nightgown as well as the smeared food on the walls. It was bizarre.' This element of Heard's evidence was not challenged in court.

think he took them down or somehow showed me and he said, "Look what you made me do. I did this for you".'

Heard began to clock that Depp had not only lost part of his finger, but had been using it as a paintbrush. She says he was still bleeding. Heard doesn't remember who called or contacted Jerry Judge, Depp's head of security (it could have been her, Depp or the compound security team, or a combination of all three), but the alarm was raised.

Heard told the court that whilst they waited for Depp's team to arrive she made him a coffee. When she handed it to him, he threw it at the TV, and began 'screaming'. In her witness statement to the UK trial, Heard wrote: 'He got nasty again and he wasn't making any sense. He thought I had had a guy over the night before, it was so crazy, I was crying.'

The row had begun again... but this time the cavalry was on its way.

DIAMOND EXTRACTION

Gold Coast, Australia, 8 March 2015

As Malcolm Connolly was being driven from his accommodation in Broadbeach to Diamond Head he texted Depp every ten minutes, telling his boss he would soon be outside and to 'stay calm mate!'

Connolly is a big, no-nonsense Glaswegian with a white beard and an accent many in the Virginia court (including the attorneys) found tricky to negotiate. Connolly remembers pulling up outside the main Diamond Head property between 1.30pm and 2pm, but the timings of his texts suggest it was closer to 12.25pm. The first thing he saw was an SUV belonging to the compound security team. It was empty. He figured 'something' was up.

Connolly approached the house. He could hear 'muffled shouting and screaming.' On opening the unlocked front door to the property, Connolly was confronted by a scene he describes as 'chaos'.

Heard and Depp were going seven bells at each other. 'Amber's irate,' remembered Connolly. 'I mean, tenacious. It's crazy stuff. Johnny's shouting back.'

Connolly tried to get Depp into the car. In court, Connolly agreed that at the time, Depp was 'upset and angry.'

Depp, according to Heard, did not want to leave, and decided at that moment to pull out his penis and announce: 'I need to take a fucking piss, it's my house.'

Writing in her witness statement, Heard claimed: 'He peed just outside the front door... then he went back in... He said he was trying to write my name, peeing on the walls and carpet, walking through the house.'

Heard said 'they' (the estate security? Connolly?) watched with 'nervous laughter' as Depp emptied his bladder. Connolly was asked about this in the US.

'Mr Depp was trying to urinate in the foyer, wasn't he?' suggested one of Heard's lawyers.

Connolly paused, a little incredulous. 'No-o...' he replied.

'Mr Depp had his penis out of his pants, didn't he?' insisted the attorney.

'I think I would remember seeing Mr Depp's penis,' Connolly deadpanned, to laughter in court.

Heard must have walked off at that point, but despite his injury, Depp was still reluctant to leave the house. According to Connolly, Depp wanted to 'say his piece' before departing.

'Eventually,' Connolly told the US court, 'I get him out. I managed to get him outside the door... but Amber appears from somewhere... and she's screaming, you know, screaming, berating him.'

In his witness statement in the UK Connolly said Heard was wearing 'a sort of green silk night thing... a slip.' In London Connolly agreed Heard had bare arms. At the US trial he said she was wearing long sleeves. Although admitting he only saw her for a short time and at a distance, Connolly was certain she did not appear to be suffering from any injuries whatsoever, but he does remember Heard being furious at Depp for being dragged away mid-argument.

'She's saying to Johnny, "Yeah... fuck off. That's what you do all the time. That's all you ever do, is fuck off. You fuck off with your guys. You're a fucking coward. That's what you fucking do. You fucking coward. You fuck off with your guys. You're a big man".'

Connolly told the court he eventually got Depp to the car and they drove back to Broadbeach and from there, to hospital. The security guard told the UK court that Kipper met him at their accommodation in Broadbeach.

This isn't correct. At 1pm on Sunday 8 March, Kipper and Nurse Debbie Lloyd were requested to attend Diamond Head by someone from Depp's security team because, as Dr Kipper's notes state, Depp 'was having a hard time leaving the house.'

By the time Kipper arrived, Depp had managed to get out of the house and was sitting in a car ready to leave. Kipper examined Depp's hand and sent him on his way. He then went into the house with Nurse Debbie to look for the rest of Depp's finger, enlisting the help of Depp's house manager, Ben King, who had also just pitched up.

King found Depp's fingertip on the floor of the bar area, wrapped in kitchen roll. It was put on ice and reunited with Depp in hospital.

During the US trial, both Depp and Heard each enlisted the services of eminent surgeons (both earning hundreds of dollars an hour) to give expert evidence about Depp's finger and how it might have been injured. Heard's eminent surgeon felt the bottle-throwing theory was 'unlikely'. Depp's eminent surgeon felt the bottle theory was 'reasonable', but concluded 'nobody can definitively state' how the injury had occurred.

The contemporaneous evidence was muddied by the need to keep the story under control and prevent Depp from being sued for being unable to fulfil his *Pirates 5* filming commitments.

Depp's security team suggested telling people he had cut the tip of his finger off with a knife whilst chopping onions. This idea foundered on first contact with the hospital doctors who examined Depp and told him his finger had been crushed, not (just) sliced. Depp says he didn't tell the doctors at the hospital Amber Heard had thrown a bottle at him in order to 'protect' her. Depp told the *Pirates* production company that he'd slammed the finger in a heavy 'accordion' door[1] within the rental house (a theory Heard's US expert felt was more plausible than the bottle theory). When it became apparent filming was going to have to be delayed, one of the executive producers of the movie circulated a press release saying Depp had injured his hand whilst racing around the Diamond Head compound's go-karting track with the property's famous owner, Mick Doohan. This is a reminder that in Hollywood, lying comes as readily as breathing.

Much has been made of the 11am text Depp sent to Kipper on the Sunday morning, which states: 'I cut the top of my middle finger off.' Depp had no reason not to be honest with Kipper. Tantalisingly, during the US trial, one of Depp's lawyers, Camille Vasquez, told the jury that during his recorded deposition, Dr Kipper remembered Depp telling him *verbally* that Heard was responsible for the damage to his finger. This section of Kipper's testimony was not played to the jury in the version of the deposition we watched in court.

The confusion over who was responsible for Depp's injury is matched by the confusion as to how and where in the timeline of events it happened. Heard originally believed that Depp smashing the wall-mounted telephone receiver caused him to lose his fingertip, but that had changed by the US trial. Depp remembers 'ripping the phone off the wall' but says this was because he was angry at having 'just lost' the tip of his finger to Heard's bottle-throwing. According to Heard, the alleged sexual assault happened *after* Depp smashed the telephone. She described Depp holding her by the neck on the countertop as he raped her with a bottle. This required two hands, one of which was carrying a relatively severe injury. It is possible that neither of them noticed this,

---

[1] An accordion is a musical instrument. An accordion door is an interior door which concertinas back and forth in sections – that is, it opens and closes by folding and unfolding. The door's folds in this way resemble the expanding and contracting folds on a concertina or accordion.

and/or that Depp was capable of carrying out the assault despite the damage to his finger. Or the rape happened before Depp injured his finger, or it didn't happen at all.

LET'S BURN AMBER!

Johnny Depp subscribes to a notion of himself as a well-mannered Southern gentleman. In his second witness statement to the UK trial, he said this persona was based on concepts of 'integrity, dignity, honesty, and respect for women.' It doesn't quite square with the counter-culture-worshipping gonzo side to his personality. The man who would never hurt a woman has a facility for conjuring dark, violent and misogynistic imagery in his writing. He has done this for comic effect, and he has done it in anger.

During his relationship with Amber Heard, Depp was friends with the actor Paul Bettany. Bettany did not see eye-to-eye with Heard (Depp alleged she once publicly humiliated Bettany's teenage son), but the two men got along famously, with Depp testifying in the UK that they took cocaine and other drugs together. Depp has a private island in the Bahamas, and Bettany's family holidayed there.

One text exchange in June 2013 between Depp and Bettany (presumably after they had both got a little fed up with Heard) came to the fore when it was raised at the High Court in 2020 and again in Virginia.

'Let's burn Amber!!!' texted Depp.

There was a 53 minute gap before Bettany responded:

'Having thought it through I don't think we should burn Amber – she's delightful company and easy on the eye, plus I'm not sure she's a witch. We could of course try the English course of action in these predicaments – we do a drowning test. Thoughts? NB I have a pool.'

Depp picked up the idea, rolled it into his own, and pushed it further:

'Let's drown her before we burn her!!! I will fuck her burnt corpse afterwards to make sure she's dead.'

Bettany responded: 'My thoughts entirely! Let's be CERTAIN before we pronounce her a witch.'

The language and tone is that of two puerile schoolboys articulating absurd and grandiose revenge fantasies. They are making each other laugh by saying the unsayable in the certain knowledge of their own impotence.

Others may read it differently, especially as the text exchange was made the same day as a pained Heard wrote herself an email lamenting the 'many times you have hurt me, physically and emotionally from the things you say and did while fucked up... you become mean and horrible.'

Depp's desire to push things to extremes linguistically may serve a purpose in a private message or conversation, but when seen by a worldwide audience, the words he uses become harder to justify.

In an August 2014 text to Dr Kipper, Depp wrote: 'Forgot to tell you, had a hopefully very positive and free of ego squawk with Amber last night that went very well... And then I shot a few negroes in a club on Sunset Boulevard. So far so good...'

Depp could be talking about negroni cocktails. During his recorded deposition to the US trial, Kipper speculated this may have been Depp's 'attempt at humor'. At best it is inadvisable wordplay.

The same month Depp put his linguistic flair to good use, this time in a text to Amber's mum, praising her for helping him detox. It read:

'My dearest Paige, how unbelievably kind and pure your message was. I am beyond thankful to have you in my life. There is no luckier man on this earth to have the strength that Amber gives me and the full support of each of you individually, that I've gotten, helps immeasurably. I don't need to explain the horrors to you. You know as well as I. What you do need to know that your daughter has risen far above the nightmarish task of taking care of this poor old junkie. Never a second has gone by that she didn't look out for me or have her eyes on me to make sure that I was okay. My words are truly feeble in attempting to explain her heroism in a text, suffice to say that I have never met or loved a woman or a thing more. She has the strength of a thousand men. And that is due to no one or nothing but you, sweetheart. Thank you. I love you. Your son out-law.'

But when Depp doesn't want to toe a line, he can lash out. Depp once called Heard a 'lesbian camp counsellor' for trying to modify his behavior. When Depp is really angry, the invective becomes visceral. On 15 August 2016, the same day he signed his divorce settlement with Heard, Depp texted his former agent Christian Carino to tell him:

'She's begging for total global humiliation. She's gonna get it. I'm gonna need your texts about San Francisco brother... I'm even sorry to ask... But she sucked Mollusk's[1] crooked dick and he gave her some shitty lawyers... I have no mercy, no fear and not an ounce of emotion or what I once thought was love for this gold digging, low level, dime a dozen, mushy, pointless dangling overused flappy fish market... I'm so fucking happy she wants to fight this out!!! She will hit the wall hard!!! And I cannot wait to have this waste of a cum guzzler out of my life!!!

---

[1] Presumably a reference to Elon Musk, who Heard was dating by this stage.

I met fucking sublime little Russian here... Which makes me realize the time I blew on that 50 cent stripper... I wouldn't touch her with a goddam glove. I can only hope that karma kicks in and takes the gift of breath from her... Sorry man... But NOW I will stop at nothing!!! Let's see if Mollusk has a pair... Come see me face to face... I'll show him things he's never seen before... Like the other side of his dick when I slice it off.'

The 'waste of a cum guzzler' vibe was not a one-off. In October 2016, Depp contacted his friend Isaac Baruch, who was at the time living in Penthouse 2 of the Eastern Columbia Building. Depp had already moved out after his split with Heard. In the first text, Depp asked Baruch:

'Is the slippery whore that I donated my jizz to for a while staying there?'

During the US trial Depp was asked to read this sentence out in court, which he did, giving a full actor's weight to the words, making it instantly meme-able. One Facebook post repeatedly played the video of Depp reading the text out loud, suggesting he could make anything sound like poetry. The phrase can also be found on several t-shirt designs for sale online.

The next day Depp wrote to Baruch: 'Hopefully, that cunt's rotting corpse is decomposing in the fucking trunk of a Honda Civic!!'

Depp told the court he was 'not proud of any of the language' he used in anger.

There is more. During the US trial Depp was shown two texts sent from his phone to Stephen Deuters in 2017. The first said:

'Molly's pussy is rightfully mine. Should I not just bust in and remove its hinges tonight?'

and:

'I want to change her understanding of what it is like to be thrashed about like a pleading mackerel. I NEED. I WANT. I TAKE.'

Depp refused to accept responsibility for these texts, telling the jury, 'there's not enough hubris in me to say anything like that.' He was reminded that this was evidence his own legal team had disclosed to the court.

A TORTUOUS KATE BUSH ANALOGY

In the first few chapters of this book I attempted to get across the nature and scale of Johnny Depp's fame, including how and why he has touched so many lives. Johnny Depp is not alone in having legions of fans who care passionately about him, but there are many factors which have transformed his battles with Amber Heard, key among them the way social media has been utilized to support and help him. Fans, who were once – at best – worried spectators, were given *collective agency* by their virtual proximity to Depp and each other.

There are several million people who identify on some level with Johnny Depp. They see him as a good person, because something about his public persona or his creative output (often combined) has moved them and made a difference to their lives. Woe betide, therefore, anyone who attempts to paint Johnny Depp not just as a flawed human being, but as the very opposite of a good person: a monstrous, violent abuser. For you won't just have Johnny Depp, his money, his lawyers and the people who protect him to deal with; you will also have an army – possibly numbering in the tens or hundreds of thousands – who see your attacks on Johnny Depp as an attack on them.

Aside from those touched by his creative output, there are people who identify with Johnny Depp because they see him as an innocent man who has been abused, or wrongly accused, or cancelled in an unfair trial by media. They may share similar experiences and want to see a person who they previously perceived as a good man (or even a hero) win a righteous victory against the powerful forces arraigned against him.

This is a relatively recent phenomenon. If I were a Kate Bush fan in the days before social media, and someone had won a temporary restraining order against her, pleading domestic violence, I would feel troubled. Before we go any further, I should stress I have selected Kate Bush as an example on the grounds she is the least likely person I can think of who could or would ever be accused of domestic violence and that, in the UK at least, she was very much a big deal in the days before social media. But let's imagine, in an alternate universe, that UK pop superstar Kate Bush, *the least likely person anyone could think of in this regard*, had been accused of domestic violence.

The way these things work, some people who weren't Kate Bush fans might assume Kate Bush *was* a perpetrator of domestic violence, or that at least there was no smoke without fire. Radio and TV producers might stop using her records on their shows, people who like her music might not go to her concerts. As a fan, I would still want to listen to Kate Bush's music and see her sing live, but I would feel conflicted. I might be concerned the allegations were true, and that my love for Kate Bush and belief she was a good person was misguided. I was either a fan of a bad person, or Kate Bush had been falsely accused of domestic violence and was always the good person I thought she was. But how would I know the truth? It would be quite an important truth to me, because I got a lot out of listening to Kate Bush records, I liked supporting her work, and I didn't want to stop. Whilst the allegations might be enough for her to be shunned or (at the very least) treated with caution, they were still only allegations. There was no video of her beating up her partner. No proof.

In my pre-social media world, I would have to trust due process, filling the information vacuum with the reports of broadcast or newspaper journalists assigned to the story. Eventually the matter would come to some sort of conclusion, which would be reported, and that would be that.

As a fan of Kate Bush in the twenty-first century, I might act a little differently. I might start looking for more information about the allegations against her on an active fan forum, or just sigh my disappointed disbelief on Twitter. Within minutes someone might confidently reply, 'there's no way Kate Bush is guilty of DV.' This bold and intriguing claim might entice me into a conversation with people who think Kate Bush is great (people like me!) who are far more certain of her innocence than the rest of the world appears to be.

Even if I am not initially convinced, I am going to give their arguments and 'evidence' the time of day. If I start to believe Kate Bush is the victim of false allegations, I might very quickly find myself outraged on Kate's behalf at the injustice she is suffering. I might become righteous, believing I am fighting powerful forces who have conspired to bring my hero down.

Community agency now comes into play. Me and my fellow Kate Bush fans are actively participating in a just cause by publicly advocating for our hero online, occasionally using vitriolic abuse to torch those with opposing perspectives out of the picture. The anger comes from the righteousness – we're the ones doing the research and seeking out the evidence to prove #katebushisinnocent. A movement is born.

The people who initially drew me in and persuaded me of Kate Bush's innocence become my friends and guides. With the fervor of true believers we evangelize and convert in growing numbers. Soon after, the creators move in, chasing clicks and eyeballs with content generated to satisfy an insatiable appetite for the Real Truth – stuff the lamestream media refuses to give us. Their work becomes a self-vin-dicating circle, auto-reinforcing the #katebushisinnocent narrative. Eventually, by sheer weight of numbers, our voices spill over into the public discourse. We are no longer ignored.

This phenomenon is one of the defining dynamics of our age, and it is not limited to individuals with large fan bases. It is happening to everything, everywhere, all at once. Pick any cultural sphere and you will find a controversial topic over which due process is struggling to function in the face of online outrage and denunciation. That's not to say due process always delivers the correct result. Sometimes due pro-cess sucks. But democracy by online mob is not healthy. The mentality behind it is nothing new – we've always loved having our biases con-firmed by people who share a similar mindset. It's just the whole thing has been amplified, exacerbated, and gloriously monetized by social media. With unpredictable results.

A STRANGE RECORDING

Welcome back to the Diamond Head compound on 8 March 2015. It is some time between 11.30am and 12.30pm. Amber Heard and Johnny Depp are alone in the house. Depp has a badly injured finger.

Help is on its way. Jerry Judge has sent Malcolm Connolly to get Depp out of the house. Dr Kipper has been made aware that his client has broken his sobriety pledge and suffered a significant injury. Nathan Holmes has apparently agreed to make a delivery of cocaine and ecstasy and Ben King is about to magically appear.

Depp and Heard moved to different locations within the property after the alleged cup-throwing incident which smashed a TV. They will soon be reunited to pick up their argument as Connolly et al arrive.

At some point during that 11.30am to 12.30pm period (or possibly sooner), either Depp or Heard encountered Heard's phone and used it to start an audio recording. Heard denies doing it, telling the UK court she saw Depp 'picking up the phone and saying he was going to record, but I could not possibly imagine that he would actually have figured that out in the state he was in.'

The recording ran unchecked for several hours. Heard said she only became aware of its existence when she handed over her phone for data extraction as part of her divorce proceedings in 2016. In 2020, Heard told the UK court she understood the recording was 'seven or eight' hours long, and immediately became suspicious when Depp's lawyers said it comprised two separate recordings, the first five hours long, the second just 27 minutes.

We don't know Depp's position on whether or not he started the recording as he hasn't been publicly asked about it. It doesn't really matter. The significance of this tape is that most people we hear speaking don't know they are being recorded. We are treated to a wide range of voices.

Frustratingly, the Australia recording has not been *formally* made public by either party. Two official transcripts approved by the respective lawyers for Depp and Heard have also not found their way into the public domain either via the parties or the courts. Snippets of the recording have been played in both the UK and US trials, and lawyers for both Depp and Heard have read sections of the transcripts out to various witnesses. The tape did fall into the hands of a YouTuber and rabid Johnny Depp supporter, known on Twitter as ThatBrianFella[1]. Brian has published an edited and 'cleaned up' version of the tape on his YouTube channel. Brian's personal transcription is heroic, but perhaps a little hopeful. He also leaves out some sections of the tape which have been quoted elsewhere. That said, I am certain as I can be that the source material he is working from is genuine. A different and much shorter version of the same recording has also been published by the Daily Mail. In what follows I have only used sections of the tape where the words being spoken are incontrovertible and, to my mind, relevant. Where possible, I have cross-referenced those words with what I can find in court documents (and the excerpts played during the US trial) to ensure that everything quoted below is *definitely* on the tape. If I'm not sure who is speaking or exactly what they are saying, I have said as much, or left it out. I have left out some dull bits, too.

The first thing we hear of note is Depp shouting: 'I wish you fuckin' understood what you are, and who you are. And how you fucked me over, and make me feel sick... OF MYSELF!!' Depp then adds, in a bizarre, slurry, sing-song voice. 'There's still a lot left in the day. Maybe you should dye your hair. I see ROOTS!!'

Depp sounds pissed, in both the American and British sense. Malcolm Connolly was played this section of the recording during the US trial and was asked if it reflected the condition Depp was in when he arrived. Connolly replied: 'Yes.'

Shortly after his tonsorial advice, Depp leaves the house and does not feature in the remainder of the tape. We next hear Dr Kipper thinking aloud. He, Nurse Debbie and Ben King are looking for Depp's fingertip whilst also getting to grips with the state of the property.

'There's still time to get this put back on,' Kipper says, referring to Depp's finger, 'otherwise he's going to need a skin graft, probably.'

'Ho-oly fuck,' says Lloyd, presumably assessing the destruction. 'Wow, wow, wow.'

As they continue to search, Kipper says: 'The majority of the blood, Debbie, is downstairs. But I went through that really carefully.'

Later, he says: 'You know I'm really concerned because he's got a lot of paint...'

'A lot of pain?' asks Lloyd.

---

[1] I first met Brian in the toilet on the fifth floor of the Fairfax County Courthouse. Given the circumstances, we didn't shake hands.

'Paint,' corrects Kipper. 'He's got a lot of pain, also.' Kipper is concerned the finger is 'going to get infected' and repeats his opinion that Depp is 'going to need a skin graft.'

Kipper starts talking about Heard.

'Amber's got to take care of herself,' he says. 'We're gonna take care of him. They *can't* be together now... [indistinct]... I think she should be in Los Angeles with her support system... This has to run its course.'

Lloyd says: 'I think somebody needs to fly with her.'

Kipper replies: 'Jerry can fly with her.'

'She won't have Jerry', Lloyd says.

'She doesn't have a choice,' says Kipper. Lloyd says something indistinct.

'I don't give a shit,' replies Kipper. 'I mean... [he chuckles]... I don't mean to invalidate what you're saying, but...'

'No but I was wondering if there's another person,' interrupts Lloyd. 'That's what I'm saying.'

'Well, I asked those same questions earlier,' says Kipper, who mentions Jerry again, saying: 'He's not going to be manipulated. He's a strong guy.'

There is more indistinct conversation. We begin to hear Amber Heard sobbing in the background.

'How big a piece of skin are we looking for?' asks Lloyd.

'You're looking at this,' says Kipper, presumably making some sort of visual indication. 'You're looking at a third of a tip of the finger... he's going to get a cellulitis.'[2]

As Heard continues sobbing, Kipper and Lloyd appear to discuss medicating her.

'Can I give her 50 of Seroquel?' asks Lloyd. Seroquel is an antipsychotic medication which Kipper also prescribed for Depp.

'Exactly,' replies Kipper.

There is another indistinct question from Lloyd involving the number '300' to which Kipper responds: 'Yeah.'

'She only usually takes 25,' says Lloyd. 'You want me to give her 50?'

'Of the Seroquel?' asks Kipper.

'Yeah.'

'I'd be okay with 100,' says Kipper, 'but give her 50.'

---

[2]   Cellulitis is an infection caused by bacteria getting into the deeper layers of your skin. It usually needs to be treated with antibiotics. It can be serious if it's not treated quickly.

Lloyd disappears. Kipper is talking to someone else. 'This is guilt,' he says.

Lloyd returns. 'She won't take 50,' says the nurse. 'I gave her 25 and 300 and said we'd reassess in a little bit.'

Eventually, Jerry Judge's voice crops up. He is talking to Heard, who is distressed. They appear to be discussing Heard's departure from Australia, but it's not possible to be certain what they are saying. Heard disappears. Judge moves closer to the phone.

'I'm staying,' says Judge. 'David [Kipper]'s still not letting her speak to John [Depp].'

'She called Christi,' he adds. 'Because when I told Christi... that she called him a fat old man...'

Heard reappears, sounding far less distressed. She has a disjointed but indistinct conversation with Judge. The next thing we hear on Brian's version of the tape is a telephone conversation between Judge and a woman who must be Depp's sister, Christi Dembrowski. Dembrowski's voice on the other end of the line is loud enough to hear, but the words are unclear. Heard has disappeared.

Judge tells Dembrowski that Depp is no longer on the premises: 'He's in Malcolm's room. He's asleep. He's sleeping like a baby.'

Judge updates Dembrowski on Heard. 'I'm talking to her and hopefully... she hasn't given me a final answer that she'll go... she wants to stay here and see him.'

Dembrowski talks calmly on the other end of the phone before Judge says: 'Ben is saying... he's happy to go with her, but so you know... she's talking to me, she keeps crying... she keeps holding my hand. She's made it quite clear to me... she said "I thought I trusted you and I don't because you told Christi that I called Johnny a fat old man." And I said "yes, I did".'

The quality of the recording dips again but Judge appears to be telling Dembrowski the 'fat old man' situation appears to have led to some kind of breakdown of trust. Judge moves on to Heard's state of mind and tells Dembrowski that she has been medicated to help her sleep. Judge tells Dembrowski Kipper has given him an extra pill to give to Heard if she wakes up too early. In reference to keeping Depp and Heard separate, he tells Dembrowski:

'I'm hoping she'll crack,' expressing again his desire to 'get her on that plane in the morning.'

'What we also need to do,' he adds, perhaps superfluously, 'is get this place cleaned up.'

Judge informs Dembrowski that he's told 'Stephen' (presumably Deuters) that the next day's *Pirates* filming schedule has to be cancelled, saying Depp is 'in no fit state'.

The conversation with Dembrowski continues, with Judge telling her: 'I've seen Johnny hurt. I've never seen him this hurt. And honestly... he wrecked this place. I mean... it's wrecked. The window's broken, there's a TV... there's been bottles thrown. And she admits to me that she threw the first one – she threw a bottle at him. She did it first.'

Judge warns Dembrowski Heard has 'scratches' on her arm and tells her that Debbie Lloyd has already clocked them. Judge says: 'I've seen those scratches before on other people... and as far as I'm concerned, they're self-inflicted. I'm convinced of that. Self-inflicted.'

Judge explains his plans. He is going to do 'a deal with the devil and calm this lady down.'

The sound of Dembrowski's voice disappears at this point. It's not clear if Judge is still talking to her or somebody else. We hear him relating details of his conversation with Heard.

'She admitted also that she hit him first,' he reports. 'She actually hit him in the face.'

Judge says Depp has 'a small burn on the right-hand side of his face' and says Heard told him that Depp 'was so out of it' he put a cigarette 'onto his own face' on the Friday night.

On Depp's condition, Judge says: 'He's not well. We need to help him out in every way we possibly can... and I'll try to convince her she can't do any good here... I said: "You can't help him. You can't. You two need to be separated. You can speak to him on the phone, but you need to leave him alone".'

Finally, Judge reports some good news. The tip of Depp's finger has been found. 'It's packed in ice,' he says. 'I've already spoken with Malcolm... it's on its way back now...'

Later on in the recording Judge is on another phone call, almost certainly to Stephen Deuters.

He tells Deuters: 'There's fifty to seventy-five thousand dollars worth of breakages here... there's blood everywhere... we'll clean it up... he drank *everything* in the last week.'

An unclear section of dialogue becomes clearer as Judge says: 'Within two hours, he took ten – *ten* – ecstasy tablets.' He appears to be reporting his conversation with Heard. Judge goes on to state what sounds like Heard's description of Depp breaking the window by throwing a bottle. In response to something Deuters says, Judge lays down his position:

'I'm not going to say she did it. I'm not going to say he did it... but when I was here yesterday, she was stone cold sober. She doesn't smell of booze... I don't fucking know... all she wants to do... all she needs to do is – look, Stephen, I'll admit, I'll give her anything to get her *the fuck* out of here.'

A further part of the tape is very hard to discern. ThatBrianFella transcribes it as Judge warning Ben King to be careful around Heard. There is also some speculation about cocaine, who might be taking it and who supplied it. Nathan Holmes' name is mentioned again.

Later in the tape, Judge is on the phone to a woman, possibly Christi again. His voice is clearer than before.

'He's awake... they just left the hotel. So I'm assuming he's awake for them to take him down there and have it done... the quicker you get it done, the quicker it takes. It'll heal up a lot quicker, okay?'

The conversation switches to Heard. 'Get... two rooms... using my name and then we'll see what she wants to do. Don't get me wrong, she's changing her mind every five minutes, okay?'

Heard's intentions and state of mind are again called into question. 'I'll be honest,' says Judge, 'she's breaking down and crying, and at the same time packing a bag. So she knows what she's doing. I don't think she intends to do anything stupid. She keeps saying, "I don't want to lose him, I don't want to leave him", and we're saying, "Look, he needs some time on his own, and then when he's on his own we'll remind him and then you two can talk on the phone and you can come back." But... no matter what happens, she needs to leave Australia, to get the fuck outta here. She really does.'

Time passes. There is another phone call between Jerry Judge and Christi Dembrowski. It seems Heard is now content to travel to LA with Ben King. Judge says:

'Christi... I'll be honest with you. She knows exactly what she's doing. She knows exactly what she's doing... I've asked her if she would go and see her shrink. She said she would.'

Finally, Heard comes downstairs.

'I was upstairs, ready to pack,' she tells Judge, 'and I found baggies of coke, and whatever else.'

'How much did you find?' asks Judge.

'Empty bags,' replies Heard.

'Empty bags...' ponders Judge. 'May I ask how many did you find?'

'Two,' replies Heard. 'One that looked like... used to be crushed up coke.'

There is a further indistinct exchange about drugs, including Xanax, Adderall and ecstasy before Heard switches tack. The dialogue is hard to follow and interspersed with indistinct words, but Heard can be made out saying:

'I hate that he hates me... I hate that I'm the element that really... sets it off.' She *may* then say, 'I feel like I'm not going to get him back.'

Judge responds: 'I don't believe that for a second.'

Heard laments. 'But I feel so stupid Jerry. I brought all my stuff over here. I shipped things... I feel so stupid.'

She becomes tearful. There is a further gap of time and Ben King appears on the scene. It seems like they are prepping to leave the house. Heard appears to apologize to them both. Judge puts his best face on it.

'It's all part of the job, sweetheart. It's all part of the job.'

Whilst Heard is being coaxed out of Diamond Head, Johnny Depp was somewhere between Connolly's accommodation in Broadbeach and the local hospital. He would later be photographed out cold on a gurney with an improvised bandage around his finger. The photograph shows a mark, which could be a cigarette burn, on Depp's right cheek. He is wearing sunglasses, and his mouth is partially open. He does not look well.

On 9 March, Depp saw a specialist, who allegedly told him the crush injury to his finger was a 'wound of velocity'. Heard flew back to LA with Ben King. Much was made of an exchange (which Heard says she does not recall) toward the end of their flight, during which King claims Heard asked him:

'Have you ever been so angry with someone that you just lost it?'

King says he replied it had 'never happened' to him. Heard was apparently so incredulous that she asked him again. King also said he noticed two 'cuts in uniform lines' on Heard's arm which he mentioned she might want to hide on arrival at LAX, 'as there might be paparazzi in the airport.' King says Heard 'chose' not to do this.

In both the US and UK, an extensive amount of time was dedicated to describing the extent of the damage to the Diamond Head property caused by Depp and Heard. There was paint and blood dripped and daubed all over the walls, floors, mirrors and furnishings. There were a large number of glass breakages, a TV worth more than ten thousand dollars had been smashed, wine had been spilt, a window was broken. Heard also alleged Depp had covered a large number of her clothes in paint. Getting things straight required more than simple replacements

and cosmetic repairs. Sections of the house's interior wall needed
re-plastering, a wooden floor needed to be sanded and re-varnished
and, according to Ben King, there was 'chipped stone on the countertop
in the bar area and on the staircase down to the bar, where a flower vase
had been launched from the floor above.' The eventual cost of repairing
all the damage was fifty thousand US dollars.

Whitney says she saw Amber shortly after she arrived in LA. Heard
apparently 'sobbed', telling Whitney about the fight and what had
happened. Whitney said Heard 'was not hiding the abuse' from her by
that point. She says she saw Heard's injuries: 'Her lip was swollen and
busted up a bit, and she also had these horrible cuts on her arms – like
gashes.'

THE GREAT TABOO

As well as the five alleged incidents detailed[1] so far, Amber Heard has also claimed Johnny Depp gave her a 'whack' in the face after the Met Gala in New York in May 2014 and subjected her to another sexual assault in the Bahamas over Christmas 2015 ('he... shoved his fingers inside me... through my bathing suit'). Heard also claimed to be the victim of a beating in Tokyo in January 2015, when Depp allegedly grabbed her hair, and started 'whaling' her from behind, wrestling her to the ground and kneeling on her back. Heard also claims she saw Depp assault an air stewardess on a private plane to Russia in June 2013, and claims that the same evening he smacked her about in a hotel room, allegedly giving her a nosebleed. Heard has also given details of a luxury train trip on the Orient Express through south east Asia in July 2015, during which Heard claims Depp tried to strangle her with a shirt in a sleeper car. Depp is also alleged to have punched his wife in the jaw in August 2015 in France during an argument about nudity and sex scenes.

Depp has repeatedly claimed to be the victim of Amber Heard's abuse. The only potential evidence of assault from any of the above incidents can be seen in a photograph of Depp and Heard taken on board the Orient Express as they pose with staff in the train's dining car. Johnny Depp has what looks like a black eye. Depp said in court that during an argument with Heard on the train he 'took a pretty good shot to the face, to the eye.' Towards the end of the US trial, Heard's lawyers produced a photo taken *before* the trip, which they say shows a similar mark on Depp's face. For her part, Heard told jurors Depp did not sustain any injury, and the mark on his face in the photograph taken in the dining car 'is Photoshop', a novel line, which was not pursued by her lawyers.

So who was getting physical with who? And why is it totally unacceptable to suggest they might be assaulting each other? What exactly is at stake for either party if they admit violence on their part?

In Western society, it is not just illegal for a man to hit a woman, it is taboo. This is a cultural acknowledgment of patriarchal power dynamics which has some of its roots in medieval notions of chivalry. Chivalry was a Christian moral code chronicled by twelfth and thirteenth century European romantic writers who harked back to an ancient, bygone

---

[1] In case you've forgotten: the Tattoo Incident, Disco Bloodbath, Hicksville, the Plane Kick and Australia.

era they dubbed The Age of Chivalry – think King Arthur and the Knights of the Round Table. During this vividly imagined period (presented as historical fact), warrior knights showed valor in battle and put themselves in harm's way to help those less fortunate than themselves. Yet the fearless protagonists of these tales remained humble, adored women and valued self-control. Over decades, the ideas presented in these fables took hold across an entire continent. It became the ultimate aspiration for a nobleman to become a *gentle*man. Chivalric concepts began to embed themselves into all aspects of social convention. Over the last three or four hundred years, metaphorical pedestals were wheeled out and women were put on them. In the late nineteenth and early twentieth century, gentlemen fought wars in which defeated combatants of their equivalent class were (supposed to be) treated honorably. They dreamed of coming home to take the hand of their beloved. If a ship went down on the high seas, it was a man's job to save the women and children first. Even today it is perfectly normal in some parts of Europe and America to teach young men to rise when a woman enters a room, to open doors for her, and help seat her at a table. A gentleman has manners.

During the twentieth and early part of this century, the concept of a gentleman (distinct from a rough-born common man) has become more egalitarian, coalescing around a generalized concept of masculinity. A gentleman became a Real Man. Real Men continued to fight real wars, took dangerous jobs and sacrificed themselves for their beautiful, passive, grateful partners. They occasionally needed to be reminded that Real Men Don't Hit Women[2].

Johnny Depp explicitly allies himself to the gentlemanly ideal[3], writing in his second witness statement to the UK trial that 'as a child, chivalry was extremely important and, whether or not this is considered old-fashioned, it is still something that I consider very important.'

Depp says this chivalric ideal doesn't just inform, but governs his behavior. 'It is a strong and central part of my moral code,' he wrote, 'that I would never strike a woman, under any circumstances, at any time. I find it simply inconceivable and it would never happen.'

---

[2]   The Real Man campaign was a Women's Aid-sponsored initiative which ran in 2012. Men were asked to sign a pledge which stated: 'A "Real Man" doesn't hit, abuse or control. A "Real Man" doesn't hurt the ones he loves. A "Real Man" makes a difference. I'm supporting the "Real Man" Campaign for Women's Aid, standing up to end violence against women and children.' It was publicized by hyper-masculine exemplars like the chef Gordon Ramsay, who posed wearing a t-shirt emblazoned with the 'Real Man' logo.

[3]   Albeit one who had little choice in the matter, as it was 'beaten into' him from a young age.

Chivalry works well within a patriarchy because it serves to enforce it. In an absolute patriarchy, men have the weapons, wealth, influence and agency. Women are defenseless, and only able to operate in the space that men give them. They are vulnerable objects of lust and beauty, care-givers and child-bearers. Providing women are prepared to accept that role, men will worship and 'protect' them. Women who refuse to conform to a romantic ideal often find they are less entitled to protection from woolly male moral codes, and must instead seek equality and empowerment through changes in the law.

The first wave of feminism, between 1870 and 1900, led to greater protections for married women in law. Alabama became the first American state to outlaw wife-beating in 1871. Others followed. In Britain the Matrimonial Causes Act of 1878 allowed a woman to seek legal separation from an abusive husband, and a husband's liberty to beat his spouse was definitively removed in 1891 when Lord Halsbury ruled:

'The right of a husband over his wife in respect of personal chastisement are not, I think, now capable of being cited as authorities in a court of justice in this or any civilised country.'

From here on in, the moral code of the chivalric gentleman – or at least the part that pertained to prohibiting violence against a female partner – would be permanently and explicitly enshrined in law on both sides of the Atlantic, essentially bolstering a (let's face it, sporadically observed) social taboo by giving it legal strength. As women fought for emancipation and equality, they were able to use their voices to strengthen the taboo, whilst taking other legal steps to mitigate against the real and ever-present threat of violence, rape, murder and jealous, controlling men. Over the course of the twentieth century, men hitting women slowly became socially unacceptable, eventually finding a place on the scale somewhere between armed robbery and paedophilia.

Women hitting men, though, is still seen to be pretty much okay. In 2007 a short, jokey article appeared in the online magazine, Jezebel. It was called *Have You Ever Beat Up A Boyfriend? Cause, Uh, We Have*. The author of the piece, Tracie Egan Morrissey, asked her girlfriends and colleagues – 'Jezebels' – for their confessions, and published them.

'One Jezebel got into it with a dude while they were breaking up,' wrote Morrissey, 'while another Jez went nuts on her guy and began violently shoving him.'

There are plenty more examples: 'One of your editors heard her boyfriend flirting on the phone with another girl, so she slapped the phone out of his hands and hit him in the face and neck... "partially open handed".'

The writer's tone is deliberately provocative and not remotely disapproving: 'Another editor slapped a guy when "he told me he thought he had breast cancer." (Okay, that one made us laugh really hard.)'

Morrissey concludes: 'Let's just say that it'd be wise to never ever fuck with us.'

You are not invited to take Morrissey's article too seriously, but the knowing prose invites the reader to ingest an unpalatable truth, which is that some women nowadays feel able to hit their men without suffering catastrophic consequences. Occasionally lamping your fella is presented as a guilty secret, akin to taking drugs or drink-driving. Transgressive acts, indeed criminal offenses, but nothing *too* serious. There is a sense of honesty about the article – *we know it's wrong, but we can't help celebrating the fact we are finally in a position to do it.* Women, the logic goes, are at last free enough – in certain circumstances – to be the oppressor.

The Jezebel article was prompted by an item published in *Psychiatric News*, the journal of the American Psychiatric Association. *Psychiatric News* cited clinical research which found, 'When it comes to nonreciprocal violence between intimate partners, women are more often the perpetrators.' The piece was called *Men Shouldn't Be Overlooked as Victims of Partner Violence*.

The study underpinning the article had asked eleven thousand people between the ages of 18 and 28 about their heterosexual relationships. They found just under a quarter were violent, and in just over half of those violent relationships there was a sole aggressor. Within that cohort the majority – seventy percent – were women.

The Jezebel article also references a (now removed) Sun interview with the (now deceased) British singer Amy Winehouse, in which she apparently said of her husband: 'I'll beat up Blake when I'm drunk. If he says one thing I don't like then I'll chin him.'

Seven years later, when TMZ published footage of Solange Knowles attacking Jay-Z in a lift, there was little, if any, condemnation of Knowles' actions. Social media, which was just hitting its stride, found it funny, producing hundreds of memes and jokes. In the footage, Jay-Z looks unflustered and uninjured by the attack.

Writing in the Guardian a few days after the video was published, the columnist Barbara Ellen warned against false equivalence. Her piece was called *Solange and Jay-Z: it's simply not the same if a man is hit by a woman.*

At the top of the article, Ellen set out her stall: 'While there are exceptions,' she wrote, 'in the majority of cases, FOM violence is different to MOF violence, in myriad ways, ranging from context, scale and intent to self-defense, sexual attacks and death rates.'

Ellen addressed the context of the video footage: 'A woman momentarily lashing out at her brother-in-law at a social event does not count as domestic violence. Perhaps it could have been assault had the bodyguard not intervened. However, even unprotected, would Jay-Z have felt under genuine physical threat from his sister-in-law?'

It's a rhetorical question, which Ellen answers in general terms: 'Most women would take it completely for granted that men are not remotely frightened of them. And that's because male physical fear of women is not the norm – there's no dominant culture of hostile matriarchy, where men need to be hyper-vigilant of female violence, or versed in ways to combat it.'

The most intriguing sentence in the column is when Ellen accepts that Solange v Jay-Z was not unique: 'Some females,' she concedes, 'might have periods in their life when they get "slap-happy", primarily when socializing, maybe when attention seeking, usually when drunk (guilty!)'

It is almost inconceivable that a male writer would have been able to file that sentence and keep his job. I am not complaining of double standards. I am just pointing out that women hitting men is seen as a bit naughty, rather than harmful, for all the reasons Ellen describes. Men hitting women is an order of magnitude more serious. Partly because of the average man's capacity to inflict damage, partly because it is an abuse of structural power, but mainly because it is socially taboo.

Social taboos often exist for good reason, and the cost of transgressing can be career-ending. A woman hitting a man is assault, but somewhere on the social scale of inadvisable to funny. In Western society, a man hitting a woman is very bad. It is almost always abuse. In 2016, on a public legal document, Amber Heard accused Johnny Depp of 'excessive emotional, verbal and physical abuse,' including 'angry, hostile, humiliating and threatening assaults' which happened 'during the entirety' of their four-and-a-half-year relationship.

Johnny Depp countered not just with a denial that it did happen, but a denial that it *could* happen: *I would never strike a woman, under any circumstances, at any time.*

The stakes were simply too high to acknowledge anything else.

And the truth?

KATE JAMES INCOMING

London, July 2020

Amber Heard's account of what happened in Australia was found to be credible by Mr Justice Nicol in the UK. He did not hear the exact same testimony as given by Amber Heard in the US, but during a private court session, which reporters were barred from attending, Amber Heard's sworn witness statement was discussed and challenged. Nicol subsequently ruled that on the balance of probabilities – bearing in mind the need for 'clear evidence' when considering an act of 'serious criminality' – Depp *did* sexually assault Heard during a 'terrifying' ordeal which put her in 'fear of her life.'

Less than two years later a Virginia jury decided Heard's testimony was either a fantasy, or a cruel and vindictive lie.

It is certainly an *easier* thing to accept that Depp is a violent rapist – unless of course you are a fan or a man who has himself been falsely accused of domestic abuse. Every court, every police officer and every woman has heard the story about the drug-addled, jealous partner with a fearsome temper and a penchant for smashing things who eventually loses control and violently assaults his wife. There's nothing new about rape or domestic violence. It happens all the time.

It is far more difficult to consider the flip side. What if Amber Heard is making all this up? Pulling the long con on the public, the UK courts and the organizations who, at the time of writing, are lining up to support her. Is that possible? Feasible? Hollywood actors don't normally fly across the Atlantic to lie consistently and repeatedly under oath for four days. It takes a special sort of person to set themselves up as a 'public figure representing domestic abuse' if the person they are accusing is actually their victim.

What then, for the US jury, didn't stack up?

My first jolt covering this story came back in London, when I was sitting in court, watching Kate James give evidence. Kate James was Amber Heard's former personal assistant. In 2020 she was beamed in from Los Angeles to be cross-examined by Sasha Wass, NGN's barrister. That afternoon did not go well for Team Heard.

Wass started by highlighting a text sent by Johnny Depp to Kate James in August 2016, shortly after Heard first accused Depp of being violent towards her.

'I'm disgusted that I ever fucking touched that scum,' wrote Depp. 'Will hit you when I get back, doll. Come over for a spot of purple and we will fix her flabby arse nice and good.'

Wass used this text as a basis for suggesting that the contents of James' witness statements were not just the lies of a disgruntled employee, but written in collusion with Depp and/or his legal team with a view to 'fix'-ing Heard's 'flabby arse'. That is, rigging the evidence.

In response, Kate James was – and there is no way of putting a finer point on this – fucking furious.

'I am here,' she said, with rising anger in her voice, 'for my own reasons. And you know what those reasons are by reading my second witness statement. I am a sexual violence survivor and it is very, *very* serious to take that stance if you are not one. And I am one.'

The ears of the journalists in court pricked up.

'And so that is the reason,' she continued, 'I am here. *Because I take offense...*'

The judge tried to intervene.

'Ms James...' he began.

James ignored him '... *at somebody...*'

'Ms James!' repeated the judge.

James stopped.

'I have understood your answer,' said the judge, back in control of his court. 'Could I ask you... please, to confine yourself to answering the questions that Ms Wass put to you?'

There was a brief period of silence. All eyes turned to Wass. Who simply said:

'My Lord, in the light of the answers I have had, I do not propose to ask any more questions of this witness,' and sat down.

Amber Heard had not, by that stage of the trial, testified in court. No one outside the parties' legal teams had seen James' or Heard's witness statements. We didn't know what was in them, but it was pretty obvious something big was brewing.

Depp's barrister, David Sherborne, got to his feet. For the benefit of the court he asked Kate James what she was talking about. Sherborne established that James' second witness statement was written in response to a specific recollection in a single paragraph of Amber Heard's fifth witness statement. The journalists in the room looked at each other like bewildered meerkats, until James was finally invited to spell it out. She told the court:

'Ms Heard referred to a conversation we had about me being violently raped at a certain point in Brazil, and she used that as her own story... She referred directly to a violent rape that occurred to me 26 years ago, and she twisted it... for her own use.'

This was a development no one expected. After James had given her evidence, her (second) witness statement was made available to journalists. In it, James had written:

'When I was 26 years old and traveling in Brazil, I was violently raped by an unknown male at machete point, having been woken by the perpetrator whilst sleeping alone in my dwelling. This ordeal went on for 5–6 hours and I narrowly escaped with my life. This torturous experience of such extreme sexual violence has haunted me ever since and permanently changed the trajectory of my life to this day. Over the years, I have shared this incident with many close friends, family and therapists. In 2013, Ms Heard became aware of what happened to me as I had talked about it with a friend of hers at her apartment. Ms Heard then summoned me to her office where we sat on her couch and she questioned me about it... On June 25, 2020, I received documents pertaining to my involvement on behalf of the Claimant in this case. As I perused the documents, much to my utter shock and dismay, I discovered that Ms Heard had in fact stolen my sexual violence conversation with her and twisted it into her own story to benefit herself. This of course caused me extreme distress and outrage that she would dare to attempt to use the most harrowing experience of my life as her own narrative.'

We still, at that point, did not know what Heard's private allegation against Depp was, but it followed it had to be something along these lines for James to cry foul.

Watching Kate James testify live remains the single most electrifying moment I experienced in covering this story either side of the Atlantic. It was not exactly a surprise to discover Amber Heard's private allegations related to sexual assault, but it was stunning to hear those allegations denounced as larcenous fantasy by another alleged abuse survivor. Who should we believe?

On the face of it, one of them was either lying, or gravely, gravely mistaken. It is more than within the bounds of possibility that Kate James had got the wrong end of the stick. The similarities between what happened to her and what Heard was claiming could just be coincidence, but James made it abundantly clear that – in her mind – there was no coincidence. Heard had stolen her story.

Almost as soon as the excitement had begun, the trail went cold. Every subsequent court interaction on the sexual nature of Depp's alleged violence was heard in private. British reporters did not find out whether Amber Heard appropriated a former employee's abuse story for her own ends, or if that specific issue was even discussed. We had to wait until November that year to find out more, and when we did, there was very little to go on. In his judgment, Mr Justice Nicol decided to disregard Kate James' explosive intervention on the grounds she was a disgruntled employee. He wrote: 'I am afraid that I did not find Ms James a satisfactory witness. She had been dismissed by Ms Heard in February 2015 and the circumstances of her termination still appeared to be a cause of rancor with Ms James.'

Of course, a disgruntled ex-employee can still be telling the truth, but it seems in the US and UK courts, their disgruntlement counts against them. This is a recurring and, as far as I can make out, unevidenced trope. Sacked employees speaking out against their former employers are routinely assumed to be primarily motivated by a desire for revenge, rather than justice. Mr Justice Nicol's evaluation of Kate James' testimony *relies* on this trope, as he gives no other reason for disregarding her evidence. Given what James said, Nicol's willingness to do this without any detailed investigation into her credibility seems a little convenient. But if Nicol accepted *anything* Kate James said or wrote in her two witness statements, he would have a serious problem with the logic of his wider judgment.

It was a different story when Kate James also gave evidence in the United States.

VAST QUANTITIES OF RED WINE

Kate James was hired by Amber Heard in March 2012. She was fired in February 2015, which meant she had a ringside view of what was going on in Amber Heard's life for the majority of her relationship with Johnny Depp. James says she took the job because she was able to negotiate a deal with Heard which allowed James to stay in LA and pick up her son from school. The downside was a significant cut to her usual terms. In fact she described Heard paying her 'very poorly... $25 an hour to start with.'

James' first witness statement to the UK trial sets out how close she got to her employer.

'In the three years that I worked for Amber,' she wrote, 'I would go to her house almost every day, including on weekends. I would not announce when I was going to attend the apartment to drop things off or pick things up, so it would regularly be without notice. I never saw any sign of an altercation, or even the aftermath of a serious and messy fight in the way that Amber describes in her statements.'

Specifically, James says: 'I never once saw any bruising, swelling, or any evidence of what could have resulted from violence. I would often see her naked, or semi-naked, when she was getting dressed or at fittings. I was around her a lot, often 7 days a week.'

Under a paragraph headed 'Alcohol abuse', Kate James wrote:

'During my time working for her, Amber would drink vast quantities of red wine each night. Meanwhile, she would ask me to buy Johnny non-alcoholic beer, as that's all that she would allow him to drink.'

Under cross-examination in the UK and US, James was asked about the aftermath of the Boston/LA plane flight on 24 May 2014. As you will remember, Heard claimed Depp kicked her, and his behavior during the flight was abusive and traumatising. Having got off the plane, Heard went to a hotel.

James said on 24 May, Heard asked her to pick her up from the airport shuttle, as she was booked into the Chateau Marmont on Sunset Boulevard. James described her 'confusion' at this as Heard had her own apartment on Orange Avenue that was 'still being paid for and maintained' by Depp.

James says she was instructed to get Heard's bathing suit, which she brought to the hotel. James says Heard was soon having a 'pool party' accompanied by her friends 'Savannah [McMillan], iO Tillett-Wright, and... Raquel Pennington.' In James' words 'they proceeded to hang out all day drinking while I sat around waiting with my son.'

Finally, said James, she went home, and Heard went back to her apartment. 'And then she wanted me to go back and pack her bags with her at about ten o'clock at night on Sunday.'

James refused. 'By that point I'd already spent the whole day sitting there. So I said I couldn't go and pack a bag because I'd already put my son to bed, and she was very angry about that.'

In her live evidence to the Depp v NGN trial, and in her pre-recorded deposition in the US, James came across as bitter at the way she had been treated. In London, when she was asked if Heard was 'the first well-known person that you have ever been employed by in Hollywood,' James replied icily that Heard was 'probably the least known person I have ever worked for in Hollywood.'

The antipathy was mutual. When Heard was asked about her relationship with James, she told the US court she had hired James 'sometime in 2012' and had 'as minimal a contact with her as I possibly could.' Asked why, Heard said James was 'difficult, troubled, and inconsistent. She drank on the job and her behavior was horrible.'

It is entirely possible that Kate James gave evidence because she was motivated by a desire to see Heard put in her place after three unhappy years in her employment, but that doesn't mean what she told the court isn't true. On one matter, at least, James appeared to have Heard bang to rights.

In her first UK witness statement, James swore on oath that an English teenager by the name of Savannah McMillan had been 'hired' by Heard in the US, 'to work as her set assistant', despite McMillan having no working visa. This is very serious. In 2014, after a tip-off, the immigration authorities detained McMillan. James says:

'Amber asked me to send a letter she had drafted to Homeland Security... Amber's letter falsely claimed that Savannah was just a friend, and not an employee, so it was correct that she only had a tourist visa.'

The letter said any allegation McMillan was working for Heard in the US was 'fraudulent'. It also stated McMillan was 'a personal friend, and to my knowledge, has never worked unlawfully or otherwise in the United States. Or for me.'

James says this was untrue, claiming in her witness statement that Heard was 'wilfully lying to the US immigration department.' Even more serious. McMillan could have been called to give evidence and cross-examined on the matter in the UK or in the US, but neither she nor Nathan Holmes, who reportedly supplied Johnny Depp with illegal drugs, were asked to.

Before she left Heard's employ, James took a photograph of the letter Heard signed. She also photographed a check from Heard to McMillan for $1,625. James attached them to her UK witness statement.

Heard's letter, James' written evidence and the paycheck appear to be something of a smoking gun, so much so that it was among the first things to come up during Heard's cross-examination in the UK. They were all duly released to journalists.

The letter to Homeland Security is loquacious. Heard addresses the tip-off, saying it 'absolutely bears no merit, worth or truth.' What's more, the allegation against Savannah was 'made from the safety of anonymity in order to satisfy a personal vendetta.' Heard adds that she regrets 'the precious time of our immigration agencies has been bastardized on such a petty personal matter.'

She finishes with a flourish:

'I would like to request that this fraudulent report be removed pending the confirmation of its baseless and false stance. I expect the same standards that we hold as pillars of our great justice system, be allied to immigration policies as they serve at the forefront in representing United States and her values. Since I expect further investigation to reveal the statements made above as true, I hope that your agency will see to it that no further inconvenience will befall my friend in her attempts to continue discovering our beautiful country.'

In court, Heard said she didn't actually write the letter – it was written by Savannah McMillan herself – but as the words of the document 'did reflect the truth', she signed it. Eleanor Laws, the barrister tasked with cross-examining Heard on behalf of Johnny Depp, was incredulous:

'You are saying that the 18-year old Savannah wrote this letter...?'

Heard gave a strange chuckle. 'I *am* saying that,' she replied. Collecting herself, Heard added: 'I only smile because it seems very much like Savannah.'

Savannah evidently had a way with words, and yet could not spell her own name. In the letter it was rendered McMillen, rather than McMillan.

During cross-examination, Heard was taken to an email from Kate James, who wrote:

'Hey there, hope you had a good flight and it's beautiful on the island. Savannah just asked me to write her a check for her pay. Just checking if that's what you want me to do and, if so, how much.'

Heard replied: 'Yes please, 1300.'

Laws asked directly if McMillan had worked for Heard as an assistant on *Magic Mike* and *The Adderall Diaries*. Heard replied:

'No, she travelled with me and she helped me out. You are working long hours... it is helpful to have somebody help you get the groceries when you do not have time in your long hours or prepare the home or help you find a rental, whatever.'

That, to me, sounded suspiciously like the job of an assistant, and it was at this point that Mr Justice Nicol intervened to ask Heard directly: 'Was Savannah McMillan ever paid by you when you were in the United States?'

'No,' replied Heard. 'Not when I was in the United States. I did loan her money when she was in the States, and I gave her money for expenses.'

The courtroom exchanges over Savannah McMillan's employment status were an attempt by Laws to impugn Heard's credibility. If she was deceiving Homeland Security and then lying about it in court, what else was she making up? From where I was sitting, it looked pretty cut and dried, but in his judgment, Mr Justice Nicol was having none of it.

Nicol referred to the explanation in Heard's fifth witness statement, which said: 'Since Savannah did not have much money, I occasionally gave her money. I would sometimes refer to the money I gave to Savannah as "payments" to minimize the discomfort and embarrassment to Savannah for receiving this money from me. The payments were partly to cover expenses for both of us, like shopping and errands.'

Nicol accepted Heard's evidence in this regard, adding, 'I do not consider that the letter to Homeland Security was a lie.'

On the issue of whether Heard was lying to court about Savannah drafting the letter, Nicol agreed these allegations have 'some force', particularly when considering Savannah's inability to spell her own surname correctly, but, he concluded, 'it takes the matter no further... the identity of the drafter of the letter does not assist in resolving whether the Department of Homeland Security was lied to by Ms Heard.'

Without conclusive proof Amber Heard lied to Homeland Security (and the judge does seem to be setting a high bar, given McMillan was required to run errands for Heard and received checks described as 'payment'), Nicol concluded the matter had 'no bearing on whether Ms Heard is to be believed in relation to her allegations that she was assaulted by Mr Depp.'

TO WHIT

Amber Heard's sister Whitney gave evidence at both trials. She seemed bright and at ease with herself in the witness box. Her style was uncomplicated and matter-of-fact. Whitney is a woman of impeccable character, notwithstanding her admissions of illegal drug-taking with Johnny Depp. On the face of it, there is no reason to disbelieve a word she is saying. On the face of it.

Whitney met Depp in 2011 during the promotional tour for *The Rum Diary*. As Heard and Depp's relationship blossomed, Whitney got to know Depp well. They became so close he would call her 'sis', and she would refer to him as her 'brother'.

In her witness statement to the UK trial, Whitney describes Depp as controlling, saying he didn't like her sister working and wanted her to stop. Depp allegedly also didn't like Heard wearing revealing dresses. Whitney says Depp was 'incredibly jealous and possessive' – red flags for abuse – 'and was threatened by her former partners and co-stars, both men and women.'

This was confirmed by Depp's former friend, Bruce Witkin, who testified to Depp's jealousy in the US trial. Witkin is Lori Anne Allison's brother-in-law – Allison was Depp's first wife. Witkin confirmed Depp had a 'jealous streak'. The younger Depp was allegedly 'jealous of Nic Cage and jealous of Adam Ant because my sister-in-law knew them.' He remembered Depp later came up with a few 'ridiculous' things about Vanessa Paradis. 'A lot of it,' said Witkin, 'was in his head' and 'not in reality.' Witkin said Depp was also jealous of Heard's co-stars, saying: 'If she was on a film or doing something that he couldn't be around to see what was going on, I think he'd work himself up, you know?'

Whitney remembers Depp and Heard getting into a huge fight in Brazil in 2015. Depp didn't like Heard 'leaving early so she could do a screen test for *Aquaman*.' Whitney remembers joking with Nathan Holmes: 'We hoped she didn't get the role because Johnny would go crazy when he saw a picture of Jason Momoa, her co-star... Many of their fights stemmed from his jealousy.'

Whitney says her filial relationship to Heard and closeness to Depp meant she was stuck with the role of mediator.

'I was often asked to intervene when they were fighting... It got to the point that my nickname became "the marriage counsellor".'

According to Whitney, the evidence of violence was there from 'early on'. Whitney says she saw 'signs of physical abuse' including 'bruises or cuts or burns' on her sister's arm. She first asked Heard about them in mid-2013. Heard 'always had an excuse: she had bumped into this or that, or she had a mark on her arm from burning herself while cooking or using her curling iron for her hair. I didn't challenge her about it initially.'

Towards the end of 2014, Whitney says she confronted Depp about the violence, having been sent to see him, once more playing the role of peacemaker.

'I remember saying to him: "Why did you fucking have to hit her?" Sometimes he would flat out deny it or downplay it by saying: "No, I just pushed her, I didn't hit her." Other times, he would acknowledge that he had hit her but would try to justify it, by claiming she hit him first or "She called me a pussy" and would say: "Sis, I just lost control".'

Whitney said Depp blamed Heard for the violence, 'saying things like, "I just love her so much but this is what she does to me" and never really took responsibility for it.'

Whitney claims that by 2015 she was 'so over' Depp's violence 'that I was no longer friendly with him... I would refuse or avoid opportunities to hang out with him or be around him.'

This did not go down well. 'Johnny accused me of leaking and selling stories to the media about him and Amber to my friend, Sara Kitnick, who is a journalist.'

Whitney told her sister Depp's allegation was not true, but Heard turned on her. 'Amber believed him and was devastated. I was upset that she believed Johnny over me, and there was a long period in 2015 when I was estranged from Amber and Johnny because of this.'

In her statement, Whitney claims she sought a rapprochement with Depp, purely out of concern for her sister. At a reconciliation meeting with Heard in January 2016, Whitney says: 'I remember being shocked when I saw her. She had lost so much weight in the months that we had not been speaking. It was awful. The stress was taking its toll. I saw that she was emaciated and she told me she had recently been suffering with shingles, anxiety attacks and heart problems. I was relieved when she finally filed for divorce and a restraining order.'

THE CLOSED FIST PUNCH

Los Angeles, 23 March 2015

In her witness statement to the UK trial, Amber Heard deals with what she claims happened on 23 March 2015 relatively perfunctorily. It began when Heard confronted Depp after she 'found messages that showed he was cheating on me.'

The alleged affair was with a woman named Rochelle Hathaway, memorably (if not wholly accurately) described by Info Guide Nigeria as a 'well-known actress and Contract Corporate Flight Attendant.'

Heard says: 'I knew that he had cheated on me before, but I did not think he would have carried on after we were married. I confronted him about it – and he reacted badly. He started smashing things up all round the apartment, including possessions of mine in my closet.'

From Depp's perspective, the fight began because 'Ms Heard was in an extremely argumentative mood and kept trying to provoke me to have an argument with her.' Depp, conveniently, could not 'remember precisely what this particular rage was about.'

The argument began in Penthouse 5 of Depp's apartments at the Eastern Columbia Building in downtown LA. At the time Whitney lived next door[1] in Penthouse 4. The two apartments have interconnecting doors on their upper levels.

Whitney says during the argument:

'Amber came in [to PH4 from PH5] and she was crying and screaming: "Can you fucking believe this? Your brother is fucking cheating on me."... I went to find Johnny to talk to him to figure out what was going on. I was sober because Amber woke me up and got me out of bed.'

The time was around 4.30am. Whitney entered PH5 from PH4 and saw from the upper level that 'Johnny had an almost empty bottle of whiskey in one hand,' which he was 'drinking in the kitchen downstairs.' His sobriety nurse, Debbie Lloyd, was with him. Whitney walked down the stairs towards Depp. 'He was not making much sense but was shouting denials and making it about Amber, saying: "She was fucking so and so"; "she made me do it".'

---

[1] For a full reminder of who lived in which apartment and how the apartments connected up, see the *Reader notes* at the front of this book and the floorplan diagram at the beginning of the *The Phone Incident* chapter.

According to Whitney, Depp was also accompanied by two security guards. Everyone else seems to think there was just one, Travis McGivern.

Heard followed Whitney back into PH5 and went down to the mezzanine level 'screaming' at Depp. According to Whitney, Depp was 'screaming' back, 'saying she was a "whore", that she was "an ugly old cunt", and that "no one would find you attractive if they knew how many men you went through".'

Whitney says she went back up to Heard on the mezzanine level 'to try to calm her down and de-escalate the situation.' Nurse Debbie appears to have joined them.

As Whitney stood on the mezzanine level of PH5 with Heard and Lloyd, Depp allegedly threw a can of Red Bull at them. Whitney says the can hit Nurse Debbie. This is partially corroborated by Heard during her evidence to both the UK and US trials. In Virginia she told the court: 'Debbie came up the stairs... to kind of comfort me. And while I was up on the mezzanine floor... he threw the Red Bull can up at me... but it either hit or narrowly missed Debbie.'

Debbie Lloyd gave evidence in the US trial and was asked about her recollection of the evening. Lloyd remained frustratingly vague about many aspects of events she apparently witnessed, answering, 'I do not recall' a hundred and fifteen times to the questions put to her. Whilst Lloyd remembers being present in the apartment on 23 March, and witnessing an argument taking place, when she was asked if she remembered Depp throwing anything at Heard or Heard throwing anything at Depp, she replied: 'I do not recall.'

Thankfully the text message Lloyd sent to Stephen Deuters following the incident survives. It says:

'Bad night last night. They got into it and it got violent again... He said she was trying to start. He took his meds and went to bed but then she found the texts to Rochelle and all hell broke loose!! He had Travis get me back there around 4. Good thing he called or they would have hurt each other. We had to physically restrain both of them.'

Travis McGivern gave evidence in both the UK and US trials through a long and magnificent grey beard. He says a can of Red Bull *was* thrown, but it was thrown by Amber Heard from the mezzanine level at Depp. McGivern says the can hit Depp in the back. The can was followed by a 'purse', which McGivern says Heard also threw at Depp. Again it was on target, but McGivern batted it away before it hit his client.

McGivern said: 'I recognized that Ms Heard had access to a variety of other items that she could throw from her position. I therefore moved next to Mr Depp to ensure that he would not get hit by anything else. At this point, Ms Heard was standing on the landing above Mr Depp and I witnessed her spit on Mr Depp' (something Heard, when asked about it in the UK trial, denied).

Whitney described Depp shouting 'Fuck you bitches, you cunts.' She says he then 'started coming up the stairs towards us, yelling at us.'

Whitney was between Depp and Heard.

'When he got to the top of the stairs,' she wrote, 'he was pulling me backwards so he could get to Amber... I was worried that I would fall backwards and fall down the stairs. Johnny reached out to shove me out of the way to lunge at Amber – reaching out to try hit Amber – and instead struck me, hitting me in the arm.'

This provoked a response from Heard: 'Amber suddenly lurched forward and hit him and said, "Don't hit my sister". I didn't see exactly how Amber hit him but it didn't seem especially hard; it was just enough for him to lose momentum.'

Whitney says the blow led to a struggle. 'He really went for Amber,' she wrote. 'Somehow I was pushed out of the way so I wasn't between them, but I was standing right there next to them when Johnny grabbed her by the hair with one hand.'

Whitney states unequivocally: 'I saw him punch her really hard in the head with his other hand multiple times.'

The fight was stopped when Travis McGivern intervened. Whitney says she took her sister back into PH4, to make sure she was okay. 'From my apartment,' she wrote, 'I could hear someone breaking and smashing things, and Johnny screaming "fucking cunt", "you fucking whore, I hate you". At some point the noise stopped, but I didn't go and see what happened.' Whitney took Heard back to the main apartment – PH3 – 'so she wouldn't have to listen to what was happening.' She describes staying with her sister until she got to sleep.

It is undisputed that after Heard and Whitney left PH5, Depp went on the rampage, tearing into Heard's possessions, but both Depp and McGivern say Heard was the *only* aggressor when it came to violence between them.

McGivern's timeline is different to Whitney's. He acknowledges Depp 'rearranged' Heard's closet, to the extent of throwing around 'probably every rack of clothing and shoes' and 'at least one down the stairs', but he says this was precipitated by the spitting and the can-throwing.

McGivern says Heard and Whitney were absent during Depp's attack on Heard's stuff, but suggests they came *back* into PH5 because Heard 'must have heard what was going on and not been too pleased.'

Memory bends. We don't know whose is the most reliable. Or who is telling the truth. Of the key moment, McGivern says he, Depp, Heard and Whitney were all assembled on the mezzanine level of PH5 (Lloyd's position, at this point, is unclear). Heard and Depp were both 'agitated'. McGivern decided 'it was time to get Mr Depp out of the situation', so he 'stepped in between Ms Heard and Mr Depp, telling Mr Depp that we were leaving and that it wasn't up to him anymore.'

Before McGivern could put his plan into action he saw 'a fist and an arm come across my right shoulder.' The fist and arm belonged to Amber Heard. McGivern says he saw Heard's 'closed fist' make contact with the left side of Depp's face.

Asked how Depp responded to the punch, McGivern replied:

'The initial look on his face mirrored mine, a look of shock, like, "What just happened? Where'd that come from?" At that point, I wasn't going to let Mr Depp get hit anymore, so I moved him down the last flight of stairs to the lower level and told him: "We're leaving".'

McGivern's main emotion appears to be one of embarrassment. 'I had let him get hit by a Red Bull can. I let him get punched. My job is to ensure the safety and well-being of my clients and I felt like I hadn't done that.'

McGivern is adamant that Depp did not lay hands on Heard, or Whitney, at any point.

Heard, like Whitney, says the violence happened immediately after the can-throwing. She told the US court she was 'screaming at him angrily. I at least called him a fucking pussy... And when I did that, he bolted up the stairs... I don't know how he managed to get his hand in my hair so fast, but he had his hand on the back of my head, my hair, and was yanking me down.'

Both sisters say that before Heard lamped him, Whitney was pushed and Heard was punched repeatedly by Depp. The allegation of punching is complicated by Depp's injury. At the time, Depp's middle finger was pinned and half his hand was set in an unclenched, naturally open position by a solid plaster cast. It is feasible a drunken Depp could have decided to use the cast (and therefore the fragile finger within it) to hit someone repeatedly, but as he was not capable of forming a fist, it could not have been a punch.

No mention was made of the cast in the initial witness statements presented to the UK courts by Whitney or Heard. Asked why in

London, Heard said: 'I did not include every detail of every thought or every item of clothing or accessory that was used in the violence. There were so many.'

In her US testimony, Heard describes the punch from her perspective. She said that after beating on her, Depp turned his attention to Whitney: 'Johnny swings at her, and I just see my little sister with her back to the staircase... I don't hesitate. I don't wait. I just in my head think of Kate Moss and the stairs, and I swung at him. In all of my relationship to date with Johnny, I hadn't landed a blow. And I, for the first time, hit him, actually hit him, square in the face.'

The perceived danger was averted. Whitney did not get pushed, or fall down the stairs. Either Depp left with McGivern and Lloyd and the incident ended, or Whitney took Heard back into PH4, leaving Depp to trash Heard's closet in PH5 before leaving.

There is a coda to this tale which involves one of the most celebrated closed fist *pumps* of 2022. But before we get to Benjamin Chew and Kate Moss, I need to introduce you to Jennifer Howell.

Jennifer Howell is the LA-based founder of the Art of Elysium charity. She, like Whitney, is a woman of impeccable character. Howell says she wrote a declaration for the US proceedings after being made aware of Whitney's evidence about the events described above. Howell was 'made aware' by way of subpoena from Johnny Depp's lawyers.

In her declaration, Howell called Whitney a 'dear friend' who was essentially lying to protect her sister. Howell remembers Whitney coming to her house in 'a mess' shortly after 23 March. Howell wrote: 'Whitney told me she tried to stop her sister Amber from hitting and attacking Johnny on the stairs. Whitney said when she tried to intervene to stop Amber from going after Johnny, Amber nearly pushed Whitney down the stairs. She told me she was worried Amber "was going to kill Johnny." She told me she had endured that kind of abuse her entire life, first from her father, and then from Amber, who she said was extremely violent.'

Howell says she took Whitney in. 'She lived with me because she did not feel she could go back to live at the Eastern Columbia Building.'

Howell wrote: 'While Whitney was living with me, she told me Johnny kept checking in to see how she was doing and that he called her "sis" and she called him "brother". Whitney said to me on multiple occasions that she did not know why he was staying in the relationship nor why he was putting up with Amber's abuse. Whitney shared with me the damage endured by both her and Amber as children and the injuries she had suffered from Amber both psychologically and physically. Whitney was devastated during this time, and my heart broke for her.'

During an edited deposition played for the jury during the US trial, Howell was shown an email letter she had sent to Whitney after she discovered she would be giving evidence to support Heard in the UK trial. The letter's content was not revealed in court, but the text has been leaked.

In the letter, Howell put her feelings on the line. She told Whitney: 'My allegiance in all of this is to you and you alone.' Howell wrote she had, 'never been more upset during any of this drama than I am right now at the thought of Amber asking you... to go to London and entangle you in all of this. If you feel that you have been asked or compromised in any way to do anything that might perjure yourself, I beg you to recant and, for once in your life, think of yourself first.'

When asked during the deposition why she had sent the email, Howell replied: 'I've struggled very much with what to do... I love someone who I know is doing something very wrong, and I know that they're doing it because they're trying to protect their sister... I'm just trying to get her to wake up and do the right thing. Which is tell the truth.'

KATE MOSS

During cross-examination at the High Court in London in 2020, Johnny Depp's barrister, Eleanor Laws, picked up on Heard's admission that she had hit her husband on the evening of 23 March 2015 and invited her to elaborate. Heard did so, saying:

'I did strike Johnny that day in defense of my sister. He was about to push her down the stairs. And the moment before that happened, I remembered information I had heard very recently, which is that he pushed a former girlfriend, I believe it was Kate Moss, down the stairs. I had heard this rumor from two people and it was fresh in my mind.'

Laws was momentarily taken aback. Kate Moss?!

'You just added that bit in,' suggested the barrister.

'I have never changed my story,' replied Heard.

Laws was quite certain Heard had changed her story. The barrister asked Heard why she had not mentioned Kate Moss in her witness statement, or during the lengthy deposition she had given as part of the US proceedings.

Heard replied: 'I have not had every opportunity to list every thought that went through my mind before any or all of the many instances in which Johnny beat me up.'

What was Heard doing bringing Kate Moss into the picture? It is plausible that two people in 2016 had told her that back in the nineties Depp had pushed Moss down a flight of stairs. Given the state of Heard's relationship with Depp when she heard the rumor, it is plausible she might believe it could be true.

It also remains plausible that this 'rumor' popped into Heard's mind during a stressful and fraught moment and that it was a genuine motivating factor in her decision to punch Johnny Depp. And it is perhaps plausible that she either forgot, or didn't think it was relevant enough to mention in preparation for the UK trial until she got into the witness box. Unfortunately, Laws did not ask the identities of the two people who revealed the information about Kate Moss to Amber Heard.

Mr Justice Nicol does not mention Kate Moss in his judgment and the matter may have ended there had Heard not brought it up again, two years later, at the US trial. During her testimony (describing the same incident) Heard told the Virginia court: 'I just in my head think of Kate Moss and the stairs, and I swung at him.'

This time, at the mention of Kate Moss, Depp's lawyer, Ben Chew, glanced in amazement at Johnny Depp and then turned back to his fellow attorneys. With a smile of a man who knows he has just heard his opponent put their foot in it, Chew gave a little fist pump before regaining composure. The TV cameras picked it up, and the moment went viral.

Depp's lawyers knew Kate Moss had nothing bad to say about Johnny Depp. What they needed was a way of presenting that knowledge to the jury. Prior to the trial, Kate Moss could not be listed as a witness for Johnny Depp, mainly because the defamation accusation had nothing to do with her. Heard's two-second witness box reference to Moss had, as they say in the US, 'opened the door'. She could now be brought into play.

If Depp *had* pushed Kate Moss down a flight of stairs in the nineties (or someone was claiming he had) there's a good chance there would be some digital imprint of this, but there isn't. There's nothing online pre-2020, when Heard first made the accusation in public.

Whilst Depp was with Moss he was arrested for causing thousands of pounds worth of damage to a New York hotel room. Depp spent a few hours in jail[1] and was subsequently arraigned, but the matter was dropped when he agreed to pay for the room damage and the rest of his scheduled stay at the hotel. Save for sketchy reports of a few public arguments, the Depp/Moss relationship seemed uncomplicated. It finished when he left her.

During a post-verdict TV interview, Benjamin Chew said Heard's decision to mention Kate Moss in the US trial 'put a lot of pressure' on his team, as they had to 'come up with the goods.' Fortunately Ms Moss 'came forward' as Chew described it, and during the final week of the trial, she was duly lined up as a witness. To an overheated media machine this was gold. Rumors Elon Musk and James Franco might be giving evidence during proceedings had come to naught. The prospect, therefore, of a celebrity witness (other than Depp and Heard themselves, of course) giving evidence at the climax of the trial cranked the anticipation up to eleven.

I was finding it hard to get too excited. Partly because I was in a state of exhaustion (the judge, in an effort to get the trial finished on time, was running nine-hour court days), and partly because Chew's fist pump suggested it was unlikely Moss would come out with confirmation that Johnny Depp had indeed thrown her down any stairs.

---

[1] As Depp was being taken to the local police station, he was recorded suggesting that the arresting Officer Perez didn't like him, 'but if she saw me at a mall, I bet she would ask me for an autograph.' Officer Perez is reported to have responded, 'No Johnny. I don't think so.'

In fact, the most interesting thing about Kate Moss giving evidence is the fact we would hear her say anything at all. Despite being one of the most famous models of the last 30 years (and very much a British icon), Moss spent much of her career avoiding interviews or putting anything substantial on the record. Now she was going to be asked questions – and cross-examined under oath. Anything could happen.

The big day – 25 May 2022 – came. Kate Moss was called up on the court video screens and asked to count to five so the techies could check the sound levels. Moss appeared to be speaking into a webcam from someone's empty spare room (which she confirmed was in 'Gloucestershire, England'). This was, nonetheless, An Event, and like most Events involving Kate Moss, the pivotal issue for some was not what she was saying, but what she was wearing.

The normally sober Guardian newspaper in England declared Moss's decision to give evidence wearing a light-spotted pussybow blouse and black satin-lapelled jacket was their 'fashion moment of the week.' The pussybow is, according to Guardian fashionistas, 'subtly subversive' as it apparently symbolizes the encroachment of feminine sensibility on male space. Whilst most of us may have just thought Kate was looking quite nice, fashion historian Dr Bethan Bide told the Guardian's readers Moss was attempting to 'evoke defiance' with her semi-undone pussybow, which apparently 'feels more rebellious. It's like she's saying, "I'm not going to perform for you here". It's a refusal to deliver for the media circus.'

As to her testimony, having established the dates of Depp and Moss's 'romantic relationship' (1994 to 1998), Chew dived straight in:

'Ms Moss,' he asked, 'did there come a time while you and Mr Depp were a couple that the two of you took a vacation together to the GoldenEye Resort in Jamaica?'

Ms Moss agreed that such a time had come. The model was asked to describe what, if anything, happened in Jamaica.

'We were leaving the room,' she replied, 'and Johnny left the room before I did. And there had been a rainstorm. And as I left the room, I slid down the stairs and I hurt my back... I screamed because I didn't know what had happened to me, and I was in pain. And he came running back to help me, and carried me to my room, and got me medical attention.'

'Did Mr Depp push you in any way down the stairs?' asked Chew.

'No,' replied Moss.

Chew asked again, to make sure: 'During the course of your relationship, did he ever push you down *any* stairs?'

'No,' replied Moss, again, laughing at the need to labor the point. 'He never pushed me, kicked me, or threw me down any stairs.'

And so ended the evidence of Kate Moss. Invited to cross-examine Depp's witness, Heard's legal team declined. The whole thing took four minutes.

In court the next day, Amber Heard found herself back on the stand giving rebuttal evidence. She was asked again about Kate Moss, Johnny Depp and The Stairs. Instead of acknowledging she may well have got the wrong end of the stick, Heard doubled down:

'Everybody who was around in the '90s and the early oughts knew that rumor,' Heard told the court. 'I had heard that rumor from multiple people.'

In his closing arguments on the final day of the trial, Chew tried to make a go of their star witness, telling the jury:

'Ms Heard lied to you... when she suggested to you that Mr Depp pushed Kate Moss down the stairs. You heard [Moss] say, just two days ago, that Mr Depp never did that. And he never hit her. And he never kicked her.'

Well, not quite, Mr Chew. Amber Heard told the court she'd heard a *rumor* that Depp had pushed Kate Moss down a flight of stairs. She thought her sister was in danger of being pushed down some stairs by Depp and (because she believed the rumor) hit Depp in the face.

Yet the episode remains extraordinary because it demonstrated Heard's capacity to take unfounded information, mark it in her mind as Probably True and then act violently on her assumptions. The jury were being invited to wonder – if she could do that, what other fantasies had become fact in her mind?

THE HOSTAGE VIDEO

One of the more memorable sights of 2016 was a video of Amber Heard and Johnny Depp sitting side-by-side on wooden chairs in a hotel room, looking for all the world like they had been taken captive. Heard is wearing all black, with her hair down. Depp is dressed in a black jacket over a white formal shirt. He is slouched. The backdrop is an uninspiring double set of folded net and beige curtains which partially obscure the light from a window behind them.

As the video begins, Depp and Heard are staring down at the camera, set for no obvious reason well below their eye-lines.

'Australia is a wonderful island,' starts Heard, leaning in, 'with a treasure trove of unique plants, animals and people.' She gives a small smile at the end of her opening sentence. She's making a go of it.

Depp seems less enthusiastic. 'It has to be protected,' he says, eyeing the camera suspiciously.

'Australia is free of many pests and diseases commonplace around the world,' continues Heard. 'That is why Australia has to have such strong biosecurity laws.' She turns to look at Depp.

'And Australians are just as unique, both warm and direct,' drawls Depp, putting in the minimum effort. 'When you disrespect Australian law, they will tell you firmly.'

Heard turns back from looking at Depp and delivers an apology to camera. 'I'm truly sorry that Pistol and Boo were not declared. Protecting Australia is important.'

'Declare everything when you enter Australia,' says Depp, nodding at the camera. 'Thanks.'

The screen fades to black.

The video was published on the Australian Government Department for Agriculture's YouTube channel. Most of their videos have fewer than ten thousand views. This one has six million. It's a hit. And its twin aims: drawing attention to Australia's strict customs laws and making it abundantly clear no one is above those laws, are achieved.

The story behind this 42-second piece of public service broadcasting is fascinating, but you might wonder what place it has in a book about domestic violence. Well – here we go...

The excerpt is part of a legal negotiation. On 21 April 2015 Amber Heard and Johnny Depp flew by private jet back from the US to Australia after Depp's finger was injured at the Diamond Head compound in

March. He and it were on the mend. On their 21 April flight, the couple were accompanied by their two teacup yorkies[1], Pistol and Boo.

On arrival in Brisbane, Depp and Heard were met by quarantine and customs officers. When replying to the question on her passenger card – *Are you bringing into Australia animals, parts of animals, et cetera?* – Heard answered *no*. That was false.

Pistol and Boo's cover was blown by social media. On 9 May the terriers were taken to Happy Dogz grooming parlour in the small town of Maudsland on the Gold Coast. Shortly afterwards, the owners posted pictures of Pistol and Boo onto Facebook with a caption stating: 'It's an honor to be grooming Johnny Depp and Amber Heard's two Yorkshire Terriers'. The post went viral.

Questions were asked. According to court documents, on 12 May, someone who identified themselves as a representative of Johnny Depp contacted the principal veterinary officer for the Department of Agriculture in Australia, informing them that there might be a problem. There was.

The authorities were provided with Pistol and Boo's veterinary records, told where they would be able to find them and advised they had been isolated. On 13 May, an official was dispatched to the Diamond Head compound, where Depp and Heard were once more staying. Pistol and Boo were examined and their records were checked. It transpired no permits allowing the importation of the dogs into Australia had been issued by the country's Director of Quarantine. Oh dear.

Immediately, the Department of Agriculture sent out a press release stating that: 'A biosecurity officer attended a Gold Coast property on 13 May and found two illegally imported dogs. The Department is now reviewing how the dogs were brought into Australia without an import permit.'

Australia's Minister of Agriculture, Barnaby Joyce, was less circumspect. 'Mr Depp needs to take his dogs back to California or we're going to have to euthanize them,' he said. 'If we start letting movie stars, even if they've been "Sexiest Man Alive" twice, to come into our nation, then why don't we just break the laws for everybody. It's time that Pistol and Boo buggered off back to the United States.'

The colorful nature of the minister's language and Depp's fame ensured the incident became international news. On 15 May 2015 both

---

[1] Very small Yorkshire terrier dogs. So named because some are small enough to fit in a teacup.

dogs were flown by private jet out of Australia, at an estimated cost of $400,000.

On 14 July, the Australian Department of Public Prosecutions issued Heard with a criminal summons. She was charged with two counts of illegally importing animals into Australia and one count of producing a false document. Producing a false document can lead to a one-year jail sentence. Illegally importing animals into Australia is a crime with a maximum penalty of ten years in prison. This was serious.

At the time, Kevin Murphy was Johnny Depp's US estate manager. In a pair of witness statements produced in support of Depp for the UK trial, Murphy gave some background to Pistol and Boo's arrival in Australia. He had some authority on the matter, telling the court that he was involved 'from start to finish.'

It seems like it was not a straightforward process. Murphy had 'concerns' towards the end of March that timing constraints were not going to allow the dogs to be vaccinated before Depp and Heard left for Australia. Murphy says he 'expressed those concerns to Ms Heard in person, by phone and in emails.' Heard apparently responded by asking if there were any other way to take the dogs. Murphy raised the possibility of them flying cargo, but Heard would not allow it. Murphy said they were therefore 'out of options.' He says Heard 'appeared to accept that there was nothing else that we could do and that the dogs would not be able to travel to Australia in time for her flight.'

Murphy says he explicitly told Heard 'several times' that 'trying to take the dogs into Australia without completing the mandatory process was illegal and could result in very harsh penalties including euthanizing the dogs, fines and potential jail time.'

Being thorough, Murphy said he notified all the key members of Depp's team, including his head of security, Jerry Judge, telling them specifically that Pistol and Boo were not allowed to be taken to Australia. Murphy said he was keen to make this point 'because Ms Heard had brought the dogs into the Bahamas without paperwork and vaccinations in another instance in July 2014' despite having 'knowledge of the risks.'

Murphy says Depp was left in the dark about all canine consignment plans 'because he never wanted the dogs to travel on any occasion' as he apparently felt 'they would have better care in Los Angeles with staff.'

The way Murphy tells it, Heard went ahead and took the dogs with her into Australia anyway. When he found out, Murphy claimed to be 'shocked'. Murphy says he contacted Jerry Judge shortly afterwards.

Judge apparently acknowledged the dogs had been smuggled into the country, and according to Murphy, told him: 'Ms Heard had insisted on bringing them to Australia.'

Amber Heard remembers the debacle differently. In her fifth witness statement to the High Court in London, she said: 'Johnny wanted Pistol and Boo to come to Australia, and knew they were on the plane with us. It is untrue, as Mr Murphy has said, that Johnny wanted to keep the dogs in the US.'

When Murphy's witness statement was brought to her attention in court, specifically the assertion that he had told her unequivocally that the dogs could not travel, Heard said: 'I was told many things... It was quite confusing.'

Heard said that when she joined Depp's party on the plane for the flight to Brisbane on 21 April, she had only been in LA for 'a matter of hours' and Depp had told her, with regard to the dogs, 'it was all taken care of.'

Pushed on this, Heard told the court: 'We brought the dogs in plain sight... We both filled up the same entry cards. We both signed the same things, and yet I was the only one that took the charges. Because if Johnny got charges, it would have further compromised *Pirates*, which was already compromised.'

In October 2015, Kevin Murphy signed a witness statement for the Australian court proceedings, dropping Kate James in the do-do. It read:

'Although Mrs Depp initially instructed me to make arrangements for the dogs to travel to Australia in April 2015, it was Ms James, an Australian citizen, who assumed the primary responsibility for preparing the necessary travel-related paperwork to permit the dogs to travel with Mrs Depp to Australia.'

He added: 'Per the household policy, Mr Depp and Mrs Depp would not have travelled with the dogs to Australia if they didn't believe all the necessary travel-related paperwork had been completed and approved.'

In his witness statement to the High Court in 2020, Murphy claimed both elements of this declaration to the Australian court were not true.

Precisely what anyone thought blaming Kate James would achieve isn't entirely clear. James says she found out she'd been singled out by Murphy 'many months' later when she 'woke up one morning... to find an email from my mother with an attachment of a newspaper article from my home town of Brisbane.'

James said (in her first witness statement to the UK trial) she was 'devastated' at being blamed. She 'broke down in tears' at the 'complete lie' and railed at Heard 'apparently perjuring herself in order to avoid responsibility.'

Whilst it was Murphy's statement which named and shamed James, it was offered in Heard's defense, and organized by lawyers working on her behalf. It is perhaps understandable that James thought Heard was responsible and had personally pointed the finger at her.

By the time the matter eventually came to an Australian court in April 2016, there was no need for a trial. Heard agreed to plead guilty to the lesser charge of producing a false document. The two more serious charges of illegally importing animals into Australia, were dropped.

Before it came to sentencing, lawyers successfully persuaded the court that Heard had no idea the passenger form she filled out on arrival in Brisbane covered pets. She apparently believed some other paperwork had been completed for the dogs and provided separately. The court accepted Heard's view 'that she did not set out to deliberately deceive the Australian authorities.'

Despite the guilty plea to the false document charge, Heard's legal team argued she should not be saddled with a criminal conviction, and Bernadette Callaghan, the presiding magistrate in Southport, Queensland, did not take much persuasion.

Callaghan told the court that she had read several references which spoke of Heard's 'generosity, commitment and kindness'. This, said the magistrate, demonstrated that 'she is just not another celebrity on the charity bandwagon... She is clearly a good person.'

Callaghan also noted Heard's assistant – Kate James – 'one of the staff responsible for that documentation' had been 'dismissed from her employment in acrimonious circumstances.' Callaghan noted: 'There were difficulties associated with this, and that had repercussions on the preparation of the documentation concerning the importation of the dogs.'

The magistrate was also at pains to recognize Heard's 'genuine remorse' and 'high degree of cooperation'. Rather than a conviction or a formal sentence, Heard would have to promise to behave for a month, or face a thousand dollar fine. The hostage video, recorded as part of the negotiations, was played in court.

Perhaps anticipating criticism, Callaghan drew attention to the benefits of her approach, saying the Department of Agriculture was 'better off using that video... that's of far more benefit to this country than anything else that I may do with regards to recording a conviction on Ms Heard.'

It was a compromise which saw Heard (and Depp) walk away from the whole farrago without any formal marks against their reputations or consequent restrictions on their ability to travel internationally. It also gave the Australian government a worldwide publicity coup which allowed them to ram home their fierce biosecurity message. Murphy and James were collateral damage.

Mr Justice Nicol had little sympathy. He devoted an entire section of his judgment to what the Aussie media dubbed the 'War on Terrier'. Nicol had already decided he would give no weight to Kate James' evidence because she was a disgruntled employee. Now he declared he would likewise give no weight to Murphy's attack on Heard's credibility – partly because Murphy had already lied in his witness statement to the Australian court ('not an encouraging starting point') and partly because Murphy had revealed himself as an 'enthusiastic' Depp supporter. This was evidenced in a 2019 email from Murphy to Depp in which Murphy said: 'I'll always have your back... anytime/anywhere... Continued relentless exposure of the fraud and the scamber bandits [a reference to Amber and her friends' alleged scam against Depp] is key.'

CRUEL INVECTIVE

The Diamond Head tape we dealt with in *A Strange Recording* is an anomaly, but it is by no means the only piece of audio evidence used in both trials. Somewhat unusually, Johnny Depp and Amber Heard spent a lot of time making recordings of each other.

'I was the first person of the two of us to record conversations,' Depp told the US court in 2022. His intention was to remind Heard of the 'demeaning, berating insults' she used in their arguments.

Depp says he needed evidence 'because she would deny having said those things... It was surreal. She had completely denied things she said directly to my face in a heated and volatile way... So, I went to her and I said, "I'm going to record us". And I did.'

This happened multiple times. At first, whoever started the recording would signal they were doing so. But then Depp said Heard started recording their conversations 'without telling me that she was recording something.' Depp described this in court as 'fine but not so fine, if you know what I mean.'

The result is a rich archive, charting the cruel invective Depp and Heard were capable of throwing at each other. Many Depp supporters I spoke to in the US told me that it was the audio tapes which had convinced them as to what was really going on in the relationship. This extended to a woman called Michelle, a survivor of domestic violence at the hands of her ex-husband. When we met outside court, early in the trial, Michelle told me she supported Amber Heard, and had come to Virginia to try to help abused women. She was committed enough to give me a passionate, if slightly disjointed interview on the matter. Unfortunately, Michelle's microphone packed up, and the interview was unusable. The message she spent most of our conversation trying to get across was related to her direct experience – Michelle wanted to tell other women that finding the courage to ask for help can change everything. Contact the authorities, or call one of the many charities running domestic abuse hotlines[1]. They will help you get out of your relationship, and start taking the relevant action against your abuser. I was gutted about the microphone not working, and felt awful for letting Michelle down, particularly as I could tell it took a lot of courage for her to go on camera. I saw Michelle at the courthouse on two more occasions. By the third she told me she had come to the conclusion it was

---

[1] There is a list of organizations and helplines at the back of this book.

Heard who had been abusing Depp. The main reason for her change of heart came from listening to the audio tapes.

Versions of the many recordings have been posted on various fan sites online, and many were played in both the UK and US courts. Whilst there is no doubt the people we hear on tape are Depp and Heard, the recordings were rarely played in their entirety. Of the tapes posted online, there is simply no way of knowing if or where they have been edited. No transcript, court or otherwise, is 100% accurate. I have listened to various recordings and personally transcribed the exchanges below after repeated listens. I have marked the sections where I am not precisely sure of what is being said. Longer versions have been played in court.

The conversations which stick in my mind primarily relate to Heard's language towards Depp and the tacit or explicit admissions of violence between the two. There are times when Heard seems to be taking a vindictive pleasure in taunting Depp. During some of these occasions, Depp sounds half cut and confused. It's not pretty. It's also very much at odds with the image Heard presented to the world during both court cases – that of a proper, wronged and decent woman. This is a good place to start:

AH: Fucking. Suck. Your own. Dick.

JD: Everything's fine until it doesn't go your way.

AH: You hear me?

JD: And when it doesn't go your way...

AH: Suck your own dick.

JD: ... I'm in trouble. And you know what, I don't need you.

AH: Suck your own dick.

JD: I don't want your kind of woman.

AH: Suck my dick.

JD: I don't want your kind of woman. I don't want your kind of woman.

AH: Suck my dick.

JD: I...

AH: Hey...

[indistinct exchange]

JD: Suck my dick, or yours?

AH: [indistinct conversation with possible tape edit] I wish I fucking hadn't bought into any of your fucking lies, your bullshit, your sober fucking presence, your fucking goodness, your sweetness. All the lies. I wish I hadn't bought into the months of you being you. I wish I hadn't bought into your [crosstalk] I wish I hadn't fucking thought I could have kids with you. You are a fucking kid yourself. I wish I hadn't bought into any of the lies you sold. Talk about a fake bill of goods.

[Continues in a similar vein with more fellatio-related invitations. Heard begins laughing maniacally, taunting Depp]

AH: [sarcastically] You can write a book!

JD: ... for another...

AH: You can write a book! Yeah! I know! You can write a book! Oh, is this gonna be gooood for your booook?! Aw! Should I sign an NDA for your booook?

JD: [mumbles inaudibly]

AH: Your book. Is this gonna be good for your book? Is this gonna be good for your book?

JD: [more mumbling]

AH: Hey,hey! I have a good idea. [Indistinct]... your journals. You don't wanna sell out or anything. Let's sell your journals. Oh... wait...

JD: Hey.

AH: Hey, you know what? No, no, no, you're not selling out.

JD: You don't wanna sell out. You don't want to sell out with *Magic Mike*. You don't wanna sell out.

AH: Yeah, no one does *21 Jump Street* when they're in their twenties. No, you're right. That's not selling out. No-oo. When you're in your twenties, you should really know what you want, like selling your journals. A-ha-ha-ha-ha-ha-haaaa!

[...]

AH: You're a joke.

JD: Yeah, I'm the joke in the industry, Amber. I'm the joke. I'm the joke in the industry.

AH: [laughing] I'm sorry, I can't really hear you. I'm sorry. The reruns of all my bullshit are playing too loud for me to hear you [indistinct] Sorry! I can't hear you.

JD: *Aquamaaaan!*

AH: Oh, oh! *21* whatever it was... or whatever who you were.

JD: I was twenty...

AH: [across him] No one cares! [laughs derisively] You fucking washed-up piece of shit.

JD: A washed-up piece of shit.

AH: Oh, what? What?

JD: Washed-up piece of shit.

AH: I can't hear you. I can't hear you!

JD: [laughs sarcastically]

AH: Oh, what? I can't hear you *again*.

JD: Your jealousy is so tragic.

AH: I'm *sorry*.

JD: Your jealousy is so tragic. Fucking like...

AH: I can't hear you!

In one long conversation, recorded in September 2015 after the alleged 'closed fist punch', Depp is on the defensive, listing the times he's either been attacked or pursued by Heard. Depp reminds Heard she threw 'pots and pans' at him, which she admits to. Eventually we get to what happened on the ECB penthouse stairs.

AH: I didn't punch you, by the way. I'm sorry that I didn't, er, er, hit you across the face in a proper slap, but I was hitting you. It was not *punching* you. Babe, you're not punched.

JD: [slurring] Don't tell me what it feels like to be punched!

AH: You know, you've been in a lot of fights, you've been around a long time. You know, yeah, I get it.

JD: No. When you fucking have a closed fist...

AH: You didn't get punched. You got hit. I'm sorry I hit you like this. But I did not *punch* you. I did not fucking *deck* you. I fucking was *hitting* you. I don't know what the fo... motion of my actual hand was. But you're *fine*. I did not hurt you. I did not punch you. I was *hitting* you.

JD: [indistinct]

AH: What am I supposed to do? Do this?

JD: [indistinct]

AH: I'm not sitting here bitching about it, am I?! You are. That's the difference between me and you. You're a fucking baby!

JD: Because you start...

AH: YOU ARE SUCH A *BABY*! Grow the fuck up, Johnny.

JD: Because you start physical fights.

AH: I did start a physical fight.

JD: Yeah, you did, so I had to get the fuck out of there.

AH: Because... Yes, you did... [sarcastically] So, you did the right thing, the big thing. You know what? You're *admirable*.

Later in the same conversation, Heard says: 'I can't promise that it will all be perfect. I can't promise you I won't get physical again. God, I fucking sometimes get so mad, I lose it. I can fucking promise you, I will do everything to change.'

In another tape, Depp and Heard are discussing an occasion when he pushed a bathroom door onto Heard's foot.

JD: Accidentally, I swear, when I was trying to close the door, I guess it scraped your toes. And I didn't... you know, I didn't mean to do that. And I bent down and you either pushed or you kicked. I think you kicked the door open. I mean, caught in the door. It got more open so that it would hit me, and it hit me.

AH: No, I didn't mean to.

[...]

JD: It hit me in the fucking head.

AH: But I did not mean to do that. I don't know what happened.

JD: I was bent down behind the door.

AH: I did not do anything to... I did not kick a door or push the door so that it would hit you. I did not. I swear. That did not... it was not my intention. I think I remember when the door scraped my toes, I reacted, but the door thing, I never did that. That wasn't on purpose. I might have done it on accident.

JD: Okay. So let's say that was an accident. I then stood up. I don't even know if I said... I mean, I might have said like, "What the fuck?" You know, whatever. Because I just been hit in the head with the fuckin' corner of the door.

AH: I'm so sorry. I didn't know. I'm sorry.

JD: And then I stood up, and then you fucking clocked me.

AH: I remember hitting you as a response to the door thing. And I'm really sorry about hitting you with the door or hitting your head. I did not mean to, nor...

JD: You didn't mean to hit me in the head with the door, but you meant to...

AH: I didn't mean...

JD: ... punch me in the jaw?!

AH: I meant to hit you, and I did not do this thing with the door. I do remember I did mean to hit you.

JD: So that, you didn't mean?

AH: The door? No. God, no, I didn't.

JD: But punching me in the jaw.

AH: Okay. I'm sorry, I hit you. I did mean to hit you, but it was in response. I just reacted in response to my foot. I just reacted. And I'm sorry, it's below me.

In another piece of audio, towards the end of their relationship, Depp references being hit again.

JD: I don't want to be with you. I don't. I *really* don't.

AH: Then if you don't want to be with me in life...

JD: Goodbye...

AH: ... then you need to actually do it. You need to actually take off your ring and forget that five hours ago you said the opposite. Otherwise, you can't keep throwing that around. You can't keep saying to me that this is something you care about.

[There is the sound of something small and metal hitting and bouncing along the floor]

JD: There you go.

AH: Is that what it's worth to you?

JD: Yeah. Yeah. For you, from all this bitching, from all these rules, all these...

AH: Rules? Because I asked you to stay? Because I asked you to stay?

JD: No, because you're a fucking...

AH: What was it when you asked me to stay?

JD: Because you're a pain in the ass.

AH: What was it when you asked me to stay?

JD: I can't stand it no more.

AH: What was it when you asked me to stay? In Australia, you said: 'You promise me not to leave,' you said. 'You promise me not to leave.' What did I do?

JD: I thought you would change.

AH: What did I do?

JD: Not change.

AH: What did I do?

JD: Not change.

AH: Did I stay or did I leave?

JD: You...

AH: *Did I stay or did I leave?*

JD: You stayed and you didn't change and you were a fucking pain in the ass and you were a cunt.

AH: So, I stayed and I've been a cunt ever since, which is why you told me about every other day how you couldn't imagine your life without me, including today. So... does that seem normal to you? Does that seem normal to you? You told me *tonight* that you couldn't imagine your life without me and now you're throwing your ring on the ground. Does that seem normal?

JD: That's how you tell me...

AH: Does that seem sober? You seem normal?

JD: You give me the definition of normal. You.

AH: Does that seem normal?

JD: You.

AH: Does that seem normal to you?

JD: Borderline Personality Dis-or-*der*.

AH: I am Borderline Personality Disorder now?

JD: Without question.

AH: When I've been consistent all night saying, 'Don't go, don't fuck this all up.' I'm not fighting with you anymore. I've been saying this to you the whole night, I'm really sorry we disagreed. You're not perfect. I said this two hours ago. I'm not perfect. You're not perfect.

JD: I love that you put me [indistinct] first.

AH: But we don't have to do this every time we disagree.

JD: No. No we don't. But we do.

AH: Please.

JD: But we do.

AH: Please, come here.

JD: And you have every insult...

AH: Please, come here! I'm not insulting you now! I have not been insulting you. I love you. Johnny, what do you need me to do? I love you! Stop!

JD: You want to smack me in the ear again?

AH: No.

JD: You want to smack my ear again? So it... fucking... *resounds* in my fucking cranium. Would you like that?

AH: I love you.

JD: Huh?

AH: I love you. I'm sorry I hit you. I love you. I love you.

JD: I love you too [indistinct] I don't love you that much.

AH: You do love me.

JD: No. I don't.

One recording Depp made whilst Heard was on speakerphone took place in the summer of 2016, after Heard had secured the DVRO but before their divorce was finalised. Reference to violence on both sides is made, but what resonated is the challenge that Amber Heard put down to Depp. She asked him if he thought he would be believed if he went public about her violence.

JD: This has been going on too long and we're just gonna stop this. We've just gotta stop it.

AH: I don't know how to get my reputation back.

JD: We write a letter together saying that we're going to take this out of the public eye. Saying that we're going to try to work this out on our own. Saying that the media has created such a fucking hateful storm. That it's sickening. That we love each other, and that we want to make sure each other is okay. Have we had fights in the past? Have we had this or whatever, fuck it, they already know all that shit. It don't matter. Here's the deal...

AH: It matters. I have been... you have no idea, every ounce of my credibility has been taken from, I mean, and done so in a dishonest way. You know?

JD: Amber... the abuse thing is... we've got to deal with that, yeah. We've got to deal with that, Amber.

AH: They don't have any way of... My credi... it's my credibility, you know...?

JD: Then why did you put that out there?

AH: I did *not*! You *forced* me. Your team forced me to, by going on the offense...

JD: I didn't force you to...

AH: [crosstalk]... beginning. I *promise*. Look up the timelines for these things, everything is... forget it. Forget it. You don't believe what I say. You don't believe what I say, but... I did not... I did not choose this. Every step of the way, it's been an offense...

JD: I did not put this anywhere. I didn't... let me talk to the fucking team.

AH: I did not call the cops. I gave them no statement... [crosstalk]

JD: iO called the cops.

AH: I did not call the cops.

JD: You told iO to call the cops.

AH: I did not call the cops and I did not give them any statement when they came. I've been trying to protect you...

JD: You told iO to call the cops.

AH: When? With what... what was happening?

JD: Yeah.

AH: Oh, I'm sorry. I'm sorry because the last time that it got crazy between us, I really did think I was gonna lose with my life. And I thought you would do it on accident. And I told you that. I said, "Oh, my God, I thought the first time..."

JD: [cuts across] Amber, I lost a fucking finger, man. Come on. I had a fucking, I had a fucking mineral can, a jar... a can of mineral spirits thrown at my nose.

AH: You can please tell people that it was a fair fight and see what the... see what the jury and judge thinks. Tell the world, Johnny... tell them: "Johnny Depp... I, Johnny Depp, a man, I'm a victim too of domestic violence...

JD: ... yes!...

AH: ... and, you know, it's a fair fight," and see how many people believe or side with you.

JD: It doesn't matter. Fair fight, my ass...

AH: Exactly!

In the US, Depp's legal team were all over this exchange, with Camille Vasquez raising it in her closing statement to the jury, telling them that Heard 'never thought that Mr Depp would tell you, the jury, and the world, that he was the real victim of domestic abuse. She said it in her own words.'

Snatches of audio conversations were also played in the US court in which Depp tacitly appears to acknowledge the possibility of violence on his part. In one snippet played to the US court, in which Heard makes a serious allegation, Depp chooses not to deny it.

AH: Well, I fucked up and cry in my bedroom after I dumped you a fucking week prior, a fucking week prior after you beat the shit out of me. And then a week later, you show in my... show up at my doorstep in my room saying you want to say goodbye. Okay, say goodbye.

JD: Oh, I said it?

AH: Yes, you did say it.

The same sort of allegation without denial can be heard in another audio clip also played to the US court. In it, Heard is talking, as Depp murmurs in the background:

'Yes, you do because you wouldn't have used that as a way to hit me. I was pouring my heart out to you and what did you do? We get it, oh we get it. *Stab* in here. That what you saw, huh? You listened to me cry...

and you're like... "now I can get her". Is that what you think? Or you just do without thinking? You do without thinking, huh? [inaudible] You... [inaudible] get a stab in where you can. You throw a swing where you can. And what [inaudible] better than doing it when I'm on the floor? Because that's when it's really good to hit someone.'

Depp also admits to having problems with Heard working, saying on one recording: 'I get irrational when you're doing movies. I become jealous and fucking crazy and weird, you know, and we fight a lot more.'

There is also a July 2016 exchange (again post-DVRO, pre-divorce), recorded when the pair are in a hotel room in San Francisco. Depp is holding a knife. He instructs Heard to cut him. When she refuses he threatens to start cutting himself. A distressed Heard begs him not to.

Depp fans, and many female victims of abuse I spoke to, were not alone in finding the audio tapes conclusive. Amanda de Cadenet, a confidant of Heard and women's rights campaigner, listened to at least one audio tape and subsequently refused to testify in support of Heard either in the UK or US. Instead, in 2020, just before the UK trial was about to begin, de Cadenet made a legal declaration in support of Johnny Depp. The declaration was then obtained by the Daily Mail.

In her declaration, according to the Mail, de Cadenet says: 'When Amber told me her version of the conflict between her and Johnny, it was my inclination to believe her and support her.' De Cadenet then heard an audio tape of 'Amber being verbally abusive to Johnny' and was 'horrified'.

De Cadenet wrote: 'I was appalled and shocked to hear how Amber was speaking to Johnny... it was not ok with me. When I confronted Amber concerning the recording, she informed me it was edited by Johnny's team. I had hoped Amber would take accountability for her behavior but she did not. I have not spoken with Amber since this exchange and have come to the very painful realization that someone who I advocated for and believed so wholeheartedly, was not entirely forthcoming with me.'

THE HEADBUTT

Los Angeles, 15 December 2015

There is one act of unwanted physical contact between Depp and Heard which Johnny Depp does admit to. The headbutt. This happened at the Eastern Columbia Building on 15 December 2015, the day before Amber Heard appeared on *The Late Late Show* with James Corden. Heard describes it as 'one of the worst and most violent nights of our relationship.' In a text to Heard's father, Depp says: 'I fucked up and went too far in our fight!!! I cannot and WILL NOT excuse my part inside these dramas!!!'

Depp does not tell David Heard how he fucked up or where he went too far, though in an audio recording of Depp and Heard made in San Francisco in July 2016 (a portion of which you read in the last chapter), Depp admits the headbutt, but disputes where it landed:

JD: I headbutted you in the fuckin'...
AH: I couldn't believe you did that.
JD: ... forehead. That doesn't break a nose.
AH: I don't know if you were aware, I don't think you did. I don't think you broke it.
JD: Don't think I broke it, I didn't touch it!
AH: Oh please, you didn't touch it? You don't know.

On this occasion no one seems to know what started the argument. Amber Heard says her recollection of the evening comes in 'flashes'. She told jurors in the US:

'I remember him chasing me in the kitchen. I remember throwing something in his direction to slow down his momentum. I remember him screaming. I remember him getting on top of me, at some point toppling me, mostly at that moment downstairs. He was hitting me on my face.'

Heard says she got away and made it halfway up the second set of apartment stairs towards their bedroom: 'I think I said something on the stairs. And I just remember how quickly he shot back up those stairs and grabbed me by the back of my hair, my head, and slammed his hand on my head.'

Heard says she fell onto the steps. 'I remember him grabbing my hair, my head, and kind of dragging me up the stairs the rest of the way... And we had this argument that was a shoving match that I was losing.

By the second or third shove, he sent me toppling over this chaise lounge, a little low-lying sofa seat. And I hit my head on the brick wall. There was an exposed brick wall.'

Heard says she got up 'and I remember Johnny asking me if I wanted to go. And he did that thing where he's... challenging me to stand up and get back up. And when I did, he said: "Oh, you really want to go now, tough guy?" He shoved me back down. "Oh, you really wanna go, huh? Oh, you're so tough." I stood back up again. This time he hits me in the face.'

Heard told jurors there was a moment of stillness as she stared Depp down. 'I just looked right at him, just looked right at his face. And he balled up his fists, leaned back, and headbutted me square in the nose, just right as I stood in front of him. I was a foot from him. He slammed me right in the nose.'

Heard remembers feeling instant, 'searing' pain. But it wasn't over. Heard says she told Depp she was leaving him and went to get some of her stuff. 'We had another struggle. He overtook me. I was trying to hit him off me... I was trying to get his body off of me, and he was just pummeling me.'

Heard says Depp then dragged her from PH3 into the bedroom of PH4 'and kind of wrestles me down onto the bed. And he kneels on my back with one leg... And he's punching me, punching me with a closed fist, punching me repeatedly. And I don't remember even feeling the pain. I just remember the sound of Johnny's voice. He got next to my ear and he was screaming over and over and over again. Each time, it sounded louder and more desperate: "I fucking hate you. I fucking hate you. I fucking hate you." Over and over, "Fucking hate you." And then pounding the back of my head, pounding it with his fists. And I don't even remember feeling pain. I just could hear myself scream until I couldn't hear myself anymore.'

The beating continued. 'I got really still,' said Heard, 'and it felt in my body, quiet, and I thought this is how I die. He's gonna kill me now, and I'm not... He's going to kill me and he won't even have realized it. I couldn't breathe. I remember trying to scream and I couldn't scream. I was suffocating in this pillow top with him holding me down, punching me over and over. And I don't have any memory after that until I woke up.'

Such was the force of Depp's alleged attack that the bed in PH4 was apparently splintered by his boots. We know the bed was damaged as there is a photo, one of many, taken by Heard, Rocky Pennington and Depp's house manager, Kevin Murphy. The bed in PH4 is alleged to have been damaged deliberately in Depp's absence. There are two photographs of a clump of blonde hair on the floor, one taken by Pennington, another by Murphy. There are also photos of injuries to Amber Heard's face and head. These pictures, taken by Pennington, show what appear to be significant, if not spectacular injuries. There is a shot of Heard's head with some hair missing. She has the beginnings of bruises around her eyes and nose. One photo shows a definite cut to Heard's lip, which is bleeding.

What the pictures demonstrate is a matter of dispute, except for a photo of a message stating Why be a fraud? All is such bullshit... agreed to be written by Depp with a sharpie on the PH3 kitchen countertop.

Johnny Depp takes issue with Heard's description of events. In his initial witness statement to the UK court, Depp did not mention headbutting Amber Heard, accidentally or otherwise. It came up under cross-examination. Depp said it was more of a 'collision' than a headbutt, and it happened accidentally in the process of trying to restrain Heard.

'She was swinging wildly at me and from behind,' Depp told the court. 'As I was walking away from the argument to my office, she is hitting me in the neck, ear, back, head, everything... the only thing I could do in that situation was to either run or try to get my arms around her to stop her from flailing and punching me. So, I did so. When I did so, it seems that there was a collision.'

Depp said when his head made contact with Heard's 'she immediately said: "You headbutted me! You broke my nose!" and screamed and then ran away.'

Depp is certain that his head did not make contact with the bridge of Heard's nose. 'The collision was head to head, forehead to forehead... I do not see how that could break a nose.'

In the US, Depp told the jury: 'After she'd made the remark about the fact that I headbutted her, which was just impossible, she split, she huffed off. I let her go, she huffs away, and she was gone for about seven or eight minutes. And then when she came back... about seven or eight minutes later, she had a Kleenex or a tissue to her nose. And she pulled it away from her nose, and she showed it to me. And there was red. There was indeed like red color on the tissue. But me, I know that there was no connection to her nose. No part of my body made connection to her nose, or eyes, or anything like.'

Depp was suspicious. 'She said, "Way to go, Johnny, you broke my nose. You broke my nose." And I knew I hadn't... And she wouldn't let me see anything. And so, I just tried to calm the situation as best I could. All the while I was waiting for her to dispense with that Kleenex because I didn't trust it. And so, I waited. And she dropped it into the wastebasket in... and left the room, went somewhere, downstairs I think, I don't know. And then I pulled the Kleenex out of the trash bin, and I inspected it pretty closely, and realized that it was nail polish. It was nail varnish or polish.'

Depp denies the graphic and lengthy attack described by Heard, saying he was 'not violent' towards her 'in any way'. Depp contends it was Heard who 'violently attacked' him 'as she had done many times before.' The violence, said Depp, left him with 'a number of scratches and swelling around my face.'

Depp's injuries were documented by Sean Bett, Depp's security guard, who took a photo of his boss on the same day. The photos show Depp with the beginnings of a black eye and some minor scratches.

Under cross-examination in the UK, Depp agreed that the photos of Heard showed bruising, but that he was not responsible. He speculated that the photo of the injured lip showed 'a cold sore' or 'chapped lips'. When asked to accept it was an injury, he again said he wasn't responsible. He also said that when he texted David Heard to admit he had gone 'too far', he meant only in terms of the nasty things he had said to Heard. Depp told the court: 'When you are being screamed at, you react and you scream back. And these hideous exchanges did happen and they happened quite often.' Depp was therefore 'apologizing for in any way upsetting him... I was being as honest with Mr Heard as I can be.'

NGN's barrister noted that Depp had not told David Heard that he had accidentally headbutted his daughter. 'No, I did not say that. I, again, the... no, I did not say that,' Depp agreed, floundering a little.

When Heard came to that evening, she contacted Pennington and asked her to come over. Heard had been due to go bowling with her makeup artist and friend, Melanie Inglessis. When Heard didn't show, Inglessis got in touch to see if she was okay. Heard replied that she very much wasn't okay, so Inglessis also dropped by. Inglessis told the UK court she remembers finding Heard 'a little erratic... in between being sad and upset and furious... quite distressed.' Inglessis said Heard told her Depp had 'beat on' her and 'that he tried to suffocate her... with a pillow. She felt he tried to kill her that night and she said he dragged her by her hair.'

Shortly before midnight on the fifteenth, Heard texted her publicist, Jodi Gottlieb, to say she had suffered an 'accident' which had left her 'really bruised'. Heard said she 'might have a black eye or two tmrw – same with my nose. Nurse on the way to make sure I don't have a concussion. There's a chance I might not be fit for tomorrow. But won't know how bad the bruising is until the morning. Giving you a heads up.'

Heard was more explicit when contacting her psychologist Dr Connell Cowan, stating baldly: 'Johnny did a number on me tonight. I'm safe and with my support tonight but need some real help... I called earlier because I thought I had a concussion and didn't know if I should have called police. But I have a nurse close to me – and rocky and her have been here for me.'

The nurse was Erin Boerum, who was in a difficult position. She was paid for by Depp (as was Cowan), and instructed by Dr Kipper, but she had also become Heard's friend.

The two had at least one phone conversation. Boerum texted to tell Heard her experience 'sounds scary'. Heard later texted Boerum to say she had 'found a bunch of Coke. Which explains it.'

In the early hours of the morning Heard texted iO Tillett-Wright to say: 'J beat me up pretty good. Rocks on the couch with me now. When r u back. I'm hurt. Don't know what to do. Need you.'

Rocky Pennington said Heard's most memorable injury was the clump of hair missing from her head. She said Heard also had 'a very swollen nose' and 'a bloody lip'.

The following morning, Heard texted Kevin Murphy, Depp's estate manager, to say: 'I just wanted to let you know that the maids will be needed downtown today. Even though Johnny didn't sleep [here] last night, he left quite a dent on the place before he left.'

By the time Murphy arrived later that morning, the maids were already on the scene. Heard was upstairs in bed. She called Murphy up to her room.

'When I went upstairs,' said Murphy, 'I found her sitting at the edge of the bed crying. Ms Heard said that Mr Depp had hit her in the face several times and pulled out her hair. I remember standing roughly four feet away and becoming suspicious, as Ms Heard did not appear to be wearing any makeup on this occasion and there were no marks, bruises, cuts, redness or swelling to Ms Heard's face, nor was there any area on her head where her hair appeared to have been pulled out.'

About an hour later, Heard and Murphy were downstairs. Heard told Murphy she wanted to show him something. Murphy remembers following Heard 'to the upstairs bedroom of Penthouse 4.' There, Heard pointed to 'a tuft of hair that she claimed Mr Depp had pulled out of her head the previous evening.'

Murphy took a photograph of the hair. Depp's side have made much of the fact that the photograph of the hair does not show any obvious roots. When Pennington returned later that morning, she began documenting Heard's injuries. She also took a picture of the hair on the floor. Pennington's picture doesn't appear to show any roots either.

Despite her condition, Heard decided she would go ahead with *The Late Late Show* appearance. The penthouses soon became a hive of activity. Pennington described the scene:

'Amber and I were exhausted, and Amber was shaken, upset, and trying to pull herself together for the show. Samantha was styling her, Melanie was doing her makeup, and Adir was doing her hair. Everyone was in damage-control mode and appeared to be aware of Amber's injuries. I remember Adir telling Amber not to touch her hair because he had styled it to cover up where the clump had been pulled out, and Melanie telling Amber she was going to do a certain kind of lip to cover the swelling.'

In the UK, Melanie Inglessis described preparing to work on Heard's face, under good lights, on the top floor of Penthouse 5. Heard, she told the court, had 'minimal discoloration... on the inner corner of her eyes, by her nose. I recall her left eye being a little more bruised than the right eye. I remember the bridge of her nose being a little red and swollen.'

For Inglessis, dealing with the cut lip was relatively straightforward: 'Amber's signature lip is a red lip, so it is not uncommon for her to have a red lip. I remember having a discussion that day that we had no other choice but to do a red lip... to cover the injury.'

Later that afternoon, Heard texted Dr Cowan again: 'Connell, sorry haven't called because rocky came over last night. Then dealt with security and called nurse for medical help and went down to sleep. Today has been filled with work (I'm shooting a late show appearance today – with 2 black eyes)... Can you please please make time for me?? Johnny beat me up pretty good last night. He's using again.'

iO Tillett-Wright also came by that day. He confirmed during his deposition in the US that he saw injuries on Amber Heard consistent with those in the photographs of her face and scalp.

The stylist that day was Samantha McMillen, who is easy to confuse with Heard's friend and definitely-not-US-assistant, Savannah McMillan. McMillen has been Johnny Depp's stylist for many years. In a witness statement, McMillen wrote that on 16 December 2015, she saw Heard 'throughout the day... in good light, at close range, wearing no makeup.' McMillen remembered seeing that Heard 'did not have any visible marks, bruises, cuts, or injuries to her face or any other part of her body.'

Heard and Inglessis, for their part, claim McMillen only saw Heard's face *after* Inglessis put her makeup on, effectively concealing any injuries.

Heard's performance on *The Late Late Show* passed off without incident. She appeared coherent and uninjured. Afterwards, McMillen recalled Heard saying to her: 'Can you believe I just did that show with two black eyes?' McMillen believes Heard 'did not have any black eyes, and had been visibly uninjured throughout the day.'

After the show had been recorded, Erin Boerum visited Heard at home. Her notes report Heard looking 'dishevelled... weepy... sad' and was drinking red wine. Boerum noted Heard had 'visible bright red blood appearing at center of lower lip.' When Boerum mentioned this, Heard 'stated it was from the injury sustained in the argument between her and her husband, and that it continues to bleed actively.' Boerum recorded Heard telling her that her head was 'bruised' and that she had 'lost clumps of hair in the altercation.' Boerum performed a quick examination of Heard's head, but could not find the 'hematomas' (bruises) Heard described. She recommended Heard stop drinking and get properly checked out, either by attending A&E or going to Dr Kipper's practice.

Rocky Pennington and her partner Josh Drew were due to fly out to the Bahamas to spend the Christmas holiday with Depp and his family. On hearing Heard's account of what happened on 15 December, they decided they were no longer interested. Heard was conflicted. She texted Lily-Rose, Depp's daughter, to say: 'here's the thing mini balls... I might not be able to go to the island for Christmas this year with you guys!! I might have to be with my family instead... (Long story I won't bore you with right now)... I'm worried that I won't get to see you and meet your man! Maybe I can see you guys soon?'

Heard also told her mum what she said had happened and sent her the photos Pennington had taken. Paige Heard reported back, telling her daughter: 'Your dad sent Steve[1] a scathing text message. I'm sorry – I told him he should have asked you but you know men on men anger. He really reamed him. He compared you to Lily-Rose and how JD would feel. Your dad's blood is boiling.'

---

[1] Heard's name for Depp. He called her Slim. Both names are taken from the film *To Have and Have Not*, starring Humphrey Bogart and Lauren Bacall. Bogart was considerably older than Bacall. By taking the names Steve and Slim, Depp and Heard were (among other things) referencing the age difference in their own relationship.

Depp's response to David Heard has not been made public, but Paige forwarded it to Amber, who replied:

'Jesus I just read that long text message... Can't believe how crazy he sounds. Nail polish?! What the fuck is he talking about?! He sounds out of his mind.'

On 17 December, Heard spent two hours with Dr Connell Cowan. His record of the session includes the note: 'Some spark ignited an argument that escalated and got violent. Shoving and screaming. Amber related that he started the physicality – pushed her down. Amber got back up.'

Cowan adds it is 'hard' for Heard 'to de-escalate a fight. Her strategy (despite our conversations) is to try and fight back (not protective of self and very self-defeating).'

On 21 December, David Heard sent Depp the most extraordinary text. It read:

'I'm not mad. I understand. A man has got to be a man, and I'm not saying that you were completely justified... but the main thing is that Amber should never hit you or call you another name, and same goes for you... I know that Amber needs help with her temper the same as you need help with your problem with drugs and alcohol. Mixing [them] together... causes you to lose control. Even though it's not one-sided, she's not blameless and I know that, but she's my kid and I love her unconditionally, but I think you do too!!!'

A few days after the fight Depp got in touch with Heard and asked her to go to spend Christmas on the island with him, Lily-Rose and his son Jack. Heard decided to go. It was, in her telling, a difficult decision:

'Every single time I went back, or allowed him back after this sort of thing would happen, I lost a piece of myself. A piece of my self-confidence, my trust in myself to leave and move on... it was somehow easier to stay. I didn't want to stay in the violence... I wanted to stay with Johnny, the good Johnny that I loved... This time was the last time because it couldn't be worse than this, right? It couldn't be worse...'

Heard says Depp told her what she wanted to believe – that this time 'he was going to be clean and sober... He wasn't going to drink any more [and] he wasn't gonna use any more. He'd never lay a hand on me again. He'd rather die than do that, is what he was saying.'

Heard describes herself as 'scared. My friends were scared. But I decided to go. After a few days of having the plane and the kids waiting... I got in the car with Johnny and we picked his kids up and left for the island.'

Unsurprisingly, things went badly in the Bahamas. After a peaceful Christmas, on 29 December, there was a blazing row.

The argument started at Depp and Heard's living quarters on the island. Contrary to Depp's promises, Heard said he was high on something, nodding off and spilling wine. Jack was present. When Heard obliquely admonished Depp for spilling his wine by thanking Jack for his concern about the spillage, Depp apparently flew off the handle. Jack was either told to leave, or left of his own volition. Depp allegedly said to Heard: 'If you ever embarrass me again in front of my kids, I'll fucking kill you.' He then, by Heard's account, proceeded to attack and sexually assault her in the bathroom of the house:

'He just grabbed me... shoved his fingers inside me, but through my bathing suit. He didn't, like, move my bathing suit out of the way, and just kind of held me there and asked me if I was so fucking tough, if I thought I was so fucking tough. He said, "Are you tough like a man now?"'

Heard said Depp was 'taunting me while jerking me around.'

Although this incident was raised as part of the confidential allegations against Depp in 2020, the parties decided the judge was not required to rule on whether it happened or not, so he didn't.

Depp says none of this happened, but did allege that during the argument, Heard threw a 'quart sized can' of 'mineral spirits' (or 'lacquer thinner') directly at Depp, hitting him square on the nose. This, according to Tara Roberts, Depp's island manager in the Bahamas, caused a 'red, swelling gash' and according to Depp, 'hurt'. The wound was not photographed.

Roberts did not witness the can being thrown, the beginning of the argument or anything that happened in the house, but found herself involved when Depp arrived at her office during the row, apparently to escape Heard, who arrived shortly afterwards.

Roberts says Heard was 'pleading' with Depp, trying to get him back to their house. Eventually he complied, but Roberts was concerned. She followed them, calling Christi Dembrowski to tell her what was happening. Roberts says she witnessed Heard berating Depp 'with increasing ferocity', saying 'specifically: "your career is over", "no one is going to hire you", "you're washed up", "fat", "you will die a lonely man".'

According to Roberts, Depp tried to extricate himself from the situation again, witnessing Heard 'lunge at Johnny, clawing, tugging and aggressively pulling him... When he stepped back to leave, her onslaught would start again. During this entire incident, I never saw

Johnny hit Amber, or push her back, nor did he physically react to the attacks. She would calm down and hug and apologize. Then he would say he needs to leave and it would start again.'

Roberts says eventually she physically intervened, stepping between them to stop the fight. She took Depp back to her office, put some ice on his wound and let him sleep there.

DEPP LOSES IN THE UK

London, 2 November 2020

Once the High Court press office had informed journalists that the Depp v NGN judgment would be made public 'remotely' at 10am on 2 November 2020, there had been some to-ing and fro-ing about what that actually meant. Judges have a number of options when it comes to making their findings public. They can decide to have physical copies 'handed down' from their bench in court, a ritual they might preface with a short oral summary of their ruling(s). Sometimes there is no hearing, but physical copies of the judgment are handed out by clerks and/or ushers to journalists and interested parties from a specific court. More frequently, judgments are posted up without ceremony on the official Judiciary website.

Under normal circumstances, Mr Justice Nicol might have chosen to say a few words before handing down his judgment in open court, but events dictated otherwise. London was still in the grip of coronavirus. Asking anyone to gather indoors for non-essential matters was considered unwise, if not dangerous. The judgment, we were told, would be posted on the Judiciary website. There would be no courtroom ceremony.

Given the public interest in the trial, I had some concerns with this approach. Promising to hand down a physical judgment in court at an allotted time gave journalists the opportunity to be there when it happened. Waiting for something to appear on a website seemed arbitrary. What if it didn't? Furthermore, there was worldwide interest in this document. Posting it on the rickety UK Judiciary servers might crash them. The judgment might appear for a few seconds and then become completely inaccessible, or accessible to some and not others.

Representations were made. The High Court press office acknowledged journalists' concerns and told those with queries they would be placed on an email list. We were promised the judgment would be circulated to those on the list the moment it was made public.

Sitting at home waiting for an email also felt a bit off. Plans could change without warning. Things could go wrong. To mitigate this, on the morning the judgment was due, I travelled up to London by train. At least by being physically closer to court I might be able to make face-to-face enquiries if the email containing the judgment didn't land in my inbox.

At 9.45am I parked myself in a coffee shop opposite the Royal Courts of Justice, opened my laptop and connected to the internet. From around 9.55am I began checking for new emails every five seconds. At 10.01am an email from Amy Baker, clerk to Mr Justice Nicol, appeared in my inbox. I opened the email, found the attached judgment and by 10.02am I had located the relevant paragraph within the 129-page ruling and tweeted:

BREAKING: Johnny Depp has lost his libel claim against NGN newspapers[1].

After sending the tweet, I checked. I was the first to publish the news. Good. I had a little preen, then began a thread, copying and pasting paragraphs from the judgment into 280 character chunks and releasing them into the twittersphere. After half an hour of this, I got bored and wandered out of the coffee shop to see if anything was going to happen outside the court buildings. It didn't look like it. Amidst a mini adrenaline-crash I sat on one of the concrete benches in front of the Royal Courts of Justice to read the judgment properly. As I was doing so an excitable reporter of my acquaintance bounded up to me.

'Well!' he exclaimed, hopping from one foot to the other. 'We all thought we knew libel law. Turns out we didn't!' He scampered off.

My journalist friend had a point. Mr Justice Nicol's judgment seemed a bit... odd. I was surprised at the certainty with which he'd come down in favor of Amber Heard's description of events, but I put that down to my lack of understanding of the law, libel, domestic violence and probability. I trusted that Mr Justice Nicol, a renowned libel expert, who must have repeatedly gone over all the evidence, knew what he was doing.

Depp's lawyers, Schillings, had no such ambivalence. They released a statement calling the judgment 'perverse' and 'bewildering'.

'Most troubling,' said Schillings, 'is the Judge's reliance on the testimony of Amber Heard, and corresponding disregard of the mountain of counter-evidence from police officers, medical practitioners, her own former assistant, other unchallenged witnesses and an array of documentary evidence which completely undermined the allegations, point by point.'

---

[1] As mentioned earlier in this book, NGN stands for News Group Newspapers, so my tweet essentially said 'Johnny Depp has lost his libel claim against News Group Newspapers newspapers.' Being the internet, I am astounded no one saw fit to pull me up on this.

Heard said the whole experience had been 'incredibly painful', but gave thanks for the 'tremendous and overwhelming outpouring of support and the many messages' she had 'received from around the world.'

HAPPY FUCKING BIRTHDAY

Los Angeles, 21 April 2016

The evening of Thursday 21 April 2016 marks a significant turning point. It was the date of a dinner held at the Eastern Columbia Building on the eve of Amber Heard's 30th birthday. The celebrations were due to start between 8pm and 8.30pm. Around twelve people were invited. That same evening Johnny Depp attended a meeting called by his new business manager, Ed White, who had been running the rule over Depp's finances. Depp says he 'desperately tried to get out of the meeting', but Mr White had serious and evidently urgent information to impart. Depp agreed to see White at 7.30pm at his Infinitum Nihil production office.

During the meeting, also attended by Christi Dembrowski, Depp was handed some good news and the worst financial news of his career. The good news was that since *Pirates 2*, he had made $650m. But the bad news was that due to what Depp continues to claim was a mixture of mismanagement and theft by his former business managers, he 'had not only lost the $650 million, but I was $100 million in the hole, because they had not paid the government my taxes for 17 years[1].'

The meeting concluded between 9pm and 9.30pm. Depp did not go straight back to the ECB to attend Heard's birthday party. One of his security guards, Sean Bett, describes taking Depp to Sweetzer, which was a short drive from Depp's office.

'We had to go inside the house and retrieve something,' said Bett. 'I don't know what it was. We were only there a short period of time. And we were kinda rushing because we had been running late.' Having got what he wanted from Sweetzer, Depp left with Bett for the ECB.

Over the course of the evening, Depp texted Heard multiple times to tell her he would not be able to get to the party on time. Responding to one text, in which Depp suggested he was ten minutes away, Heard wrote:

'Hey baby, bring something up to drink and a joint. I'm in if you are. See you in a minute? xx'

---

[1] Depp's former managers deny failing to pay his taxes for 17 years, deny mismanagement and deny stealing any money from him. The legal case brought against them by Depp was settled out of court.

One of the birthday guests at the ECB was Nurse Erin Boerum. At the time, Heard was a client of hers, and despite the social nature of the occasion, Boerum kept a professional eye on her charge. Boerum arrived at the party at 9pm. She made notes, recording that Heard appeared 'irritable and upset' due to Depp's no-show. Nurse Boerum 'provided reassurance' that Depp would arrive, and encouraged Heard to 'distract herself by socializing with friends.' According to Boerum, Depp finally made it to the party at around 10.15pm. According to Starling Jenkins, a member of Depp's security team, Depp had not arrived by the time he went off shift at 11pm.

There is considerable disagreement from those present as to what sort of condition Depp was in when he arrived. Rocky Pennington, Heard's then best friend, described Depp as 'coherent' but told the UK court he was neither sociable nor affectionate. Pennington's boyfriend, Josh Drew, catered the party. In London he agreed that Depp was in 'a coherent, sociable, friendly mood', 'slightly inebriated' and 'affectionate' towards Heard. Two years later in the US, Drew described Depp as 'very obviously intoxicated'. Nurse Boerum's notes from that evening describe Depp as 'coherent, oriented and sociable'. Whitney Heard told the Virginia court he was 'drunk'. Kristina Sexton, Heard's acting coach, agreed Depp was 'sociable', but also 'clearly inebriated. His speech was slurred, he could not hold himself up properly, and he kept interrupting or speaking at inappropriate moments.' Depp admits to drinking a glass of wine during the meeting with Ed White and a couple of large glasses at the party. He agrees it was 'likely' he'd smoked some cannabis in the car after the meeting with White.

Heard's state of inebriation that evening was not discussed to the same extent in either the US or the UK trials but Depp, in his UK witness statement, says Heard had been 'drinking heavily'. Josh Drew agreed she was 'intoxicated'.

The evening appears to have become a train wreck. According to Drew, Depp 'put on a show for everybody.' Whitney Heard went into more detail. She told US jurors that guests took it in turns to share their favorite memory of Amber. When it came to Johnny, he volunteered the story of how they first met. Whitney remembers Depp describing how Heard 'came into his office and she sat on the couch, and her perfect ass left a perfect imprint on the couch and he wouldn't let anyone sit there after she left that day.'

It was not necessarily what the guests wanted to hear. 'You know,' said Whitney, 'we had all gone around the table saying really nice things... and it gets to him and he's talking about her ass. We were all kind of embarrassed.'

Sexton was watching her client. In her witness statement to the UK trial, she says: 'Amber was clearly horrified and humiliated by his story. I found it to be so inappropriate and disrespectful. Until that point, she had been trying to be happy and keep the party going, but after he told that story, it was like she gave up.'

The party wound down. All the guests were gone by half past midnight. Then it kicked off. According to Depp, Heard started an argument by 'voicing how upset she was that I was so late for her birthday dinner, and that I had made a fool of her, and that I did not care, and everybody was talking about how awful it was of me to do such a thing.' Thereafter, Depp says, things 'ramped up'. Heard became 'much more aggressive. She was very, very, very upset and very angry.'

Depp says that to avoid 'yet another confrontation' he took himself off to bed in Penthouse 3 and started reading a book. Heard joined Depp in bed. She denies she was aggressive, instead claiming she was more 'sad' and 'upset' about Johnny's lateness, which she wanted to discuss. According to Heard, Depp began the argument using words to the effect of 'What's your fucking problem now?' Heard says in response, she chose her words 'carefully' as it was 'important for me not to make him feel attacked.'

The matter escalated.

Heard said she got out of bed, followed by Depp. In her witness statement to the UK trial, Heard claims Depp 'picked up and threw a magnum sized bottle of champagne at me, which missed and hit the wall.' Either the bottle broke, or it broke something else. Heard was not completely sure. 'But I remember that bits of flying shattered glass hit me.'

In the US trial, Heard says the bottle 'went through a painting' and 'left a giant hole in it.' After that the argument moved outside the bedroom to what Heard called the 'salon' area. 'Johnny picked up my phone...' she told the court, 'and threw it out of the open window of the salon area out onto the street.' Heard grabbed Depp's phone from the countertop and retaliated in kind.

The argument returned to the bedroom. Then it got physical. In her witness statement to the UK trial, Heard says Depp 'grabbed me by the shoulders, pushed me onto the bed, and blocked the bedroom door when I tried to leave.' Depp then allegedly grabbed Heard by the hair and pushed her to the ground. Heard wrote: 'I scraped my knees on bits of broken glass. He was screaming at me and taunting me, asking if I thought I was a "tough guy" or something like that, and he said that he wouldn't let me leave... Then he squared up to me and bumped his chest into mine, making me stumble backwards onto the bed. I tried to plead with him not to be like this on my birthday, then I tried to walk past him to leave the bedroom, but he pushed me to the floor again.'

In the Virginia trial, Heard augmented her recollection, saying that whilst Depp shoved her down, 'taunting' her, 'he grabbed me by the pubic bone' and 'kind of just pushed me down and held me down by it.'

Depp denies any kind of sexual assault, or throwing a bottle of champagne. He says the violence was started by Heard. According to Depp's interpretation of the evening, Heard 'was still rattling off all the wrongs that I'd done to her in that particular day. And how unreliable I am, and what a horrible person I was.' Depp says he refused to engage, so Heard got out of bed, and as he 'lay reading' came round to his side and began 'throwing multiple shots' at his face and head – 'anything she could hit.'

Depp says in response, he got up out of bed and grabbed her by the shoulders.

'I sat her down on the bed and I said, "I'm leaving. Please don't get off the bed. Please don't follow me. Please don't try and stop me. I'm leaving".'

Depp says Heard did more than try to stop him.

'She squared off at me in the doorway of our bedroom. And I said, "What do you want to do? Hit me again? Would you like to hit me again?" And I said, "Go ahead. Hit me".'

Depp alleges he allowed Heard to hit him twice. Then he again grabbed her by the shoulders, walked her to the bed, sat her down, and said: 'Don't follow me. Leave me alone. I'm out. I'm gone.'

Depp left. Heard says as he walked out of the apartment he was 'smashing things – pictures and photographs.'

Depp denies smashing anything, but agrees it is entirely possible (as Heard alleges) he found the time to leave a note which read: '*Happy Fucking Birthday*'.

Three months later Amber Heard made a secret recording of a conversation between the couple in a hotel room in San Francisco. Heard had already publicly accused Depp of domestic violence and secured a restraining order against him. The meeting was at Heard's insistence. During a long conversation about whether the relationship was at an end – something Depp seemed quite keen to ensure – Depp brings up the early hours of 22 April. He says:

'I left you because you... you were fuckin'... you fuckin' *haymakered* me, man. You came around the bed and fuckin' started *punching* on me.'

Heard replies: 'I'm so sad. I'm so sad. I love you so much, Johnny.'

Depp's lawyers noted that at the time, with every opportunity to do so, Amber Heard did not deny the 'haymaker' allegation. Heard says it was because 'that is not what I was having a conversation with him about.' Depp's barrister believes it was because Heard 'knows that the tape recording is whirring away' and therefore cannot give 'even a hint, not even an attempt at denying it, because she knew if she did, Mr Depp would go further.'

WALDMAN'S WORLD

One of the most important people in this story is Johnny Depp's personal consigliere, Adam Waldman. Waldman hovered like a spectre over the 2020 High Court proceedings and briefly made it into the spotlight in Virginia in 2022, but his sphere of influence envelops many aspects of Johnny Depp's life.

In his Twitter profile photo, Waldman sports a black suit, shiny shirt and a dark grey tie. He sits legs crossed, palms resting downwards on a black surface. It is a standard corporate power pose. *This* world, says the body language, is *mine*.

Waldman's 'living the dream' image is publicly maintained via his Instagram account which treats us to a series of stylish family pictures taken in exotic locations. They occasionally feature Waldman's glamorous partner, the skincare specialist Dr Barbara Sturm.

Waldman and Depp first met in October 2016, when Depp was looking for new advisors. His finances were a mess and his former wife had accused him of domestic violence. If Depp was going to change direction he needed people around him who were going to deliver. Waldman impressed, and was hired almost on the spot.

Before taking on Johnny Depp, Adam Waldman was working in Washington DC as an attorney and reported lobbyist for two men with close links to the Russian president, Vladimir Putin. The first was Oleg Deripaska, a billionaire oligarch who, when Waldman picked him up in 2009, was banned from the USA over his suspected links to organized crime. In 2020 a United States Senate Intelligence Committee report found Deripaska conducted 'influence operations, frequently in countries where he has a significant economic interest. The Russian government coordinates with and directs Deripaska on many of his influence operations.' Insider magazine revealed that Waldman's Endeavor Group consultancy had been put on a $40,000 monthly retainer with the aim of lobbying the US government on Deripaska's behalf to provide 'legal advice on issues involving US visa as well as commercial transactions.'

Shortly after he started working with Waldman, Deripaska visited the US, where he reportedly met with FBI agents and the head of Goldman Sachs. Waldman's progress on behalf of Deripaska presumably won approval in Russia, because in 2010, he started working with Sergey Lavrov, the Russian foreign minister, a direct proxy of Vladimir Putin.

There is no suggestion Adam Waldman has ever been involved in anything illegal or against the interests of his country. In 2018, two years after starting a working relationship with Johnny Depp, Waldman stopped working for Deripaska. The political lobbying appears to have wound down. The Endeavor Group's web domain currently redirects to a fictional electronic wargaming community calling itself the 48th Mechanized Infantry.

Waldman was introduced to Depp at a dinner hosted by Ed White, the man who now manages all Depp's financial affairs. He had been recommended to Depp by a lawyer in the UK. Depp was in dispute with his personal attorney Jake Bloom, and was looking to hire a fresh face from outside Hollywood. Waldman wasted no time in becoming one of Depp's trusted lieutenants.

Waldman's approach was new to Depp. He came from the world of politics where the rapid rebuttal of any allegations is essential to stop them taking hold. This differs from the Hollywood method, which prefers minimal engagement. A star who directly addresses an allegation with a press statement can feed and amplify the allegation (whilst elevating the person making it), dragging the protagonist into more unwelcome media noise.

Waldman seemed to inherently understand that Depp was not involved in a standard Hollywood scandal which could be tidied up on the quiet. He recognized Depp needed someone highly visible, acting with authority and fighting in the trenches on his behalf. Waldman went to war, leveraging his privileged position to gain influence amongst Depp fans. His currency was his legal credibility, access to Depp, and a knack for generating media (and, importantly, social media) coverage.

Waldman began to build relationships with people he called 'internet journalists', specifically ThatUmbrellaGuy, Laura Bockov (TheRealLauraB) and ThatBrianFella (known on YouTube as IncrediblyAverage). These were people who could propagate and amplify the scraps of information he fed them. Twitter was a crucial weapon in this. Waldman built alliances with fans, answering their questions about the UK and US cases, and complimenting them on their 'detective work'. In one instance, he admired a piece of fan art and told the poster he'd passed their picture to Depp himself; in another he took note of what looked like a potentially useful piece of witness information and told the poster: 'Please go to my dm [direct messages] and I will receive your narrative statement and other evidence on this.'

Waldman quickly and successfully positioned himself as Depp's representative on earth, a direct and effective conduit between a star and the fans who were desperate to help. At the same time, he began to wage a campaign against newspaper and magazine reporters who he felt were spreading a false (i.e. Amber Heard's) narrative. He did this in multiple ways, telling his followers to look beyond the words journalists were writing and try to think about who was paying them to take a specific editorial angle.

All Murdoch media was fair game (after all, one of their publications had called Depp a 'wife-beater'). Variety, Deadline and Rolling Stone were dismissed as 'Saudi Arabia-owned' (true in so far as the Saudi sovereign wealth fund PIF had a minority stake in PMC, the magazines' owners). He also appeared to share Depp's personal animus toward Elon Musk, who Waldman accused of being less than truthful about the timing of his relationship with Amber Heard (Musk maintained they got together *after* she split from Depp).

'Rachel Abrams,' wrote Waldman in response to one Twitter query. 'NYT [New York Times]. But more importantly, Ex writer for both Saudi-owned Deadline and Variety. Has written puff pieces on Elon Musk, Ari Emanuel and Ms Heard's talent agency WME. 5 mins to catch who she is, who sent her, and what her game is.'

Waldman's techniques came straight from the populist playbook – don't play the game, attack the agenda. He also broke convention, sharing reporters' correspondence online and delighting in their reactions. On one occasion, a Sunday Times journalist from the UK contacted Waldman to offer him the right of reply in a piece she was writing about Depp. Instead of declining the request or obediently supplying a quote, Waldman published a screenshot of the reporter's email, adding the hashtags #murdochclowns and #keeptrying.

When the reporter responded with a rather pearl-clutching 'I have never had a lawyer tweet out an email giving them right of reply in my 13 years as a journalist', Waldman tweeted: 'If you don't like it, maybe you and your Murdoch empire colleagues should go back to smearing people that don't fight back.'

Waldman was relentless. Journalists were either corrupt or stupid – in his words: 'propaganda tools supporting the agendas of the powerful.' In Waldman's world, Depp's fans and *real* victims of abuse knew the truth. Heard's claims were a hoax and he had the evidence to prove it. The enemy was the mainstream media: 'they refuse to report the highly newsworthy facts,' he tweeted, 'although YouTube videos are replacing traditional investigative reporting and getting millions of views. Ask yourself why.'

When newspaper commentators (and Heard's lawyers) began suggesting that the viciousness of Depp fans attacking any pro-Heard position had the hallmarks of an orchestrated or even automated campaign, Waldman was sarcastic. Marianna Springs, the BBC's 'Disinformation and Social Media Correspondent', was given the treatment when she contacted self-described 'truth-seeker' Laura Bockov, asking why Bockov tweeted exclusively in support of Johnny Depp. Waldman weighed in with: 'Ms Springs your British taxpayer-funded "investigation" of abuse victims is important to us. For a "cyberbot" narrative, press 1. For a russian disinformation narrative, press 2. For any other hoax stories, please stay on the line.' The hashtag #notabot was gleefully used and shared by Depp fans.

For Depp supporters, Waldman was a godsend. Finally, someone with authority and acuity was not just putting Depp's case, but going on the front foot, building a wall of protection around Depp and pulling his followers in behind it. Waldman became the de facto leader of Depp's online army, described by Amber Heard as 'Wald-mignons', a name they took to wearing as an ironic badge of honor. Waldman didn't just give Depp supporters a voice, he gave them *authority*, and they, in turn, amplified the pro-Depp signal.

Despite his righteous war against the mainstream media, Waldman wasn't going to ignore every newspaper journalist. The Daily Mail is a popular tabloid in the UK, which has a wildly successful website known as the MailOnline. As well as giving the Mail several on-the-record quotes calling Heard's claims a 'hoax', Waldman secretly supplied the Mail with two audio tapes.

The Mail published a number of recordings of Depp and Heard which were subsequently used in both the US and UK trials. Excerpts from the lengthy Australia tape appeared on the Mail website in April 2020 alongside a quote from Waldman saying the recording 'further exposes' Heard's 'big and little lies'. In early 2021 the Mail published two tapes in two weeks under the headline 'Amber Heard admits to 'hitting' ex-husband Johnny Depp and pelting him with pots, pans and vases in explosive audio confession' and 'Amber Heard scoffs at Johnny Depp for claiming he's a domestic violence victim, suggesting court would take her side because she's a slender woman'. The relationship between the Depp camp and the Mail developed to the extent that at least one meeting between Waldman and the Daily Mail was attended in February 2021 by Johnny Depp himself.

When it came to his day job – overseeing the legal cases against NGN and Amber Heard – Waldman had to find the right witnesses.

Some gave evidence willingly. Others needed persuasion. When the interior designer Laura Divenere (who variously worked for Heard, Depp and Elon Musk) appeared to be vacillating about giving evidence in the case, Waldman sent her the following text:

'I heard from Johnny and others that you are a nice person and more importantly, I have you all over the surveillance video immediately after the May 21 faked abuse claims, have witness testimony about you, and possess other written and testimonial evidence of your constant interactions with amber and acting on her behalf after she claimed to be beaten... So the question for you to consider is: do you want to speak with me off the record and we can consider together it and now to use any eyewitness account you provide, regarding which I would be very respectful of your wishes and sensitivities, or do you want to remain on the side of the hoax and indirectly facilitate her suppression of the truth that continues to create catastrophic damage to Johnny Depp? If it's the latter we will send you a subpoena to compel your appearance in a sworn deposition.'

According to court documents, Waldman told Divenere she would need to find between $15,000 and $20,000 in legal fees if she wanted to go down the deposition route. Divenere said she felt 'threatened' by Waldman, and then 'coerced' into signing a legal declaration which was written for her, by Waldman himself. Heard's lawyers called Waldman's methods 'harassment' and 'intimidation'. Divenere called Waldman 'the biggest asshole under the sun' and during the UK trial said she felt 'pressured' to include negative things in her declaration about Amber Heard.

By the time the UK trial came round there is some evidence that Waldman was getting under his opponents' skin. Over three weeks at the High Court, his name came up more than sixty times – quite extraordinary for a non-participant. It seemed one or two lawyers were getting a little fed up with Waldman's social media tactics. Divenere's UK cross-examination (via a bizarre little sub-plot) brought this to light.

In her declaration – the one she says she was coerced into signing – Divenere says she 'witnessed Amber being verbally abusive towards her former personal assistant Kate, screaming at her on the phone.' She also says she was 'aware from news articles that Amber was arrested and spent the night in jail for domestically abusing her former wife.'

After making her June 2019 declaration for Waldman, or as she would have it, approving and signing the statement he wrote, Divenere took a call from Amber Heard asking her to drop by. Heard claimed she had Divenere's full permission to record their conversation. Divenere said she knew nothing about it.

Divenere spent most of her time in Heard's company talking about the declaration, desperately trying to row back on what she'd now committed as evidence to the court. She described her experience with Waldman as 'horrible' and said she hadn't 'slept for nights'. It is during this conversation that Divenere twice called Waldman the 'biggest asshole under the sun.'

During her conversation with Heard, Divenere also claimed Kate James 'consistently screwed things up all the time, she was a mess.' She also said she didn't know anything about Heard's DV arrest until Waldman told her about it.

Perhaps in ignorance of the legal process, Divenere announced to Heard that she would like to be invited to make a declaration by Heard's lawyers in her favor, 'so it nulls anything out.'

This did not happen. What did happen was that in March 2020, just before Depp v NGN came to trial in the UK, Divenere had something of an epiphany. She told her lawyer, and Johnny Depp's lawyers, that her declaration to Waldman was '100% truthful'. Any thought of coercion was banished. 'In retrospect,' she wrote 'where I may have thought I was unduly pressured to write and sign my declaration I now believe that was not the case. My declaration went through three iterations with my complete involvement and understanding.'

Divenere's position held until she was forced to give evidence at the UK trial, when she reverted to saying she felt 'pressured' to answer Waldman's questions during the 2019 declaration session. Watching from the public gallery in the main court, Waldman tweeted: 'In Memoriam Elon Musk's decorator Laura Divenere.'

The phrase *In Memoriam*[1] was one Waldman had used in a number of tweets, usually to highlight various legal or journalistic hares which were no longer running. On this occasion it brought him to the court's attention.

Waldman sent his tweet on a Friday. The following Monday, one of NGN's barristers, Adam Wolanski, stood up in court, and asked the judge if he could raise an issue which 'relates to an individual about whom your Lordship has heard much in evidence, but who is not a witness in these proceedings – Mr Adam Waldman.'

---

[1]   Latin for 'in memory of' and usually used after someone has died.

Wolanski told the judge he was 'very concerned' because 'Mr Waldman has been tweeting extremely sinister messages about witnesses.' He handed up a copy of Waldman's *In Memoriam* tweet about Laura Divenere. This message was, according to Wolanski, 'macabre' and 'threatening'. Given that Amber Heard and her witnesses were due to start giving their evidence, Wolanski asked the judge to stop Waldman from tweeting in that way about things which were happening in court. In response to Wolanski's request, Depp's barrister – David Sherborne – began a long peroration, piling into Laura Divenere, her lawyer and her evidence.

The judge was not amused. 'The phrase *In Memoriam* is unwelcome,' he intoned.

Sherborne tried to give some context, telling the judge: 'This is not a phrase that is used for the first time. There have been a series of tweets about the lies that have been defeated... It is a tag phrase.'

Mr Justice Nicol remained unamused. 'Anybody attending this trial,' he said, 'must take care that what they put out on Twitter or any other feed is not perhaps misconstrued, but construed as a threat. That would be quite wrong.'

Sherborne agreed, saying: 'I am sure Mr Waldman knows that, as we all do... He is a lawyer in America, really. In my submission, he does not deserve the kind of attack that Mr Wolanski's clients are launching.'

Waldman dropped the phrase *In Memoriam*, but continued to tweet and continued to play his part. In the US trial Amber Heard recounted her experience of sitting next to Waldman (albeit socially-distanced) at the High Court. Heard says whilst they were near each other, Waldman thrust a newspaper in her direction. The article Waldman wanted to draw Heard's attention to referenced Kate James' evidence from the previous day. It was headlined 'Amber Heard stole my sexual assault story, ex-aide tells libel trial'.

In 2022, Judge Penney Azcarate decided the aggressive use of the newspaper was one of the reasons the 'malice' element to Amber Heard's defamation counter-claim against Johnny Depp could proceed.

Waldman took no part in the Virginia trial proceedings, thanks once again to his online activities. In October 2020, Courthouse News reported a hearing in Virginia during which lawyers for Amber Heard complained that Waldman had been leaking 'audio recordings, surveillance pictures and declarations from third-party witnesses to websites and Twitter users.'

Waldman, they said, was spreading 'false rumors' about their client. Chief Judge Bruce White found that ethical standards had been violated and revoked Waldman's permission to work on the case in Virginia.

Waldman was undeterred, and carried on tweeting. He also had another wheeze to pursue. Since 2019, he'd pushed the idea that Amber Heard might be prosecuted for the crime of perjury. This was certainly *possible*. If there was 'proof' Amber Heard had lied to the British, Australian or US courts, it followed that law-enforcement agencies in those countries might take an interest. In April 2019, after Heard lodged court filings detailing many of the alleged attacks described in this book, Waldman told The Blast website 'Amber Heard's problem is not only violence but perjury.' The same month a quote from him appeared in Hollywood Life saying Heard was responsible for 'defamation, perjury, and filing a demonstrably false temporary restraining order demand.'

Waldman mentioned the idea again in the 2020 Daily Mail article about the Australia recording. He told reporter Ben Ashford: 'The penalty for perjury in both the UK and US is prison. If you can't do the time, don't audio tape the aftermath of the crime.'

Waldman's claim of perjury related to Heard's allegations of violence, but it was Kate James' and Kevin Murphy's evidence to the UK trial about the illegal importation of Depp and Heard's dogs into Australia which made it a live issue beyond Depp supporters[2]. Barnaby Joyce, the former Australian Minister for Agriculture who had subsequently become Deputy Prime Minister, floated the idea in a *60 minutes* current affairs broadcast. Joyce asked both rhetorically and sarcastically: 'Is the defense for perjury that you have got to be able to act? What is the point of having laws if they are not pursued?'

Within days, Australia's Department of Agriculture issued a statement confirming an investigation into Amber Heard was underway. It said: 'The department is investigating if any criminal offenses under Commonwealth legislation have been committed relating to the testimony provided to the High Court in London.' An official from the agriculture department, Peta Lane, told the Australian Senate: 'There was evidence presented in the London court case which suggested false statements were provided... so we are investigating that.'

---

[2] See *The Hostage Video* chapter.

This was good for Waldman, but not quite good enough. He'd been making the case that Heard was lying about violence, not dog importation. He needed to force the issue.

On 5 July 2021 the German publication Bild magazine excitedly published news that Amber Heard was being investigated by the Los Angeles Police Department for perjury. The reason, said the magazine, was because Heard had given 'false information' to the courts about a phone-throwing incident in May 2016[3]. Their source was Adam Waldman. During his deposition to the US trial, Waldman said he had been told by the LAPD in 2021 'that they were investigating the perjury claim at that time', but the claim had subsequently been passed on to the Los Angeles Sheriff's Department, 'and that' said Waldman, 'was the last I heard about it.'

Heard's lawyer, Ben Rottenborn, became interested in this. What follows is a version of Rottenborn and Waldman's verbal exchange during Waldman's deposition, with extraneous words edited out for clarity:

'Who notified you from the LAPD that it was allegedly the sheriff's department who was investigating it?' asked Rottenborn.

'The desk officer,' replied Waldman.

'How did you come into contact with this desk officer?' asked Rottenborn.

'I brought a binder of information, including the statements that had been made and the evidence showing that those statements were false,' replied Waldman.

'So, the investigation was opened up at your request after you brought this binder to the desk officer?' asked Rottenborn.

'I didn't ask him to open an investigation. I filed a claim with the LAPD regarding these perjurious statements that Ms Heard and her best friend, Rocky Pennington, had made to a court,' said Waldman.

Unfortunately Waldman had kept no written record of his claim, nor was he sure if he signed it. Nor could he remember the name of the desk officer he spoke to. Five days after his deposition was shown to the Virginia court, a pro-Depp social media user called Jax tweeted what appeared to be an LAPD investigative report form, dated 29 April 2021. In it, Amber Heard and Raquel Pennington were listed as 'suspects'. The crime was of 'perjury', specifically presenting 'false evidence in court'. The victim in this case was listed as 'Los Angeles Superior

---

[3] See *The Phone Incident* chapter.

Court'. The 'involved person', acting in this capacity as a witness, was: 'Waldman, Adam'.

Maybe he had time on his hands. Waldman's report to the LAPD was made nine days after he was suspended by Twitter. His last tweet in 2021 was on 20 April. Until that date, Waldman had been posting scraps of transcripts and media articles, pointing out what he saw as the hypocrisy of his opponents and/or inconsistencies in their statements. He would occasionally append a song lyric to his tweets. In April 2021 alone we were treated to couplets from Bob Dylan, Duran Duran, Dire Straits, Violent Femmes and UB40. Twitter apparently told Waldman he had been permanently suspended due to 'multiple violations' of the platform's 'private information policy'.

No further clarification was forthcoming, but a clue might be found in Twitter's 'private information and media policy', which makes it clear the company doesn't just consider the factual content of information being shared, but the 'intent' of the person sharing it. The policy states: 'If we believe that someone is sharing information with an abusive intent, or to harass or encourage others to harass another person, we will take action.'

Although Waldman was out of the frontline picture, he'd done enough to prepare the ground. By the time of his suspension, Waldman was known to a network of trusted influencers who would post up any half-truth they thought might help Depp's cause. They in turn had energized a constituency of justice-seekers, hell bent on finding the smoking gun(s) to nail Heard's lies. Proving the lazy, lying mainstream media wrong was an incentive. Shitposting Heard and anyone who tried to stand up for her was a given.

Other YouTubers caught on. Insight and opinion from legal commentators found a huge audience. Each snippet of 'evidence' and opinion thrown into the confirmation bias machine grew and monetized the followings of their creators. Millions of casual social media users got sucked into the narrative: *The truth is out there. The #justiceforjohnnydepp community is hunting it down. Together, we will save a wronged man.*

The dynamite which caused this volatile market of consumers and creators to explode was the hours and hours of live footage being generated by the US trial. This was nothing to do with Waldman, but he had undoubtedly primed the pump.

Of course, Waldman can't take all the credit for leading the Depp fightback. Indeed, there might be some on Depp's team who think he was more a hindrance than a help. Waldman went into the UK trial all guns blazing on social media, and in the process managed to irritate the decision-making judge. He got thrown off the Virginia case for allegedly acting unethically, and was then suspended from Twitter. Depp's success in 2022 only came after Waldman had been formally removed from proceedings. Furthermore, the online Depp community were active well before Waldman started tweeting, and they did a lot of work themselves. One person close to Depp's team told me:

'I'm not going to try to excuse different things Adam did or how he went about it. There were points in time where, from the legal side, it was really not helpful. There were elements of what he did that may have had a positive impact because of the way it rallied the troops, but there were also things that were potentially very dangerous to Johnny's cause, specifically where he shared information from conversations that were privileged. By sharing them publicly that potentially opens up the team to anything else related to those conversations to be put in play in open court. And while it didn't come to that, it was a legitimate potential issue.'

That said, Waldman's willingness to take on journalists, his combative statements and the information he fed pro-Depp online propagandists undoubtedly had an effect, helping ensure everything hit critical mass for his client at the perfect moment.

There is a little postscript to this. On 26 November 2022 Waldman's Twitter account was reinstated – possibly part of new owner Elon Musk's general amnesty for suspended accounts (though, given Depp's publicly stated antipathy towards Musk, I doubt the Tesla billionaire had any direct involvement). Waldman wasted no time in picking up where he left off, calling Amber Heard's former lawyer Jennifer Robinson a liar, quoting George Orwell, De La Soul and Gang Starr in his tweets and obliquely suggesting an Amber Heard Instagram post contained more than a hint of narcissistic self-regard. Waldman was back, and his mignons cheered.

THE GRUMPY

Come on, then. Let's dive into the poo. During an early telephone conference with my publishers about the draft plan for this book I mentioned some of the events which would likely be given stand-alone chapters. As I listed the Boston/LA plane flight, Australia, Kate Moss's appearance in court and the Battle of the Forensic Psychologists (the latter still to come), a female voice on the other end of the line piped up: 'Are you not going to do one on the poo?'

Of course I am going to do a chapter on the poo. How could I avoid it? None of us can avoid the poo. It has been smeared all over Amber Heard's reputation since April 2016.

Although it helped put the skids on their relationship, the feces in question only has tangential relevance to domestic violence, or libel. Yet the Legend of The Grumpy has captivated millions and kept some of our finest legal minds occupied for many hundreds of billable hours. It has progressively become one of the most expensive plops on the planet. It has a claim to be the most famous.

After Depp's departure from the ECB in the early hours of Friday 22 April, Heard was, as far as we know, in bed asleep. At some point between 10am and 10.30am, Rocky Pennington entered PH3 and went up to Heard's bedroom. Heard had messaged Pennington earlier that morning, asking her to come round to wake her up. In her messages to Pennington, Heard explained that she and Depp had thrown each other's phones into the street. Among other things, this meant Heard had no way of setting a sleep alarm. How she messaged Pennington without a phone has not been formally explained, but Heard has, in the past, referenced using an iPad for similar tasks.

Pennington did as requested, letting herself into the penthouse at the appointed time with her master key. She opened Heard's bedroom door. In her UK witness statement, Pennington wrote:

'I saw that there was shattered glass all over the floor. I stopped where I was. I saw that a lamp was broken and that pictures had been ripped down from the walls.'

She continued: 'I made my way carefully around the broken glass and climbed into Amber's bed and gently woke her... At no time did I see any feces in the bed and at no time was this topic discussed.'

In her US deposition, Pennington says both dogs were present in bed with Heard at the time, and when Heard woke up, 'she started crying'.

The two women were due to begin packing for Heard's birthday trip to Coachella[1], but there was a problem. They needed to retrieve the lost phones.

Starling Jenkins from Depp's security team arrived at the penthouse at 10.45am. Jenkins is a serious-looking man of few words. He carries an air of authority, possibly developed during his years of service with the US Marines.

Jenkins told the Virginia court that Heard was already in possession of her phone by the time he arrived and was in the process of 'redownloading' her information onto it.

Locating Depp's phone was a different matter. Jenkins told the court he 'formulated a plan' which was 'to use the *Find My Phone* app. Hit the streets. Try to get lucky.'

Lucky they got. Depp's phone was located in the possession of an 'unhoused gentleman' who surrendered it in exchange for a $420 reward, supplemented with food and drink.

Searching for Depp's phone caused a three-hour delay. Once it had been recovered and left at the guard hut (or 'command post' as Jenkins, the ex-marine, called it) next to PH5, the birthday party finally took off towards Palm Springs. Heard, Pennington, Savannah McMillan and Whitney travelled in Heard's classic Mustang. Jenkins drove the dogs and luggage in an SUV. Jenkins estimates they arrived at the Parker Hotel in Palm Springs at 'around 5.30-ish, maybe quarter to 6'. The journey between the ECB and the Parker Hotel is 115 miles, which takes 2 hours 35 minutes without stops. In all probability the party left for Coachella between 2.30pm and 2.45pm.

At 3pm, Hilda Vargas, Johnny Depp's long-serving housekeeper, arrived at the ECB with a female co-worker. Vargas had spent the morning tidying up at Sweetzer Avenue. It was a well-established routine. The pair started work on the penthouses.

In a witness statement to the UK trial, Vargas describes what happened next:

'I had just finished washing dishes and vacuuming and I was about to help the other cleaning woman change the sheets, when I heard her call out. I joined her in the master bedroom. She was pointing to the bed

---

[1]   A music festival held at Coachella Valley in the Colorado Desert.

and told me that she couldn't believe what she had found. I pulled back the top sheet on the bed and saw a large pile of feces.'

Vargas was, understandably, 'horrified and disgusted'.

At the time of writing her witness statement, Hilda Vargas knew Amber Heard was claiming the feces had been produced by one of the couple's dogs, Pistol or Boo. Vargas contradicts this:

'It was clear to me that this was human feces. I knew that the feces could not have come from either of Mr Depp's and Ms Heard's two small dogs. I have cleaned up after those dogs many times and their feces are much smaller. Further, I have never known those dogs to defecate in the bed.'

Vargas was 'completely shocked' by what she had to deal with. Before removing the poo and putting the sheets on to wash, she took a number of photos, three of which were attached to her witness statement. Two are time-stamped 6.54pm.

The quality of the photos as rendered in the witness statement are not great, but others are circulating online. The photographs appear to show a single turd rather than 'a large pile'.

If the poo *is* human poo, one is forced to wonder how it got there. I find it difficult to believe anyone would crouch over the sheets and coil one out *in situ*, but I should perhaps accept that someone who might be prepared to deliberately put a poo in a bed might also be prepared to produce it (or arrange to have it produced) directly.

Vargas was called by Kevin Murphy, Depp's estate manager, to see if she had finished her work. Because Vargas was 'angry', she told Murphy about the poo.

If the order of events in Vargas' statement is to be taken chronologically, Vargas had already cleared away the poo by the time Murphy called. She also made no mention of Murphy coming over. According to *Murphy's* statement he made the call, received the pictures and then went to the ECB to inspect the scene.

'When I arrived at the penthouse,' he wrote, 'I was shocked and disgusted by what I observed as human feces on the bed.'

If that is true, Vargas had not already cleaned up, as she described, before receiving Murphy's call. Murphy, for some reason, did not take any photos of his own. Instead he sent Vargas' photographs to one of Depp's security team, Sean Bett, who forwarded them to Depp. Twenty-four hours later, Murphy spoke to Depp about the poo. He described his employer's reaction as 'sullen and disgusted', adding:

'I believe he suggested getting the feces DNA tested to see where they had come from.'

It wasn't long before Depp was seeing the funny side. He sent texts to his team calling the photographs 'hilarious', suggesting he had 'not... laughed that hard for years.' In other texts, Depp was explicit (although given the general tone, perhaps joking) about who he perceived to be responsible. 'My wife left a whopper poop on my bed,' he wrote, adding, 'I've been through a whole lot of shit with her.' Depp also coined a nickname for his soon-to-be ex-wife, which, six years later, would be chanted at her by hundreds of fans outside court in Virginia: 'Amber Turd'.

Whilst the *fact* of the grumpy is not in dispute, its origin certainly is.

In his witness statement, Kevin Murphy said 'the feces did not appear to come from either of Mr Depp's and Ms Heard's two small Yorkshire terriers.'

He wrote: 'I have walked, cleaned up after, played with and interacted with these dogs many times, and their feces have always been significantly smaller than what I saw in the bed.'

Amber Heard was convinced it was either Pistol or Boo. 'I cannot fathom what adult would ever do such a thing,' she told the UK trial. 'I cannot imagine what kind of human being would have a sense of humor like that, other than Johnny.' Heard called it 'horrific, which is why I can only imagine a dog being responsible for it.'

At the London trial, Depp believed the turd's sponsor was bipedal. 'It was a mystery grumpy,' he said, introducing a new piece of slang to the UK, 'and it was not left by a three or four pound dog.'

When asked if he really thought it was something Heard could have done, Depp replied: 'To be quite honest, iO Tillett-Wright seemed the only one that would be crass enough to commit such an act.'

There is no record of Tillett-Wright entering the ECB penthouse complex between the time Depp left the building and the poo was discovered. Rocky Pennington has said in a sworn statement that he was not even in LA at the time, though he did meet up with Heard's Coachella party later that day in Palm Springs.

When asked, Tillett-Wright told the UK trial Amber Heard was unlikely to be the culprit as she was 'fecal-phobic' and had no history of playing pranks. He did not explain how he knew Heard was 'fecal-phobic' other than to say 'she likes to pretend that she does not do that in private, much less on her own bed.'

The mystery remained hanging in the air until the following month. In a sworn statement, Kevin Murphy says he was called on 12 May by Heard, who was furious with him for forwarding Vargas' poo pics to

Sean Bett. In the course of the call, Murphy says Heard 'told me that leaving the feces in Mr Depp's bed had been "just a harmless prank".'

Murphy relayed this to Depp, who believes Heard was 'effectively acknowledging that she had been responsible, whereas she had previously sought to blame our dogs.'

Could the dogs have done it? Pistol and Boo were known shitters, Boo especially. iO Tillett-Wright wrote in his witness statement: 'Boo pooped everywhere, all the time, including in the bed, twice on my pillow – and once on Johnny while he was sitting in a chair. The dog has faulty bowels.'

Text messages between Heard and Murphy discussing Boo's inability to control his fecal emissions concluded with Murphy agreeing he needed extra training. Heard described Boo shitting on Johnny whilst he slept and said that both dogs liked to get into their bed. Heard told the UK court that, like Murphy and Vargas, she had cleaned up after both dogs on a number of occasions.

There is a conflict of evidence as to whether either of the dogs were able to get up onto the marital bed unaided. Vargas said she had never had to deal with a poo on that bed before. In his deposition to the US trial, Josh Drew said one dog was capable of doing so, but the other was not. He did not specify which dog could or couldn't by name.

Vargas definitely thought it was human poo. Murphy, if he did see it, thought it was human poo. Depp concluded from Vargas' photographs it was human poo.

In court, on oath, Kevin Murphy was cross-examined by NGN's barrister, who suggested the conversation on 12 May during which Heard allegedly took responsibility for the poo never happened.

'I can assure you that it did,' replied Murphy.

'This detail of the case has been an attempt to make Ms Heard appear disgusting and absurd in the public eye,' countered the lawyer.

Murphy was unmoved.

'It is just the truth,' he said.

When Depp confronted Heard about the poo on 21 May, Heard vehemently denied saying anything to Murphy about a prank. Putting him on speakerphone, the couple called the estate manager to straighten things out. Heard said Murphy did not volunteer any information at first, but then 'Johnny took the phone and started speaking to Mr Murphy.' Heard says Johnny put it to him that she had told him the incident was a prank. After that 'Mr Murphy made a vague blanket agreement with whatever Johnny said.'

Kevin Murphy was not used as a trial witness in Virginia, which meant the jury did not get to hear his evidence about this all-important matter. Starling Jenkins, however, did appear, live by videolink from LA.

Jenkins described arriving at the Parker Hotel on 22 April, then driving Heard and friends from the hotel to the festival site. 'Did you have any discussions with Ms Heard on the way to Coachella that evening?' asked Depp's attorney.

Jenkins replied: 'We had a conversation pertaining to the surprise she left in the boss's bed prior to leaving the apartment.'

Depp's lawyer probed further: 'The surprise in the boss's bed... what are you referring to?'

'The defecation,' replied Jenkins, solemnly.

'And what did Ms Heard say about the defecation in Mr Depp's bed?' asked the attorney.

'A horrible practical joke gone wrong,' intoned Jenkins, without elaboration.

Whether this confession was heard by the other people in the car was not discussed in court. Jenkins makes no mention of the alleged conversation in his statement to the UK trial, and was therefore not cross-examined on it.

Six years after the event I found myself outside Fairfax County Courthouse filming an interview with a young lady who had come to court dressed as, in her words, a 'sexy turd'. She wore a revealing copper-brown top, a dark chocolate-colored taffeta skirt, a blonde wig and a poo-emoji hat. Her name was Priscilla. We did not discuss the fact of the poo or its provenance. Instead we focused on the hundreds of people chanting 'Amber Turd! Amber Turd!' around the back of the court as Heard arrived that morning.

Priscilla told me she wouldn't be dressed as a poo and wandering around outside court had she not been a witness to female-perpetrated domestic violence within her family. 'It's very hard being a child of this product,' Priscilla told me, 'if it's your father or if it's your uncle you see... how it ultimately destroys them. It emasculates them... to the extent that they can't even speak of it as if it's bothering them.'

I asked whether Heard deserved the wellspring of hatred which had bubbled up online and manifested itself in the chanting directed at her when she arrived at court.

'I wouldn't say that she deserves it and I wouldn't say that she doesn't deserve it,' replied Priscilla. 'It's hard for me to sympathize.'

I asked Priscilla about the relentless abuse Heard was getting, when, depending on the perspectives put forward in court, she could be a liar, a delusional fantasist or a genuine victim of sexual abuse. Priscilla said:

'Those are things that really doesn't have to be considered when it comes to meme-ing and trolling in this day and age. That's how a lot of us cope with situations. That's how we express ourselves.'

Priscilla felt Amber Heard was adopting the language and persona of an abused woman without having enough evidence to demonstrate she had been abused herself. 'A person who is truly being abused has the photo evidence, which is not that difficult to get,' Priscilla told me. 'If you're being beat, if you're being pummelled, it is not difficult to get that photo evidence.'

Priscilla hoped the trial would encourage more male victims of domestic violence to come forward. She wanted people to take men claiming abuse 'more seriously', and see 'that they're not *pussies*, they're not *big babies*, they're not *weak men*.' She felt Depp's defamation claim was an act of vulnerability, which could inspire other men to speak out. 'They see someone as macho and manly as Johnny Depp and feel that "if he can come out, maybe I can come out, too".'

On 14 May 2022, during a period when it seemed the entire internet was dedicated to comedy memes and TikToks about Depp v Heard, *Saturday Night Live* began with a skit on what was happening in Virginia. Their way in was The Grumpy. This was not without risk. After all, the central issue was sexual violence. Nine days before the skit aired, Amber Heard had taken the stand, and testified that Johnny Depp had raped her with a bottle.

But if the world was going lol-a-minute online, which suggested there was a huge appetite for trial-related gags – why shouldn't some of the nation's brightest comedic minds try to grab a slice of the action?

The skit is passably funny. It deals with domestic violence by ignoring it completely, to the extent of taking the alleged victim out of the scene. There is a comedian playing Amber Heard's lawyer, but there is no comedian playing Amber Heard. The focus of the sketch is on the discovery of the 'dookie' and the staff who have to deal with it. The debate over who was responsible for the 'booboo' is a non-debate. The dog argument is dismissed with one line: *That mess ain't come out of no dog.*

The logic of the sketch invites us to conclude that in this comedy universe Amber Heard did shit the bed, and she did so because a) she had already cut Johnny Depp's finger off and was therefore mad enough to do anything; b) living with Johnny Depp would make anyone mad enough to shit the bed. If, that is, the bed had been shat at all. Right at the beginning of the sketch, possibly to embed the sense of unreality into what we are watching, the comedian playing Elaine Bredehoft is required to say: 'There's no actual proof that this ever happened.'

But the dookie did happen, and neither Johnny Depp nor Amber Heard have ever claimed otherwise.

Depp has repeatedly described the emergence of the grumpy as a pivotal moment in his relationship with Heard. His second witness statement to the UK trial makes it clear the day he discovered his wife had allegedly confessed to a scatalogical prank involving leaving feces in the marital bed, Depp 'resolved to divorce'.

Yet the very odd thing about all of this is that no one seems to have considered how the prank, if that's what it was, was supposed to have worked. Whilst Starling Jenkins was out looking for Johnny Depp's phone, is it suggested that Heard, Rocky, Whitney or Savannah – or all four together – conceived a plan to produce or source a lump of poo and place it in the bed? Heard has said that by this stage of the relationship Johnny was sleeping most nights at Sweetzer. Given what had transpired in the early hours of that morning, it seemed most unlikely he would return to the ECB in the afternoon for a nap. Who, then, was the grumpy for? Heard would have known that cleaning staff were due to visit the penthouse shortly after she left for Coachella. It was their routine. The cleaners would therefore be the first to discover and have to deal with the shit. Was it a practical joke on the cleaners? Or was Heard hoping it would all get back to Johnny and he would find the whole thing... er, hilarious?

It is a shame the poo was disposed of before Depp had a chance to pursue his DNA test idea. The only documentary evidence still in existence remains Vargas' photos. I sent them to Professor Chuka Nwokolo CBE, a respected consultant gastroenterologist at the University Hospitals Coventry and Warwickshire NHS Trust. He told me he was 'unable to determine' if the pictured stool 'is from man or dog.' He did say that if it was passed by a human, 'the person would be constipated.'

You may wish to chew on that. You may, on reflection, want to think about something else.

ABDUCTIVE REASONING

Judges in UK libel trials, as jurors in US defamation trials, are often described in court as 'fact-finders' (with the spoken emphasis settling naturally on the word 'fact'). This feels misleading because we nowadays tend to equate 'finding' with discovering things. Yet legally speaking, discovery of the 'facts' of a case is carried out by the parties' lawyers before and during a trial. Judges and juries have to make decisions *about* the 'facts' in evidence and testimony. It is in this way that judges and juries are actually 'fact-*finders*', with the emphasis on the second word. It is the judge's or jury's job to make *findings* of fact.

This is spectacularly difficult, particularly when the truth of a matter is bitterly contested by the only witnesses. But that is why people go to court. They want decisions which have financial and social consequences. They want their version of the truth endorsed by a higher authority, so that it is no longer contested, but vindicated. The risks (and indeed the costs) involved are enormous, but so is the prize: finality, resolution, judgment.

Going to court is therefore about getting a result. Ideally a just result based on a series of incontrovertible truths, but it is the result that matters, and the courts know this. If a judge fudges a case by finding partly for both sides, or a jury fails to reach a conclusive verdict, it can make the opportunity cost of going to court prohibitive.

Broadly, the qualifying bar for a decision about an alleged criminal offense is 'beyond reasonable doubt'. Put crudely, that's around 97% sure[1]. The civil courts in the UK require a decision to be made on 'the balance of probabilities'. In the US it is known as the 'preponderance of evidence'. In these courts, a fair-minded and impartial observer of all the evidence simply has to decide what is the more *likely* truth. Put crudely, that's around 51% sure.

In America there is a third standard, or *burden* of proof. Here a judge or jury must be satisfied the evidence is 'clear and convincing' before making a decision – around 80% sure. This comes into play in some civil and some criminal cases. In Virginia, Johnny Depp had to convince a jury he had been defamed (i.e. what Amber Heard had written in the Washington Post was untrue and likely to seriously damage his reputation) on the 'preponderance of evidence'. To be awarded damages

---

[1] I've tested this figure with several learned friends. They talked me down from my initial estimate of 99%.

for that defamation, he had to convince the jury of *malice* (i.e. Amber Heard had written her Washington Post article knowing it was untrue with a clear intention to damage Depp's reputation[2]). The malice element required a 'clear and convincing' standard of proof.

The UK does not have this third standard. However, when allegations of 'serious criminality' are made in a civil court as part of (say) a libel claim, 'clear evidence' is required. Repeated beatings and rape are matters of serious criminality; therefore the judge in Depp v NGN had to be satisfied there was clear evidence of these assaults before accepting, on the balance of probabilities, that they happened – around 80% sure.

Judges and juries are human. They make mistakes. Everyone does. To mitigate against mistakes in a jury system, you rely on collective decisions made by a bunch of reasonable people. If a single judge is making a decision, you are relying on their experience and expertize. Neither system is perfect.

Trying to work out which court made the right decision in the case of Johnny Depp is an intriguing proposition.

Before going any further, I need to address the theory that the judge in the UK was corrupt, had a conflict of interest or was biased against Johnny Depp, something I heard time and again amongst Depp fans on the ground in the US.

The idea Judge Andrew Nicol was somehow inept, paid or warned off has taken hold, particularly in America, where several thousand people have signed a petition calling for an investigation. The conspiracy theory is as follows:

The Sun newspaper is owned by billionaire media mogul Rupert Murdoch through his company NGN. Rupert Murdoch also happens to own a radio station called TalkRadio via the Wireless Group, a subsidiary of another Murdoch company – News Corp. Robert Palmer, Andrew Nicol's son, works for TalkRadio, as does Dan Wootton, author of the 'wife-beater' article in the Sun. Using his unlimited power and influence, Rupert Murdoch somehow got a message to Nicol that if he didn't find in NGN's favor, Palmer would get the bullet. If it wasn't a threat, it was a favor. Nicol and Murdoch are socially affiliated because of Palmer and other establishment connections. Nicol would therefore

---

[2]   The exact legal terminology is *actual malice* and the definition for actual malice (confirmed by the US Supreme Court) is a statement made 'with knowledge that it was false or with reckless disregard of whether it was false or not.'

be inclined to find for NGN over Johnny Depp. Either way, Nicol is in Rupert Murdoch's pocket and abused his position as a High Court judge to shape the Depp v NGN judgment in NGN's favor.

Robert Palmer's social media offerings suggest he is indeed Mr Justice Nicol's son, or at least the son of Nicol's current wife (Palmer refused to confirm his biographical details to me directly). Palmer works full time for Tax Justice UK, a not-for-profit organization campaigning for a tax system which 'actively redistributes wealth to tackle inequality'. Until recently, Palmer stated on his Twitter bio that he was a 'review regular' on TalkRadio. As a journalist who has occasionally reviewed papers on the radio, I can vouch for the fact that this is a poorly or unpaid gig involving about an hour's work once or twice a week. It is fun and serves as an opportunity to get a bit of media experience. Mr Palmer did not respond to my requests for an interview. I wanted to ask him if he persuaded his dad (if it is his dad) to find against Johnny Depp so he could keep his paper-reviewing gig on TalkRadio, but I suspect I don't need to.

I'm not saying that Mr Justice Nicol *wasn't* strong-armed by Rupert Murdoch into finding for NGN, or that he somehow felt some kind of allegiance towards him and therefore doctored his judgment. It is just that there isn't a single shred of evidence for this theory whatsoever. In the absence of evidence we have to go on likelihood, and the likelihood of a High Court judge consciously choosing to pervert the course of justice to save his son's twice-weekly gig reviewing newspapers on a radio station is a sentence I can't quite believe I'm actually typing. But YouTubers, Instagrammers and PopOptic (ranked by Google as a 'news' site) are peddling it, and people are believing it, because it fits with their own preconceptions and biases.

Just because it is unlikely Mr Justice Nicol brought a conscious or malign bias to bear on his judgment, it doesn't mean he didn't bring a whole raft of *unconscious* biases to his task, and this is perhaps where things become a little more interesting. The concept of unconscious (or implicit) bias has been around since the mid-nineties, but as a survival-related prejudicial system of thinking – it's as old as the hills.

We process and act on information consciously and unconsciously. Once we've learned how, skills like talking, walking and riding a bike become unconscious activities. We can do them 'without' thinking. The psychologist Daniel Kahneman calls this unconscious process 'System 1' thinking. It is fast, instinctive and has a hard wire to our emotional responses.

'System 2' thinking engages reason. Activities which utilize this part of the brain include writing essays, filling out tax returns and assembling IKEA furniture. Everything in this arena is slow and requires effort. System 1 thinking underpins System 2 thinking. Both inform each other. Whilst I am carefully formulating the words you are reading in this book in order to convey a series of ideas, my fingers don't require much conscious thought to pick out the letters from the keyboard in front of me. For me, spelling and typing are (just about) System 1 processes without which I would not be able to complete my System 2-oriented task, which is to write this book for you to read. My typing and spelling skills have become (more or less) embedded in my unconscious, System 1 thinking.

Humans have developed like this to enable us to deal with the world. Our senses are constantly bombarded by huge volumes of information every waking moment of every day. As Harvard psychologist Charlotte Ruhl explains in her excellent primer *Implicit or Unconscious Bias*, we use 'mental shortcuts' – rules of thumb, educated guesses and 'common sense' – to filter out irrelevant data and respond to the stimuli which keep us safe and upright. It's this which creates the time and space our conscious minds need to contemplate the slow and difficult thinking we hope will make us thrive.

Ruhl cites research which demonstrates that as we socialize, we assign positive feelings towards those within our social group and negative feelings towards those people outside our social group. These are instincts honed over millennia, and we do it as naturally as talking, or riding a bike. As we get older and discover more about who we are as individuals, we start to develop positive associations towards those who we perceive as similar to us (even if they are not within our immediate social group) and negative associations towards those who we see as dissimilar. These cognitive short cuts operating in our System 1 thinking unconsciously inform our System 2 thinking. It is perhaps best summed up by the Avenue Q song *Everyone's a Little Bit Racist*.

But it's not just race. Unconscious bias can be triggered by any of the differences between us – gender, body-shape, body-markings, class, nationality, accent and the way people present themselves. These *all* affect what we think about certain individuals, or groups of people.

Is it possible that Mr Justice Nicol, who may not have known much about Johnny Depp, and even less about Amber Heard, decided that the tattooed, drug-taking, short-tempered, cupboard-smashing, wine-bottle throwing individual before him was the *sort* of person who would beat up his wife? Could that have influenced his judgement?

The understanding that unconscious or implicit bias has been a problem for the judiciary was acknowledged by the top judge in England and Wales – the Lord Chief Justice – in a strategy document published in November 2020, coincidentally the same month the Depp v NGN judgment was handed down. It decreed that all UK judges would hence-forth receive formal training to help them recognize 'the existence of implicit bias and how to employ mitigation strategies.' This training would help them understand 'the different influences at work on them and others when hearing and deciding cases and how best to reduce their influence on the conduct and outcome of proceedings.'

Mr Justice Nicol, being a top judge and bright chap, would no doubt be aware of the concept, and perhaps the dangers of unconscious bias, but equally he will have brought his own unconscious biases to bear on Depp v NGN, just as the jury will have done on Depp v Heard. What we don't know is how much of an influence they could have had on his (or their) reasoning and what steps he (or they) took to mitigate them. What we do know is that judges and juries should only draw their conclusions from the evidence presented to them at trial. And a decent bulwark against unconscious bias (or even consciously acknowledged prejudices) is analytical investigative rigor, something Nicol did not shy away from in a 129-page judgment, which took more than three months to deliver.

The problem the judge had in Depp v NGN was one which has plagued this story from the start. There is very little direct evidence that Johnny Depp was violent towards Amber Heard. In Depp v NGN, it went back to the burden of proof – the 'balance of probabilities'. Likelihood.

Likelihood is parsed through a process known as abductive reason-ing. Deductive reasoning can come to a logically valid conclusion if all its premises are known to be true (or in logic, *sound*). Abductive reason-ing starts with an observation or set of observations which may or may not be sound and then seeks the most plausible or likely conclusion from those observations. In logical terms it does not deliver certainty, but in legal terms it very much helps a fact-finder make a decision. The strength of the result is therefore not just in the validity of the observa-tions themselves, but the rigor with which they can be shown to have been interrogated.

A simplistic version of this approach is known as the duck test: 'If it walks like a duck and quacks like a duck, it probably is a duck.'

Drawing on his forty years' legal experience, Mr Justice Nicol reviewed thousands of evidential documents and three weeks' worth of court transcripts. He put together a detailed and reasoned analysis of the claims before him, focusing on fourteen incidents of alleged violence and three (unreportable at the time) incidents of alleged sexual assault. Nicol concluded that, on the balance of probabilities, twelve incidents of violence and one of the three allegations of sexual assault reached the required evidential standard. They happened, and they were perpetrated by Johnny Depp. The Sun and Dan Wootton are therefore entitled to call Depp a wife-beater, on the grounds it is 'substantially true'.

Depp could be said to exhibit many of the hallmarks of a typical abuser. He was a victim of violence within his childhood home. He took alcohol and drugs to excess during his relationship with Amber Heard. He was jealous, witnesses said he was controlling[3] and he expressed his inner rage by defacing and destroying things.

This, in itself, is not evidence that he beat Amber Heard. Someone can be a jealous drug abuser who smashes things without being a wife-beater. But what is the likelihood?

Nicol doesn't *know* what actually happened. Nor do you, or I, or the Virginia jurors. In one strange passage in his judgment, Nicol refers to a text sent on 5 April 2016 by Johnny Depp. In it Depp begs his security guard Malcolm Connolly:

'Please get her out of this room NOW!!! She's struck me about 10 times ... Can't take any more!!!'

The judge decided that as Heard was not asked about it in court, he couldn't put any weight on it.

Is it possible that Nicol's abductive reasoning had taken him in the wrong direction? Could his fundamental premises be wrong? Could he have mistaken a harmless, innocent man for a waddling, quacking duck?

---

[3] Possibly corroborated by a text sent in October 2013 expressing outrage when Heard said she had a meeting. Depp replied 'Holy crack whores!!! NO GODDAM MEETINGS!!! NO MOVIES!!! Why??? Why do you deviate from our agreement??? What species of meeting??? Fuck it... Just tell me when you get home...' Depp said this was 'not necessarily an angry text' nor was it 'about her doing films.'

THE PHONE INCIDENT

Los Angeles, 21 May 2016

It was a month after Heard's disastrous 30th birthday party. The scene, once more, was Penthouse 3 of the ECB. On this occasion Amber Heard claimed she sustained injuries caused by Johnny Depp when he allegedly threw a cellphone, with force, directly at her face.

Heard said the phone hit her right cheekbone and caused a mark. The mark led a somewhat chequered life before appearing (if it was the same mark), along with Heard's solemn face, on the cover of People magazine, shortly after she had been given a temporary restraining order against Johnny Depp, and filed for divorce.

Depp had not seen Heard since leaving Penthouse 3 in the early hours of 22 April. Despite the violence which preceded it, and the retrospective acknowledgment by both parties (especially Depp) that their marriage was all but over, textual relations between the two remained cordial . But the spectre of The Grumpy remained unresolved. Heard told US jurors about one telephone conversation she had with Depp whilst she was in Italy on a modelling job:

'He was going on about scientists and DNA and feces, that he had had some, you know scientific analysis done and DNA analysis done... he was going on about all the scientists that he had conferred about the DNA results with.'

Heard thought he 'was out of his mind' and concluded he was on a drink and drug binge, which was bringing on 'delusions'.

Depp was in London working through most of May, but flew back to LA on the 17th when he heard his mother, who was receiving care at the Cedars-Sinai hospital, had taken a turn for the worse.

Depp was in a bad place. He'd been told his finances were in a serious mess. His marriage was on the point of collapse. He had substance abuse issues and his mother was dying.

On 18 May, Depp sent a text to Heard, saying: 'I'm with Betty Sue, this will be it, the end is nigh. I've spoken your words of love and respect for her and then some. She's ready to split. Thank you for loving her.'

In court Depp described his mother's condition:

'She was pretty much incapable of speech... her eyes were still open... she could kind of react with her eyes, but she couldn't speak. She was fighting still inside, but she was lying in the bed and... excuse this analogy, but... I knew that the one thing, as far as Betty Sue was concerned,

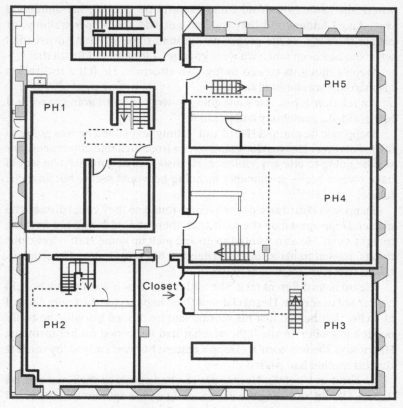

Simplified representation of the main level of the penthouses at the ECB

the last thing that she would have wanted was to have ended up lying there... on a deli platter.'

Depp brought his children to Betty Sue's bedside to say goodbye ('we all spoke into her ear'). She died on 20 May.

Depp says he had no desire, on this occasion, to cope with his grief through self-medication. He told the UK court: 'There was so much to deal with that on such profoundly important and sensitive levels that I could not escape into any drug-induced pain-free setting. I did not inebriate myself to the point of numbness.'

Depp told the US trial his mother's death made him realize 'life is a birdsong, that what feels like 100 years is, in fact, a second, millisecond.' In his grief, he 'made peace' with Betty Sue, 'because I understood where she came from. And I understood how difficult her childhood was. And I understood that she had not had the proper training, or proper teaching, or the proper background to be anything other than what she had been when we were younger. I forgave her for all that.'

Depp's thoughts turned to his own situation. He felt a realization his marriage was beyond saving.

'In relationships... if it's not going to work, it's not going to work. I had decided... somebody had to call it.'

Depp said he phoned Heard and 'calmly' explained he was going to file for divorce. He was not going to cite irreconcilable differences, nor was he going to cite any violence. He also says he promised he would 'take care of her' – presumably meaning he would secure her financial future.

Depp says Heard asked him to come round so they could discuss the matter. Depp agreed on the basis that 'there should have been nothing to fight over.' He also wanted to go and pick up some stuff – 'precious things' related to his 'children... friends... Brando, Hunter Thompson... things that were important to me.'

Heard has a different take. She told the US trial it was Depp who said he wanted to see her. Heard claimed Depp kept saying 'he really needed his wife, that he had lost his mother and he missed his wife, he really needed his wife.' In the light of what had happened on her birthday, Heard says she felt 'torn' by Depp's request but was swayed 'by the fact that his mother had passed.'

In court in Virginia, Heard says she had specified their meeting on 21 May should be during the day to 'mitigate the amount that he would be drinking', as 'night is a little bit more dangerous.'

Whether it was because he was asleep for the rest of the afternoon, or for other reasons, Depp did not arrive at the ECB until shortly after 7pm.

Aware of how volatile things could get, Depp has now told two courtrooms that he was very careful to ask his security to wait outside the door to Penthouse 3, rather than take up their usual spot in the 'command post' adjacent to Penthouse 5. He says he issued the direct instruction: 'If you hear anything, if you hear screaming... get in there.'

Depp explained to the US court: 'I had them waiting by the door... in case anything went down.'

In 2020 – his first public telling of what happened on his arrival at the ECB that night – Depp maintained he was walking into a trap. Part of the trap involved Rocky Pennington hiding in a closet, ready to leap out and do Heard's bidding. Depp told the UK court Pennington *had* to have been hiding somewhere in PH3 because there was no way she could have evaded the attention of his security detail, Jerry Judge and Sean Bett, who should have been posted outside the door to PH3, in the main hallway.

According to Heard, when Depp did walk into PH3 he was 'drunk and high', although not incoherent.

Depp describes seeing Heard sitting on their L-shaped couch in their living area. They began talking. Both Depp and Heard accuse each other of bringing up the contested turd. It certainly squelched its way into the conversation, and relatively quickly.

Depp told jurors Heard 'was trying to explain a few things about Coachella, and then the fecal delivery, and saying that it was the dogs. And I... could not agree with her.'

Heard says Depp refused to accept what she saw as the logical flaw in the human poo/prank theory: 'I tried to point out how that didn't make any sense. I'm not even going to be there, I wasn't there, and my friends wouldn't do that. That's not something a bunch of 30-year old women thinks is funny. What is he talking about?'

Depp was having none of it. It was human poo, and he wanted to know who did it. Pistol and Boo could not have been responsible. 'I lived with those dogs,' he told the US trial. 'I picked up their fun.'

The formerly 'peaceful' discussion turned (somewhat predictably), into a blazing row. Depp continued to maintain Heard had told Kevin Murphy the poo was a prank. Heard denied it. To resolve this, the couple called Murphy and put him on speakerphone. In his UK witness statement Murphy says he confirmed to the couple that Heard did speak to him earlier that month and during their conversation Heard admitted that she was responsible.

This did not go down well with Heard. Murphy said: 'Ms Heard yelled and called me "a fucking liar" multiple times. I asked her to stop yelling and swearing at me and overheard Mr Depp in the background saying "please don't speak to him that way. Be respectful." I then heard Mr Depp say that he couldn't do this anymore and wanted a divorce. When Ms Heard would not stop yelling, I hung up the telephone.'

There is a mystery at this point as to why Jerry Judge and Sean Bett did not burst into the penthouse as per their employer's specific instruction. Either his security team weren't at the door, or they didn't hear Heard (in Depp's words) 'screaming obscenities' at Murphy. Or they did hear the yelling and screaming, but decided, contrary to Depp's wishes, not to intervene. Or the 'screaming' and 'yelling' did not happen.

After the call to Murphy, Depp went upstairs to collect his things. Starting at 8.02pm Heard sent a series of texts to Murphy, continuing to deny making any admission about any prank. At 8.06pm Heard texted Pennington, asking her to come round. Heard then texted iO Tillett-Wright, who called back from New York. Heard told Tillett-Wright that Depp believed she or they were responsible for the fecal deposit. Tillett-Wright, who was on speakerphone, found this hilarious. Depp didn't. He told the US court:

'They were making a wonderful point of just how funny it was that I thought that some human being had actually dropped a grumpy, pardon the term, onto the bed. And they were yakking. They were yucking it up. They were laughing about the whole thing.'

Depp didn't like being made fun of. 'It was a tough couple of days. And I really didn't feel like I deserved that kind of treatment.'

In response to what he felt was goading, Depp grabbed the phone out of Heard's hand, telling Tillett-Wright: 'You've got what you want, you can have her, it's over.'

Depp says he then 'flipped the phone onto the couch, next to Ms Heard.' Heard disagrees. She says instead of throwing the phone onto the couch, Depp 'wound up his arm back like he was a baseball pitcher and threw the phone at my face as hard as he could. The phone hit me in the right cheek and eye.'

Heard says the speed and force with which Depp threw the phone did not give her time to react. She describes feeling as if the phone had 'popped my eye out.'

In his witness statement for the 2020 trial, Tillett-Wright picked up the story: 'I heard something that sounded as if the phone had dropped on the floor, and Amber yelped. I heard her pick up the phone and she said, "He just fucking threw the phone in my face". Then she shouted at him, "You just threw the phone in my fucking face". She even said something like, "He wound it up as a baseball and threw it at me"; and "Oh my god, that really fucking hurt".'

Tillett-Wright claims he heard Depp say: 'You think I fucking hurt you? What if I fucking peel [or pull[1]] your hair back? That will fucking hurt.'

---

[1]   In his initial statement, written and sent to Amber in 2016, Tillett-Wright used the word "pull". Under cross-examination in the 2020 trial, Tillett-Wright said 'I am not totally sure if [Depp] said "pull", "peel" or "peeled".' By 2022 Tillett-Wright had settled on Depp saying "peel".

Tillett-Wright then says: 'I heard her drop the phone... telling him to stop,' adding in court that he remembered her 'screaming'.

Heard says she 'was crying with pain'. In her version of what happened, Depp was 'yelling at me, saying he wanted to see my eye and how hard he had hit me. He said, "what if I pulled your hair back?" and charged at me, grabbing my hair and started yanking and jerking my head around. As I tried to get up from the sofa he was slapping and shaking me. I called out: "Call 911", hoping that iO might still be on the speakerphone and would hear me.'

Tillett-Wright did hear her. He has given two differing accounts of what was said – in the first he says he told Heard over the speakerphone that he was going to call the police and Heard responds: 'Do it!' In another he is instructed to call the police by Heard and before doing so, he checked to see if that's what she really wanted. According to Tillett-Wright, Heard responded by saying that it is exactly what she wanted. Tillett-Wright rang off the call with Heard and tried to call Rocky Pennington, guessing she (or her boyfriend Josh Drew who lived with Pennington in PH1) would be nearby and able to intervene more quickly. Pennington did not pick up the call, so at 8.16pm Tillett-Wright sent a text saying: 'Are you at Eastern? JD attacking Amber. She told me to call 911. I am doing it.'

Concerned it would take some time for the NYPD to contact the LAPD, Tillett-Wright phoned his friend, Lauren Shapiro in LA, asking her to dial 911 on his behalf. Tillett-Wright felt a local emergency call had a better chance of getting to the LAPD more quickly. In his 2022 deposition, Tillett-Wright told the court that as well as calling 911 in New York and Shapiro in LA, he thinks he 'may have' placed a second call to NYPD, though he doesn't say when or why.

Depp says he did not throw a phone at Heard, nor did he grab her hair. He says that after speaking to Tillett-Wright, he either 'banged', 'flopped' or, as per the quote above, 'flipped' the phone onto the couch. He told the UK trial he then started 'walking towards the kitchen to exit.' Suddenly, Rocky Pennington 'ran into the penthouse, and started [saying], "Leave her alone, Johnny. Leave her alone".' Depp was incredulous. 'I was by the refrigerator at this point. I was 20 feet away.'

During the 2020 trial, Heard was adamant that when Pennington arrived, Depp was still assaulting her:

'He was pulling me off the couch... Johnny is quite a bit bigger than me, and he wears these heavy rings on all of his fingers, and... when that hand, full of those big heavy metal rings, lands on your skull, it makes quite an impact... He had one hand in my hair and I was trying to pull my face away, so that he could not land any more blows on my face, and squeezing my chin.'

In her witness statement, Pennington made no mention of being called by iO Tillett-Wright, but says she reacted to the 8.06pm text from Heard 'asking me to come over to her apartment right away.'

Pennington claims she was in PH1 when she received the text, though Josh Drew believes he was with her in PH5 when the text arrived. How Pennington got into PH3 has never quite been nailed down. This has become a matter of fevered internet speculation, fuelled by Depp's 2020 assertion that Pennington must have been hiding in a closet, because there's no way she could have come into the apartment's front door without encountering Judge and Bett.

Piecing it together from the various available accounts (and it may help to refer to the ECB floorplan at the beginning of this chapter), Pennington either went from PH1 (or PH5) to the front door of PH3, where she did *not* encounter Judge and Bett, found the door locked, 'ran' (her word) to PH5, retrieved her keys and then entered PH3 via the front door, again without being seen by Judge or Bett. Or she could have reached PH3 from PH5 via the upstairs connecting doors. This would have taken her from PH5 through PH4 to PH3 without needing to go back into the main hallway. *Or* she went from PH1 to PH5 in the first instance, walked from PH5 through PH4 to find the door to PH3 locked, went back into PH5 to get her keys and then retraced her steps to enter PH3 from upstairs via PH4.

This was obliquely raised during Pennington's deposition for the US trial, when Depp's attorney stated (in the middle of a discussion about the events of 21 May):

'You can get from Penthouse 5 to Penthouse 3 without going out the main hallway, is that right?'

Pennington responded: 'Correct.' Unfortunately she was not asked if that is what she did on that occasion.

There remains the *possibility* that Pennington received the text whilst she was in PH5 and made her way through to PH3 via PH4, but Depp and Heard both seem to think Pennington came in via the main entrance to PH3.

Although Heard claimed Depp was still assaulting her when Pennington came into PH3, Pennington is equally certain Depp and Heard were 12 feet apart when she clapped eyes on them, and therefore she saw no assault. Heard says this may be because there is a stretch of hallway in PH3 'in which you cannot see the rest of the apartment'. This is true. Once you have got into PH3, you have to navigate a short passage before turning left, whereupon the apartment opens out, first into a kitchen area and then the living room.

The way Heard describes it: 'I heard the door, Johnny heard the door, because he let go of my head... His grip on my hair loosened. I recall pushing away from him... and he separated from me, as if to see who was coming into the apartment.'

Heard explains the difference between her and Pennington's testimony by saying that when Pennington *entered* the apartment she was being assaulted, but by the time Pennington had got to the end of the short hallway, turned left and finally set eyes on them, Depp and Heard were 12 feet apart. Neither Pennington, Depp nor Heard state anywhere that Pennington made her entrance into PH3 from the upper floor via the stairs.

You know what is in the short hallway just inside PH3? A closet!

So Pennington either secreted herself in the closet (for some, as yet, unexplained purpose) and then (according to Heard) got out so noisily she announced her presence in the apartment before she could see any violence. Or Pennington was in PH1 (as she said) when she received the text from Heard and made her way (after retrieving her keys from PH5) down the main external corridor into PH3 without being seen by Judge or Bett.

The absence of Bett and Judge directly outside PH3 could explain why neither of them entered the apartment when the alleged yelling (at Kevin Murphy on the phone) began, despite Depp saying he gave them explicit instructions to intervene the moment they heard anything.

The security team see things rather differently. According to Sean Bett's 2019 witness statement, he arrived with Depp and Judge at the ECB between 7.30pm and 7.45pm (it was, in fact, 7.02pm). Bett described Depp as 'sober and lucid'. Bett also says Depp had 'expressed his concern to us about how Ms Heard might behave.'

When the trio got to PH3, Bett and Judge entered with Depp in tow, but they did not see Heard. Bett described seeing signs – including lit candles – indicating Heard's presence, but insists she was not visible. According to Bett, Depp told his team he would go upstairs to see Heard. This contradicts Depp's own testimony to the US trial. In 2022 he said: 'When I first walked into the penthouse... I saw Ms Heard sitting there on the couch.'

There is no mention in Bett's witness statement of an instruction to stand guard outside PH3, but this is what Bett says he and Judge did.

Their position outside PH3, said Bett, allowed them to 'see into the penthouse.' This statement is very difficult to square with the basic layout of the block and each apartment's solid wood doors. Even if Bett and Judge had the door to PH3 open they would only be afforded a view of the hallway (containing the closet) leading into the apartment proper. Mr Bett may be good, but he cannot see around corners.

Depp says before they arrived at PH3 he explicitly told Judge and Bett: 'If you hear anything, if you hear screaming, you got to get in there... spring in there if you hear something.' Bett says apart from going 'very briefly' into PH4, he and Judge remained outside PH3 for 'approximately 10 minutes' before re-entering the penthouse on hearing 'screams'.

But the apparent yelling inside the apartment started some time before Bett and Judge arrived on the scene. Depp had enough time after Heard allegedly yelled at Murphy to go upstairs and start collecting his things before he came down to speak to Tillett-Wright.

Bett's statement that he and Judge abandoned their posts outside PH3 to spend a short time in PH4 may not have been for as brief a period as he remembers (a possibility given Bett's gauging of their time of arrival at the ECB – incorrect by at least 28 minutes).

Sadly, Jerry Judge died of cancer in early 2020, which meant he could not give evidence in court. He did make a declaration on the matter in 2016, fragments of which appear in Johnny Depp's first witness statement to the UK trial, with other fragments quoted in the subsequent judgment by Mr Justice Nicol. Judge asserted Depp was 'sober in all respects' on the evening of 21 May, and believed their arrival at the ECB was between 7pm and 7.30pm. Judge says he and Bett heard 'raised voices' and entered PH3 'about 30 minutes or less later.' This isn't as inaccurate as Bett's statement, but CCTV evidence shows Judge and Bett were in the ECB for more than an hour (six times as long as Bett's estimate) before they dived into PH3 to retrieve their boss. If Bett and Judge's recollections about where they were stationed are to be believed, they missed a lot of screaming.

So what happened to Rocky Pennington during the brief moments she saw Depp and Heard before the security team finally came into PH3? Pennington says when she saw her friend, Heard yelled: 'Help, please. He hit me with the phone. Please help. Please call for help.'

According to Pennington, Depp was yelling 'obscenities', shouting 'She's a fucking liar. Get the fuck out of here. Oh, poor her. A little phone hit you. Poor fucking you.'

Pennington says that when Johnny saw her, he told her to 'get the fuck out' of PH3. Pennington did not do so. Instead she says she 'started to walk towards Amber.' Pennington remembers stepping in front of

Depp 'to shield her from him, with my hands up, lightly touching his chest.' She asked him to stop what he was doing.

Pennington says Depp replied: 'Get your fucking hands off me' and 'knocked my hands out of the way. I said "stop" again and put my hands out again to stop him. Johnny yelled obscenities at me, directly into my face.'

During this moment, Heard says she 'collapsed' onto the sofa. Pennington remembers moving to join her, in an attempt to protect her friend, 'sort of holding the top half of her body on my lap and I covering her with my arms.' Pennington remembers Heard saying words to the effect of 'I didn't do anything. I just called iO to back me up, I didn't do anything.'

Pennington says: 'Johnny moved toward Amber and me on the couch. He stood right over us, not more than a foot away. He yelled words to the effect of "Get up. Get up, Amber. Get the fuck up. Get up right now. Get up," about ten times.'

Depp denies throwing a phone at Heard and says Pennington certainly did not 'enter the flat', as his 'guards who were guarding the only door to Penthouse 3 would have seen and stopped her.' Depp maintained 'she was hiding in the coat closet just inside the door, because suddenly Ms Pennington appeared and bolted past my right shoulder to run to Ms Heard's side.'

Depp says he 'did not touch Ms Pennington during the entire time she was there' nor did he verbally abuse her. He says when Pennington arrived he was already 'walking towards the kitchen to exit', and it was at this point Heard apparently started screaming, 'Stop hitting me, Johnny,' when he was '20 feet away.'

Depp believes the sudden arrival of Bett and Judge also seemed to signal a change in Heard's behavior. Apparently surprised to see Depp's security detail in the apartment, Depp says Heard began screaming 'That's the last time you'll ever hit me. That's the last time you'll ever do that to me.'

Heard remembers it differently: 'I yelled at Jerry to help me, saying I would call the police.'

In his statement for the UK trial Bett agreed Heard was shouting words to the effect of: 'If he hits me one more time, I am calling the police.'

Pennington says at this point Depp 'picked up a magnum size bottle of wine and began swinging it like a baseball bat. Wine was flying all over the walls, floors and furniture, and he began using the bottle to smash everything he could.' Heard says Depp was 'swigging out of' the bottle and 'smashing it around.'

Everyone present agrees Judge indicated to his boss it was probably time to leave the apartment. Pennington says Depp 'grabbed his bag and stormed out', still apparently 'sloshing wine everywhere.' As he left, Pennington says Depp 'knocked over a bunch of items that were on the kitchen island, fruit baskets and bottles and things like that. That was the main damage in PH3.'

Depp denies picking up a wine bottle or causing any damage to Heard or the apartment. Sean Bett says it's 'possible' Depp knocked some things over.

Whilst Heard and Pennington remained in PH3, Depp exited into the external hallway which connected the apartments, where he allegedly smashed a glass light fitting, spilled a significant amount of red wine on the floor and wall outside PH1 and used the bottle to strike the door to PH1, leaving a mark. Then he proceeded to PH5.

Pennington's fiancé Josh Drew and a woman called Elizabeth Marz were in PH5. Marz was Pennington's childhood friend. She had been helping her make some beads, which Pennington intended to sell at a craft fair the next day.

Josh Drew says he heard activity outside the penthouse, including a 'large noise' which he 'later discovered was the sound of a wine bottle being slammed into our door of PH1.' The door to PH5 had been unlocked so the girlfriends could move freely between PH1 and PH5 while they were working. On hearing what Marz calls a 'commotion' in the corridor, involving 'voices and distraction', Drew locked the door to PH5. Drew says he heard Depp come to the door of PH5 and 'shout at his security to "open this fucking door, let me in this fucking place".' Drew says Bett and Judge did this 'without hesitation'. Depp then apparently 'walked in and immediately started screaming.'

Marz says 'it all happened very fast.' Depp came 'bursting through the door' still holding the magnum bottle of wine. He looked 'wasted... really under the influence of something, drugs or alcohol.' Marz says he was spilling wine 'all over the place.' Bett and Judge stood behind him.

According to a note Josh Drew wrote the next day (for Heard's lawyer), Depp said something along the lines of: 'You motherfuckers fucking sold me out!' and/or 'Get the fuck out of my house!'

Marz remembers Depp saying: 'Get your bitch out of here.' She was frightened. 'I almost felt like he was coming towards me,' she said, 'it scared me and I just ran out past him... My heart was beating really fast very quickly and I was freaked out.'

Marz found somewhere to hide near the outdoor pool. Depp apparently remained in PH5 smashing a few more things (something he denies). Drew left the apartment and headed down the corridor to PH3 where he found Pennington and Heard. Drew took them into PH1 and dead-bolted the door. Heard was holding Depp's phone, which Drew said he took from her. Whilst in PH1 Pennington told Drew Depp had 'shoved' her. Drew became angry and left PH1 for PH5 in order to seek a confrontation with Depp, but he was nowhere to be seen. CCTV shows he left with Bett and Judge at 8.29pm. Marz remained in her hiding place until she was coaxed out by Pennington who texted to tell her Depp had left the building. Drew describes Heard's state as 'damn near catatonic after all this.'

Within minutes, Drew's phone was ringing. It was Jerry Judge. Depp wanted his phone back. Drew said he had it and would return it, but told Judge he and Depp 'could not set foot in the building.' A still angry Drew met Judge downstairs in the ECB lobby and gave him the handset. According to Drew's 2019 witness statement, Judge 'took a few steps to walk away and then turned and asked me, "Is she okay?" I said something like, "Are you fucking kidding me? He beat the shit out of her again and you guys stood by and watched it".'

Drew says Judge 'started to demur' and then said 'something along the lines of it's not his business, they are husband and wife, he barely touched her.' Drew was not impressed, telling Judge, by his recollection to "get the fuck out of here, be real proud of yourself; get the fuck out".'

Back upstairs, Heard contacted her publicist and a divorce lawyer called Samantha Spector. Spector advised them to take photos of the property damage and any injuries. She also told everyone present to make a 'contemporaneous, matter-of-fact' (Drew's words) note stating exactly what happened. Pennington, Drew and Heard got to work. Then the police arrived. Twice.

SITH LORDS ADJUDICATE

London, March 2021

As with any High Court ruling, Depp had the right to apply to appeal it. This he did, with pre-trial papers stating that Mr Justice Nicol's judgment was 'plainly wrong' and 'manifestly unsafe'. Depp's lawyers said Nicol's findings were 'bare assertions rather than reasoned decisions' and having 'uncritically accepted at the outset that Ms Heard must have been correct in her allegations,' he 'discounted evidence to the contrary.'

Depp wanted the original judgment set aside, and a re-trial with a different judge. First he had to persuade two senior judges his application to appeal had merit. If the judges deemed the application had no merit, the appeal would not be allowed.

The Court of Appeal set aside a single day – 18 March 2021 – for oral arguments. Unlike the High Court trial, proceedings were streamed on YouTube, accompanied by dire, on-screen warnings that the 're-use, capture, re-editing and redistribution' of any footage of the hearing 'could attract liability for breach of copyright or defamation and, in some circumstances... contempt of court.'

When the day came round I made my way up to London, walked through the RCJ's familiar gothic double doors and set out for the appeal courts. Soon I was seated on the long press bench, marvelling at the strange incongruity of the barristers' wigs, the black and yellow plastic hazard tape tacked all over the courtroom (coronavirus again) and the Court of Appeal judges' ludicrous robes (think Catholic-cardinal-meets-Sith-Lord).

Appeals can be allowed for a number of reasons. If it looks likely a trial judge has got the law wrong, a judgment can be overturned. Trying to get an appeal on the basis that a judge has not weighed the factual evidence correctly is a long shot. The trial judge has seen the evidence and witnessed the testimony – they are best placed to make a decision about what actually happened. An appeal court judge reviewing the facts without having been present at the trial is at a disadvantage. Depp's legal team were asking for a re-trial on the grounds that Nicol had erred in fact. No one I knew in London thought he had more than a sliver of a chance.

The first point made in the actual hearing was about the $7m divorce settlement which Amber Heard had said would be given away to the American Civil Liberties Union and the Children's Hospital of

Los Angeles. In her (fifth) witness statement to the UK trial, submitted in February 2020, Heard had baldly stated that the 'entire amount' of her divorce settlement 'was donated to charity.'

Depp's barrister, Andrew Caldecott, noted that Mr Justice Nicol had picked up on this in his judgment ('a donation of $7 million to charity is hardly the act one would expect of a gold-digger') whilst dismissing Depp's claim that Heard had seduced and married him as part of a lengthy hoax.

Caldecott pointed out that by February 2020, Amber Heard had not given away anything like the 'entire amount' of her divorce settlement, and she knew it. She was being dishonest in her fifth witness statement. Not only was she being dishonest, but by suggesting she had given her settlement away, she was giving herself 'a considerable boost to her credit as a person' whilst sending a 'potent subliminal message' to the wider public about her treatment at Depp's hands.

Whilst Heard's charitable donations would come to play a huge part in the Virginia proceedings, it seemed like a weak point on which to open an application for appeal in the UK. If you are going to go after a judge on his findings of fact about domestic violence and sexual abuse, why waste time talking about charitable donations? Caldecott argued that Amber Heard wasn't just an unreliable witness, she was a dishonest one, which made her allegations about abuse at the hands of Johnny Depp untrustworthy. According to Caldecott, Heard's decision to paint herself as a saintly victim, distributing Depp's money to charity rather than keeping any for herself was a 'tilting of the scales from the outset. It is a false plus to her and it is a false minus to him.'

Caldecott addressed some of the allegations of violence, and the way the judge treated them. Depp's team also submitted papers complaining that Mr Justice Nicol was responsible for 'serious failings', not least his 'lack of reasoned decision-making', a 'failure to test the evidence', and, once more 'the failure to test the credibility of witnesses.'

Seven days later I went back up to London for the decision. The judges filed in, wearing their Sith robes. Lord Justice Underhill informed the almost empty court that Depp's application to appeal Mr Justice Nicol's judgment had failed.

In their written reasons, the judges noted that Nicol had chosen not to make overall assessments as to Amber Heard's credibility, as the 'various submissions' challenging her credibility 'did not assist him.' Nicol, we were told, instead 'relied essentially on the evidence' relating to each specific incident. In coming to his conclusions, the judges found that Nicol correctly ascertained that when under the influence of drink and drugs, Depp 'was liable to moods of extreme anger and jealousy and could behave highly destructively.' The judges accepted that whilst 'it does not necessarily follow that angry and jealous behavior of this kind would involve physical violence' against Amber Heard, Nicol 'evidently regarded it as making her allegations more likely to be true.'

The judges also pointed towards contemporaneous texts and messages from Depp which acknowledged he had been 'out of control' and 'behaved very badly.' Whilst there are no specific admissions of violence in his messages, say the judges, Nicol was entitled to regard the apologies 'as making it more plausible that he did in fact commit such acts.'

On the issue of Heard's credibility, illustrated by the factually incorrect assertion in her fifth witness statement about donating $7m to charity, the judges note Nicol 'does not refer to her charitable donation at all in the context of his central findings' because he does not think it has a bearing on whether or not Johnny Depp hit Amber Heard. The judges write: 'In the case of many of the incidents there were contemporaneous evidence and admissions beyond the say-so of the two protagonists, which cast a clear light on the probabilities.' The Court of Appeal judgment concludes that the approach Nicol took meant 'there was little need or room... to give weight to any general assessment of Ms Heard's credibility, which is notoriously a more difficult and uncertain basis for deciding on disputed facts.'

The idea that Nicol might change his judgment if he felt that Heard was being dishonest about her charitable donations is dismissed as 'pure speculation, and in our view very unlikely.'

So that was that. Johnny Depp had suffered a serious setback to his reputation, and the matter in the UK was now closed. All eyes turned to America.

CALL THE COPS

I do wonder if Officers Tyler Hadden and Melissa Saenz have thought much about what they might have done differently when they answered a radio call to an alleged incident of domestic violence at the Eastern Columbia Building Penthouses, 849 South Broadway, on 21 May 2016. Hadden and Saenz were the first pair of officers to visit the ECB that night, and their actions have been scrutinized in a variety of legal environments. Their recollections as to what they saw are at odds with those reported by Josh Drew, Amber Heard and Rocky Pennington.

This was apparently not the first time the police had been called about an altercation between Heard and Depp. During her third day of evidence in the US trial in 2022, Heard told the court they had also been called in December 2011, sometime in 2012 and again in March 2013 'by the landlord.'

This significant piece of information seemed to pass everyone by. It certainly wasn't picked up and challenged by Depp's lawyers during cross-examination, and now just seems to be hanging in the ether. In the course of putting together this book, I asked Heard's representatives for more information on the police being called in 2011, 2012 and 2013. Sadly, no help on that issue was forthcoming. Guessing the police force Heard was referencing might be the LAPD, I asked if they could shed any light on the matter. They did a search for me, but nothing came up.

There is, however, plenty of police evidence – including LAPD dispatch records, officer testimony, witness testimony and bodycam recordings – available for the evening of 21 May 2016, so let's focus on that.

At 8.27pm an emergency call was made by a woman in LA. She wishes to remain anonymous, though it is likely Lauren Shapiro, iO Tillett-Wright's friend, who has asked her to make the call. Shapiro, if it is her, told the emergency operator a 'friend... Amber' is being attacked by her 'boyfriend' in PH3 of the ECB. This message is forwarded from the call handler to the LAPD at 8.30pm.

Seven minutes later, the LAPD received what they designate as a duplicate alert, this time from the NYPD. An NYPD officer relayed the following information: 'FEM/DECLINED CALLED AND ADVISED HER. FRIEND WAS INVOLVED IN A DOMESTIC DISPUTE, SUSP

JOHNNY HEARD, W/M 53 YRS OLD BRO HAIR BRO EYES 511 UNK IF WPNS, VICT AMBER'

In translation, this means: 'A female[1] who declined to give her name has advised her friend is involved in a domestic dispute. The suspect is named as "Johnny Heard", a white 53-year old male with brown hair and brown eyes. He is 5'11" tall. It is not known if weapons are involved. The victim is called "Amber".'

Officers Saenz and Hadden responded at 8.46pm. Although the initial caller said the attack was happening at PH3, Saenz and Hadden say they were not given a specific penthouse number in their dispatch information. They headed to the ECB.

In a deposition to Los Angeles Superior Court, made as part of the legal proceedings leading up to Depp and Heard's divorces, Saenz told lawyers for both parties that when she and her partner got out of the lift they 'attempted to door-knock the penthouse, and we did not receive an answer. So we tried to listen for possible signs of domestic violence. Glass breaking, fighting, shouting. We heard nothing.'

The two cops investigated an outdoor courtyard on the same floor, but again saw nothing of interest. When they went back into the hallway linking the apartments, they were met by someone Saenz describes as a 'generic white male'. It was Josh Drew. They did not take his name. After a short discussion during which it was established that the officers are responding to a domestic violence call, Drew was told by Saenz she needs to speak with the alleged victim. Drew disappeared into PH1 and re-emerged with Heard and Pennington. According to Saenz, Heard was crying, 'and from her body language it was very clear that she did not want to speak to us.'

Saenz says she had a good opportunity to look at Heard's face and was adamant 'she had no injuries', including bruises, marks or swelling. She nonetheless took Heard and Pennington into PH3 to have a chat, whilst Officer Hadden and Josh Drew remained outside.

Whilst Saenz was inside PH3 with Heard and Pennington, Drew spoke to Hadden:

'We knew that she did not intend to file a complaint,' Drew told the UK trial, 'and we were obviously very worried about her, and we wanted to be helpful and protect her. So, I asked him what we could do.'

---

[1] iO Tillett-Wright was born female and may have presented as such during this period.

Hadden allegedly told Drew: 'Her face is red, there is damage in these apartments, there is enough here if she wants to file a complaint, we can go pick him up.'

Tyler Hadden was due to be cross-examined via digi-link from LA during the UK trial, but lawyers for NGN decided they didn't need to speak to him. We finally saw Officer Hadden in the US trial during a pre-recorded deposition. In it, Hadden confirmed he spoke to Drew for five to ten minutes whilst the women were together in PH3, but he couldn't remember the content of the conversation.

Inside PH3, Saenz asked Heard what happened. Heard 'continued to cry' and told her nothing had happened. Heard refused to tell the officer her partner's name and indicated she did not wish to make a report. Again, Saenz is adamant there was not a hint of damage to Heard's face. When asked just how carefully she scrutinized Heard, Saenz says her examination was 'extremely thorough'.

Saenz told Heard she would still have to check the apartment to ensure it was safe. And this is where it gets weird.

In her evidence to the UK trial, Amber Heard told the court there was 'tons' of accumulated damage in Penthouses 1 and 5 and the connecting hallway, including 'broken glass, spilled wine... damaged doors, broken sconces.'

Pennington says 'Amber's belongings had been ransacked, framed photos had been smashed, and glass broken. In the hallway there were puddles of spilled wine on the floor and splashed on the walls, and a dent in the [door] of my apartment.'

Even Isaac Baruch, a loyal friend of Depp's who lived in PH2, saw property damage outside the apartments. On the evening of 21 May at around 9.30pm, he walked from the elevator to his penthouse with a friend. In the hallway he saw 'broken glass on the floor from a broken sconce that hung on the wall.' In front of PH1 Baruch noticed 'a large puddle of spilt wine along with splashed wine running down the wall directly in front of the door.'

During his deposition at the US trial, Josh Drew was shown the pictures that he and Rocky Pennington took in the aftermath of Depp's visit to the ECB. The photos of property damage do not show what I would characterize as a trail of devastation, but there are apparent liquid spills on the floor outside PH1, there is broken glass on the stairs at PH5, and at least one broken picture frame. On the floor of the living room of PH5, one picture shows a bottle of wine lying on its side with stains on the floor next to it.

Josh Drew says he accompanied both officers on their safety check of the penthouse floor whilst Pennington and Heard remained in PH3. He says he 'showed them broken glass, walking past the large wine stain in the hallway.'

Drew also says he showed them the wine bottle dent in the door of PH1, then he gave the officers a tour of PH5 showing them 'broken picture frames, smashed glass and Rocky's jewellery and other things strewn across the apartment.' Drew says the officers 'acknowledged that something had clearly happened.'

Drew is also sure that in the course of the 'tour' the officers 'pointed and made statements to the effect of noticing broken glass, noticing things strewn about.'

Yet both Saenz and Hadden are certain they did not see any wine stains, any damage to the door of PH1 or any smashed glass anywhere in any of the penthouses. Hadden agreed that Drew had accompanied the officers on their 'sweep' of the property, but contrary to Drew's recollection, Hadden says he did not see any broken glass or spilt wine.

Like Melissa Saenz, Tyler Hadden is also certain there was no visible damage to Amber Heard's face. Sitting in their patrol car outside the ECB, the two officers filed a two line report:

'MET W/ VICT, CHCKD LOC. VERIFIED HUSBAND LEFT LOC. VICT ADVISED VERBAL DISPUTE AND REFUSED TO GIVE ANY FRTHR INFO. ISSUE BUS CARD.'

In her US deposition, Saenz said this meant: 'We met with the victim, we checked the location, the husband wasn't there, and that the victim advised us that she just had an argument and that she wasn't gonna give us any further information. And because we didn't identify a crime, we issued her a business card letting her know that she could reach out to us later if she changed her mind and wanted to cooperate.'

The 242-D (domestic violence battery) case was closed at 9.22pm, three minutes after the officers had left the building.

Officers Saenz and Hadden's visit to the ECB resulted in a quite serious conflict of evidence. Putting aside any injuries to Amber Heard (and these were the alleged injuries which directly led to the divorce application and Domestic Violence Restraining Order), there was either a noticeable amount of property damage that evening after Johnny Depp had left, or there wasn't.

At 10.09pm, 47 minutes after Officers Saenz and Hadden had closed their domestic violence ticket, the LAPD received another message from the NYPD. This one came through on 'teletype'. The 'PR' or

'Person Reporting' was recorded on the LAPD police log as 'JO' or 'IO' Wright.

The report came through as follows: 'FEMALE STATED SHE WAS ON THE PHONE WITH HER FRIEND AND SHE BEGAN SCREAMING AT HER HUSBAND. SUBJ ^AMBER HEARD^ HUSBAND ^JOHNNY HEARD^ M/W 53 YEARS, 511, NFD NFI.'

NFD means 'No Further Description'. NFI means 'No Further Information'. The incident was again reported as taking place in the penthouses of 849 South Broadway. An LAPD crew was duly dispatched at 10.16pm, but then diverted away. A secondary crew, comprising Officers William Gatlin and Christopher Diener, eventually got to the ECB at 11.02pm. By this stage Gatlin and Diener were aware Officers Saenz and Hadden had been in attendance earlier that evening and had closed the call. Nonetheless, the two officers were obliged to make their check. Unlike Saenz and Hadden, Gatlin and Diener were wearing body cameras, which they activated for the duration of their visit.

According to Johnny Depp, or at least his legal proxy, Adam Waldman, this second visit by the LAPD was instigated by Amber Heard as part of the scam which led to her application for a Domestic Violence Restraining Order. Talking to the Daily Mail in 2020, Waldman told the British journalist, Ben Ashford:

'This was an ambush, a hoax. They set Mr Depp up by calling the cops, but the first attempt didn't do the trick. The officers came to the penthouses, thoroughly searched and interviewed, and left after seeing no damage to face or property. So Amber and her friends spilled a little wine and roughed the place up, got their stories straight under the direction of a lawyer and publicist, and then placed a second call to 911.'

You will remember Tillett-Wright said he may have called the NYPD twice, but it is not clear when he placed that second call. There is no evidence that it happened beyond his initial flurry of calls which began at 8.16pm LA time on the night of the 21st.

Images from Gatlin and Diener's bodycams were shown to the jury in the US trial. The cameras are worn at chest height on the police officers' uniform and we get a sense of what they are seeing as they walk from the penthouse floor elevator to the door of PH3. Something which may or may not be a glass object appears in shot on the floor in the hallway before the officers reach the door to PH1. The door to PH1 appears unmarked, and whilst it is possible there are some stains on the striped carpet outside PH1, they are not obviously red wine. When the door to PH3 opens, we see Josh Drew's t-shirt-covered belly and the tattoos on his right arm. There is a conversation about Saenz and Hadden's visit. Drew is reluctant to let the officers into the apartment.

'Does one of you know someone in New York or something?' asks Gatlin.

'Yeah,' says Drew. 'She probably called twice.'

'Can we just talk to your wife just to make sure...' starts Gatlin.

Drew cuts in. 'Oh she's not my wife.'

Drew volunteers to get the business card left by Saenz and Hadden. As he does so, he makes to close the apartment door. The officers quickly get their hands to it.

'We'll just come in here and just check,' says Gatlin. 'We need to make sure everyone in here is okay.'

As the officers walk into the apartment, we see two dogs running around. Drew is marching ahead.

'iO called twice,' he says, loudly.

'Oh, she did?' replies a female voice.

The officers turn left into the kitchen and approach the lounge area. The cameras are angled downwards which makes it hard to assess what state the apartment is in. The kitchen area is relatively bright, but the rest of the apartment is very poorly lit. There is no visible sign of any damage. In fact, it looks quite tidy.

'We just got another notification...' says Gatlin.

'There must have been a mistake,' replies a female voice from the middle distance.

Gatlin perseveres, saying the officers wanted to come in and 'make sure everybody is okay. Check you're all good.'

The officers come to a standstill, and in the bodycam footage we see three unidentifiable females sitting in the gloom about 15 feet away.

'Nobody else is in here?' asks Gatlin.

'No,' responds the female on the left of shot, quickly. She is doing most of the talking. It's probably Rocky Pennington.

'The other officers came by,' she says, 'and checked the apartment and the other apartment as well. It must have been, like, a double call.'

'All good,' says Gatlin. 'Who's Amber?'

The female in the middle of the three women raises her hand.

'You – okay,' Gatlin says. 'Johnny?'

'Is *definitely* not here,' replies Drew.

Pennington says he left 'probably, like... two hours ago.'

The mood is calm. The officers' presence is clearly unwelcome. Gatlin decides to retreat.

'Alright, then,' he says. 'If you guys need anything else, just call us back.'

'Thank you,' Pennington calls after the officers as they walk away. '*Thank you very much.*'

'You have a good night,' says Gatlin as he leaves.

'Thank you, officers,' says Drew, seeing them out.

The total amount of time Gatlin and Diener spend in PH3 is one minute, eleven seconds.

We know the LAPD's first visit to the ECB that night has assumed a greater significance in its recollection than its execution. In her 2022 deposition, Office Saenz was reminded that she initially thought she and her partner Tyler Hadden had spent thirty to sixty minutes in the penthouses responding to the emergency call. In fact they were on the penthouse floor for precisely fifteen minutes, from 9.04pm to 9.19pm.

Responding to a domestic violence call must be difficult. Perpetrators can claim to be victims. Victims can either be frightened or coerced into non-cooperation or simply decide they don't want to deal with the stress of pursuing a complaint. Victim non-cooperation makes a police officer's job significantly harder, yet non-cooperation is a hallmark of domestic violence calls.

In recognition of these complex sensitivities there is a procedure police officers should follow. According to the LAPD's Domestic Violence Standards of Review, as read to Melissa Saenz by lawyers for Amber Heard during her deposition, LAPD police officers attending a DV call must (among many other investigative duties):

– *Identify the person who first saw the complainant after the incident.*
– *Identify the person with whom the complainant first spoke about the incident.*
– *Ensure photographs are taken of injuries or lack of injury to complainant.*
– *Ensure photographs are taken of scene.*
– *Canvass location and interview all witnesses.*

None of the above happened. Saenz did not even record Drew or Pennington's names, let alone interview them.

LAPD officers are told they have a statutory duty to inform DV victims of their rights when attending a call. In LA this means handing out a VINE (Victim Information Notification Everyday) pamphlet, giving them what Officer Saenz describes as 'domestic violence resources, like shelters and phone numbers that provide help.'

This was not given to Amber Heard, because, as Saenz told the US court: 'I did not identify her as a victim of domestic violence.'

In his 2020 judgment, Mr Justice Nicol took a close look at the actions of the officers and weighed them against the other available evidence. He concluded:

'While it is not for me to criticize the methods of another police force, the absence of contemporaneous notes means that their evidence does not carry the same weight as it would otherwise... they did not note the names of the man and woman they first encountered in the penthouses... They significantly over-estimated the length of time that they were in the apartments.'

Nicol appears to insinuate that the officers thought they were dealing with a closed matter. He writes: 'In the absence of a complaint the officers would have known that no further criminal action could be taken.'

That is a subtle but crucial difference to the officers' assertion that no crime had taken place.

On the issue of property damage, Nicol says: 'I accept that the officers said there was no damage to the property, no broken glass and no spilled wine, but that evidence has to be contrasted with the spilled wine which Mr Baruch did see and the photographs of wine stains which were taken just before their arrival.'

Again Nicol appears to insinuate the officers took no notice of any damage because of 'their knowledge that no further action was likely to be taken in the absence of a complaint by Ms Heard.'

By not criticizing 'the methods' of a foreign police force, Nicol left a deliberate ambiguity hanging over his judgment. Nobody saw Johnny Depp throw a phone at Amber Heard, but plenty of people say they saw property damage in Penthouses 3 and 5 and the external hallway connecting them. Yet a pair of police officers with no apparent reason to give false information to a court remain insistent; not just that they *saw* no damage whatsoever but that there *was* no damage whatsoever. As Saenz said, they 'searched the entire flat and there was no damage and there was no broken glass. There was nothing to report and nothing out of the ordinary.'

Is that the truth?

Let's turn it round. Only a very brave or foolish police officer is going to tell a court that in retrospect their work was cursory, sloppy and unprofessional. Or that it was entirely possible a crime had taken place and they chose to do nothing about it. Such an admission would not only be career death, it would bring the LAPD into disrepute and generate headlines that would reverberate beyond the Depp/Heard case for many years to come.

In the moment, on the ground, Saenz and Hadden were not thinking about anything like this. From a practical, frontline, law-enforcement context, the alleged victim did not want to file a report. Any injuries were not obvious or pronounced. Depp's name was not mentioned. The police officers did not know the situation involved a public figure. Amber Heard was just another uncooperative Jane Doe, and by the time the police had arrived, any immediate threat had dissipated. With unlimited resources and unlimited time, Saenz could have spent the rest of the evening working to the letter of the Domestic Violence Standards of Review – taking names, interviewing witnesses, gathering evidence and seeking the alleged perpetrator's whereabouts. Even if Heard did not wish to take things further, a case could be made for a prosecution without cooperation, or the evidence could be filed and used against the alleged perpetrator if something similar happened again. But the LAPD doesn't have unlimited time or resources, and in the context of the other calls they might have to deal with in a big, bad city that evening, it didn't present itself as an urgent priority. Saenz and Hadden made a practical, pragmatic call to designate the matter as a non-crime, and move on to the next job.

The contested sequence of events that evening soon spun themselves into fully-formed alternate universes, terraformed by subpoenas, depositions and witness statements. To stop their version of events imploding under contradiction, Saenz and Hadden had to stick to the primary narrative, telling lawyer after lawyer and court after court that they only saw what they reported, and only reported what they saw, and because they didn't report anything, nothing happened. Had they attempted to volunteer anything which cast doubt on the veracity of their initial report, the chain reaction might cause correlating narratives (particularly around faith in the reliability of police evidence) to unwind. Sticking to your own reality (or unreality) can sometimes feel more important than acknowledging evidence to the contrary.

Maybe Saenz and Hadden were mistaken about what they did or didn't see. Josh Drew, Rocky Pennington, Elizabeth Marz and Isaac Baruch might also be mistaken, or wrong, about what they claim they saw. Truth is elusive and not always absolute, which is what makes this story so compelling.

THE FORMER HIM

Los Angeles, May 2016

The phone-throwing, closet-hiding, cop-visiting drama marked the last act of alleged violence between Amber Heard and Johnny Depp, and the last knockings of their disastrous relationship.

That night Heard texted her parents, attaching a photo of her cheek with the message: 'I think I'm done "being there" for Johnny, wouldn't you agree "mom and dad"?'

She later sent another, longer text to her parents, containing an ultimatum:

'If you text him or involve yourself anymore in his life I will never speak to you guys again. Dad either you understand that and respect that or you don't. But if you go against my wishes I will never speak to you again.'

Heard also texted her makeup artist and confidant, Melanie Inglessis:

'Johnny came over "to talk",' she wrote, 'His mom just died. Then he went sideways. Convinced of some CRAZY shit. Beat on me. Cops were called. They just left. Filing a restraining order. Divorce goes through on Monday. My face looks stupid and swollen. Bad night.'

At 11.52pm Heard texted her nurse, Erin Boerum, reporting that Depp was 'completely delusional and crazed. Hit me in the face several times, while on the phone to iO. She [Tillett-Wright] called the cops. Restraining order will be filed in the am. Cops just left. (Long after he did of course) Rocky and josh were here too. It was horrible.'

Overnight, Depp texted Heard, accusing her of being 'already ready to strike!!!'

He asked: 'Why did I even come there in the 1st place?? To be yelled at by you!!! I'm an idiot. PH5 is Rocky's studio?? You are shameless... I tried to make it work and you just turned more and more into a spoiled brat. All you wanted was to make me fucking miserable. Well I'm finally there. I'll never be able to understand how I fell in love with you... You're not her. I loved you more than anything... I did everything I could. But you never fucking loved me... I hope our divorce goes as quickly as possible and that it is as painless as possible. So sorry you were as unhappy with me as you were... obviously the purity of whatever was, has been gone for a long time. I will miss the moments of beauty and truth... Goodbye Amber... What the fuck was I thinking??? I wish you all you merit... The former Him.'

In the early hours of the morning, Heard texted Savannah McMillan to say: 'Shit is bad but I'm OK. Please don't text Rocky or anyone. It's OK. I'll explain later.'

At just before 8am on the morning of the 22nd, Heard texted Josh Drew asking him to put in writing what he saw happen.

'Hey Josh,' she wrote. 'I hope you and Rocky got some sleep last night... The lawyers asking for brief statements from you guys, as witnesses so that she can file the appropriate way for a restraining order... Doesn't have to be fancy or even well-written, nothing like that just a brief play-by-play of what you saw.'

Josh replied that it would be 'no problem' to put together a statement and that he would 'help' Rocky with hers. He also told Heard he was waiting for a locksmith to come and change the locks.

After the drama of the night before, iO Tillett-Wright, out in New York, was keen to know what had happened as a result of the emergency calls he made. He texted Heard.

'Are you OK?' he asked. 'Did he get arrested? Are you taking out a restraining order?'

Heard replied: 'Yes restraining order. They didn't arrest him because I didn't make a statement.'

Tillett-Wright was pleased to hear about the restraining order. 'Good!!' he responded. 'That's gonna be the only thing that will get him arrested next time.' Tillett-Wright also wanted to know why Heard hadn't allowed the police to make a report.

'Because,' she replied, 'it would have gone straight to tmz... which will happen on Monday anyway.'

Heard asked Tillett-Wright to send her a statement to use either in her restraining order application or divorce papers. He complied.

On the afternoon of Sunday 22 May, Heard attended Amanda de Cadenet's birthday party. At the party someone took a picture of de Cadenet, Heard and the supermodel-turned-actor Amber Valletta. Heard has a lock of hair covering her right cheek. The three women look happy.

Whilst Heard was at de Cadenet's party, the comedian Doug Stanhope visited Depp. In a 'guest column' published exactly a week later in The Wrap[1], a media industry magazine, Stanhope wrote that

---

[1] On publication, Heard sued Stanhope for defamation. The claim was dropped as part of Depp and Heard's divorce settlement agreement. The column is still available to read on The Wrap's website.

when he visited, he assumed Depp was in a 'dour mood' because of his mother's death. But then Depp 'opened up in the most vulnerable of ways' to tell Stanhope he wasn't just down about his mother 'but that Amber was now going to leave him, threatening to lie about him publicly in any and every possible duplicitous way if he didn't agree to her terms.'

Stanhope told The Wrap's readers he decided to stage an impromptu intervention. The comedian and his partner Bingo 'together, and then separately', told Depp 'how much we were aware of this manipulative a-hole [Heard, obvs], how his closest circle had all agreed on this since the day we met and that we all feared that telling him outright might alienate us all.'

'Other people came in and out during the afternoon,' wrote Stanhope, 'all verifying that we'd been cowardly, saying things only behind his back for so long.'

According to Stanhope, Depp 'seemed dumbstruck that nobody had ever come clean about this and he thanked everyone for being honest.'

Tellingly, added Stanhope, Depp 'still pronounced his love for Amber but was presciently aware that she was going to pull off some kind of ruse to f— him over. He hadn't slept in days with anxiety. You'd call him a paranoid if you didn't know better. But he knew better and he was right.'

Stanhope says he made sure his friend was okay and then left him to get some sleep.

After de Cadenet's party there was a text exchange between Depp and Heard, in which Heard appeared to be trying to set up a face-to-face conversation. During the exchange, Depp wrote: 'Nothing I have to say to you should elicit anything but, a sense of ease... All my love and profound apologies... J.'

Both told each other they were 'sad and scared'. At 6.55pm Depp texted 'I want you happy, i have ZERO harsh feelings... i am clear and i am me. the me that you once loved... we can cure one another of this constant misery born out of love.'

That evening Depp tried to call Heard. At 2.28am on 23 May, Heard sent four unanswered texts:

'I hope you got my message... I called you back.'

'I'm not quite sure what your last text meant, if I'm being honest.'

'I don't know what to say or do or think.'

'All I know, I've never felt so much love, pain or grief in my life...'

The pair talk, but it's late. Twelve hours after the texts, Heard sent three more. The first is at 2.34pm on the afternoon of Monday 23 May. She wrote:

'You fell asleep earlier while we were talking... I checked with security to check on you to see if you were okay.. Hope you get some rest. Can we please talk later?'

The text went unanswered. Fourteen minutes later, Heard tried again:

'Please call me when you can speak, okay? With all the love in my heart. Me.'

The text was again unanswered.

By 4.40pm, Heard had filed for divorce.

THE BRUISE

Los Angeles, May 2016

Of all the assaults that Amber Heard says she sustained, the alleged injury to her cheek on the evening of 21 May is, legally, the most important. It triggered the divorce filing and was the basis of Heard's application for a domestic violence restraining order.

But was Heard's cheek injured? Did Depp throw a phone at her face? Although iO Tillett-Wright was listening on the phone, and Rocky Pennington was quickly on the scene, no one saw Johnny Depp lay hands on Amber Heard that evening.

Remember, in the moment Heard claimed Depp had hit her in the face with the phone, he denied it. This would either be because it was true – Heard had lied to bolster her false claims of abuse and was once more crying wolf. Or Depp *had* hit her, and his first reaction was to add insult to injury by claiming it hadn't happened. Or, Depp was so off his face he didn't realize he'd hit Heard when he threw the phone, and his denials were genuine, if mistaken.

At the time, Heard's yelling that Depp had hit her with his phone seemed to provoke him further. Pennington says she felt compelled to intervene to protect her friend. iO Tillett-Wright was so concerned for Heard's safety he called the police.

Then there are the photographs. On the instructions of Samantha Spector, a divorce lawyer Heard spoke to that evening, multiple photographs were taken of Amber Heard's face. Team Depp has never put together a coherent (let alone conclusive) case that these photos have been deliberately manipulated by Team Heard to amplify the extent of any injuries they purport to show. But they don't show much. Mr Justice Nicol studied all the photographs of this injury which were submitted in evidence. He refers to one taken at 8.23pm on 21 May, several more taken around an hour later, another set taken at 11.30pm and others which were taken twelve hours after that. The judge noted the photographs were taken in different lighting conditions and said that was 'a good reason' as to why they looked so different. Nicol concluded 'they clearly show (at least) some reddening to [Heard's] cheek, as Mr Depp in the course of his cross-examination admitted.'

It's not clear where this gets us. Officer Saenz also agreed that Heard had a red cheek when she inspected her, but said it was 'flushed' and 'red from the crying.'

The mark certainly seemed to disappear for a few days. Multiple witnesses said they saw Amber Heard between 21 and 27 May without makeup and sporting no bruise. The most striking testimony came from Johnny Depp's long-time friend Isaac Baruch, who describes Heard specifically pointing out her bruised face to Baruch outside his penthouse on 22 May.

Baruch has the most outrageous Noo Yoik accent, so if it helps to imagine him speaking with one, fill your boots.

'I inspect the face,' Baruch told the US jury. 'I'm looking at her forehead. I'm looking at the side of her eye. I'm looking at a cheek. I'm looking at her chin. I'm looking at the other side of the face. I'm looking at the whole thing and I don't see anything... I don't see a cut, a bruise, swelling, redness. It's just Amber's face.'

Baruch described the pictures of Heard's swollen, bruised or just red cheek as 'phoney baloney' and surmised it was all preparation for Heard's 'fraudulent domestic violence claim' which she would use to 'extort and blackmail' Depp during their divorce.

DIVORCE PETITION AND DVRO

Los Angeles, May 2016

Amber Heard's typed petition for divorce was filed at Los Angeles County Superior Court, central district, at 4.40pm on Monday 23 May 2016. Her attorney is listed as Samantha Spector from Spector Law. Heard is the petitioner – named on the application as Amber Laura Depp. John Christopher Depp II (AKA Johnny Depp) is the respondent. Heard wants a 'dissolution of marriage'. The reason given is 'irreconcilable differences'. There is no hint of the simmering volatility between the two parties.

As part of the divorce petition, Depp was issued with a summons. He was given thirty days to file a response to Heard's application. The form reminds the recipient that failure to file their response might lead to the court making 'orders affecting your marriage or domestic partnership, your property, and custody of your children.'

Until this point, Johnny Depp and Amber Heard had managed to keep their relationship dysfunction out of the public gaze. Things were now about to go nuclear, though it took two days before anyone noticed the filing had been made. TMZ got it first – they published the document at 3.27pm on Wednesday 25 May, noting it had been filed three days after Depp's mother had died. TMZ's article was updated at 4.40pm the same day to report that Depp had filed a response via his attorney Laura Wasser, asking the judge to reject Heard's claim for 'spousal support'.

On the morning of Friday 27 May, accompanied by her publicist Jodi Gottlieb, Rocky Pennington and Samantha Spector, Heard attended Los Angeles Municipal Courthouse on Grand Avenue to apply to the Superior Court for a Domestic Violence Restraining Order against Johnny Depp (and possession of her dog, Pistol). Whilst at court, Pennington took photos of Heard, who had a very visible mark on her right cheek. In more than one photo, taken by Pennington inside the building, Gottlieb can be seen in the background speaking on her phone.

Asked what she did whilst in the courthouse, Heard said: 'I provided testimony and sat there and cried.'

Whilst Heard and her entourage were inside, camera crews and reporters were assembling outside the front door of the court building.

Heard's Domestic Violence Restraining Order request form alleged Depp had been 'verbally and physically abusive' towards Heard for 'the entirety' of their relationship. Heard put down a short description of what she said happened on 21 April and 21 May and referred to the headbutt incident in December 2015, stating on that occasion she 'truly feared' her 'life was in danger.'

Heard wanted Depp to stay a minimum of 100 yards away from her home, vehicle, job and workplace. She also wanted him to move out of the ECB, their 'marital residence'. The judge granted Heard's request and issued the court order that day.

After filing her request, Heard left the courthouse and walked straight into a media scrum. The journalists and crews present all seemed to be expecting her, and all wanted to know what she was up to. From video footage available online we see Heard respond passively. She does not change her facial expression as she is led by her team from the courthouse to a waiting SUV. At one point Heard stops briefly and moves her head around. As she approaches the kerbside we see and hear Samantha Spector striding ahead, demanding room. A minder pushes reporters and paparazzi back from behind Heard's right shoulder. 'Get her through!' commands Spector. Jodi Gottlieb is a pace or two back. Pennington brings up the rear, accompanied by two Deputy Sheriffs. Heard doesn't speak as an off-camera reporter asks: 'Did Johnny give you that bruise on your face? Did Johnny beat you up?'

Just before she gets into the SUV Heard tosses her head again, allowing the mark on her cheek to be seen. 'Did Johnny brutalise you, Amber?' badgers the reporter. 'Are you okay Amber? You look upset... Are you going to the hospital, Amber?'

A paparazzi photo taken through the glass from outside the SUV once Heard is safely inside shows her breaking composure. She is in obvious distress.

In court in Virginia, Heard described the experience:

'At that point in my life,' she said, 'I had never seen so many photographers and they just surrounded me as I walked out of that courthouse and screamed at me, screamed horrible things at me.'

This is not true. There are plenty of photos of Johnny Depp and Amber Heard at red carpet events, where there are far more photographers than there were outside court on 27 May 2016. No one was screaming. The only consistently audible voice is that of the reporter asking Heard if she had been beaten up and if she was okay. Of course, walking out of court after filing a DVRO request would have been a far more stressful environment than a celebrity premiere, and Heard's reaction in the car suggests she found it extremely upsetting, but her recollection does not match the reality.

During her testimony in Virginia, Heard also put on oath her mystification as to how so many people were outside court, ready to film her. She told jurors she was 'shocked', saying she 'didn't expect all these photographers and cameras to show up at the courthouse in real-time.'

If it is a genuinely held view, it is astonishingly naïve. According to a February 2016 profile in the New Yorker, TMZ has three reporters stationed full-time at the courthouse. One former TMZ staffer told the New Yorker he spent 'most of his days at the Los Angeles County Municipal Courthouse, searching for new filings and trying to charm clerks into giving him information.' The arrival of a Hollywood actor, her lawyer and publicist is unlikely to go under the radar. Even if all those reporters were asleep, a court employee with a side-hustle in tip-offs could get a message from inside the building to a newsroom within seconds.

The courthouse staff tip-off theory does not seem to have been addressed by either Depp or Heard's legal teams. Certainly, any single tip-off to a single newsroom would not turn the event into a circus, as the newsroom in question would be seeking to preserve their exclusive. In the videos, we can see reporters, photographers and at least four camera crews (representing X17, Fox News, ABC News and TMZ) circling Heard's party. Somehow *everyone* knew she was in the building.

During the US trial, Heard said she had brought her publicist along as 'I was told the filing was public. That... there's no way for you to do a private filing. And that the second that I filed for the TRO[1], it would be public news.'

Under cross-examination, Heard seemed to insinuate she thought Depp's side might be responsible for leaking the DVRO application process.

'When I walked into the courtroom that day,' she said, 'it was completely quiet, still, empty. Even though I had given Johnny's team notice that I was filing the TRO.'

'You told this jury that you had no idea the press was going to be at the courthouse,' said Depp's attorney.

'I said I did not have anything to do with it,' replied Heard.

There is a grey area here. Celebrities have associates either acting on instruction or unilaterally in what they believe to be their client's best

---

[1] TRO stands for Temporary Restraining Order. The specific order requested was a DVRO – a Domestic Violence Restraining Order – but Heard's team used the terms interchangeably (alongside DVTRO) throughout the trial. Depp's team tended to stick to TRO.

interests. Johnny Depp, as one of the biggest celebrities in the world, has an army of people physically guarding him, getting him from A to B, running his various business ventures, supplying him with drugs, keeping him away from drugs, fighting his legal battles and protecting his reputation. Amber Heard also has a team, and in May 2016 that included a top Hollywood divorce lawyer and a top Hollywood publicist.

During the first week of the US trial, SiriusXM anchor Megyn Kelly hosted a TV discussion on Depp v Heard. After describing both protagonists as 'deeply narcissistic, deranged people', Kelly turned to the day Heard got her DVRO. Kelly had no doubt Heard 'intentionally' walked out of the front of the LA courthouse.

'Even at my level of being a public figure,' Megyn told her guests, 'you don't have to walk in and out of the front door of the courthouse. When you're Amber Heard you *really* don't have to use the front door... she clearly wanted to be photographed.'

Towards the end of the US trial, a surprise witness came forward. His name was Morgan Tremaine. In his Twitter bio, Tremaine describes himself as a 'reformed TMZ staffer'. In 2016 he was TMZ's field assignments manager, based in LA. His job was to dispatch camera crews to specific locations on instruction from the newsroom.

At the time, Tremaine was bossing around twenty crews in LA. They would be dispatched according to tip-offs, or sent to areas where celebrities hang out – which Tremaine described as 'hotspots'.

Tip-offs would come from established news producers – journalists on the ground or in the office dealing with contacts – or via the TMZ tip line. Sources could be 'lawyers... publicists, managers, agents, or B-list celebrities'. If the information came via the tip line, a more extensive verification process would come into play. Before dispatching a crew, TMZ had to be sure who was offering the tip and how likely it was to be true.

On 27 May 2016, Morgan Tremaine was instructed by the newsroom to dispatch a crew to Los Angeles Municipal Court, where he was told Amber Heard was in the process of obtaining a restraining order. This was no speculative punt.

'It's not by any means a celebrity hotspot,' said Tremaine. 'We would only ever send people there if we had been tipped off that something was occurring and there was somebody present there.'

Tremaine also passed on instructions he received, which was 'to capture Amber leaving the courthouse and an alleged bruise on the right side of her face.'

Tremaine says he was told that, on leaving the courthouse, Heard would 'sort of stop and turn towards the camera to display the bruise.'

The tip had come from a TMZ news producer, which meant it was deemed credible. Before Tremaine gave evidence in Virginia, his former employer tried to stop him. A lawyer from TMZ argued before Judge Azcarate that the information Tremaine was due to share was somehow privileged, and that Team Depp had no business seeking to air it in court. TMZ failed in its application to gag Tremaine, but there was a clear understanding hanging over the proceedings that if TMZ wanted to sue their former employee for breach of confidentiality in a separate action, that was their business.

At the beginning of Tremaine's cross-examination, Amber Heard's attorney, Elaine Bredehoft, could not resist a little dig. Tremaine had not been listed as a witness and had only come to Team Depp's attention in the penultimate week of the trial. He was therefore something of an unknown quantity.

'You know this case is being televised, right?' asked Bredehoft.

'I'm aware that there are cameras,' replied Tremaine.

'And so this gets you your 15 minutes of fame,' noted the attorney.

'I stand to gain nothing from this,' countered Tremaine. 'I'm actually putting myself in the target of TMZ, a very litigious organization, and I'm not seeking any 15 minutes here. Though you're welcome to speculate. I could say the same thing by taking Amber Heard as a client for you.'

It might not be the sickest of burns, but it demolished Bredehoft's attempt to impugn Tremaine's credibility. It also highlighted to the jury the personal risk the former staffer might be taking by giving evidence. Having accomplished the exact opposite of what she set out to achieve with her opening question, Bredehoft spent what little cross-examination time she had left by reminding Tremaine that one of Depp's divorce lawyers, Blair Berk, 'had a very close relationship with TMZ.' Tremaine said he knew nothing about this.

Despite the obvious inferences that could be drawn from Tremaine's evidence, he confirmed to Bredehoft that he didn't know who had provided the tip-offs about Amber Heard's movements outside Los Angeles Municipal Court.

One of the most tenacious reporters on the ground at the US trial was Angenette Levy from the Law and Crime TV network. Several weeks after the verdict, she secured an exclusive interview with Tremaine. He told Levy he got into the trial by watching videos online.

'I remember seeing a TikTok in which someone felt like they had some kind of idea or evidence... and they had recorded themselves sending an email to Camille [Vasquez]. I hadn't even thought of that as a possibility and so then I started think – maybe I should just send her an email and just see if I can help in some way, because somebody's definitely lying.'

Vasquez called him back within two hours.

During his testimony Tremaine also had something to say about the infamous cupboard-smashing video[2], which was first published by TMZ on 8 August 2016.

Although Tremaine had no knowledge of where the footage came from, he told the court it was received and published within 'about 15 minutes'. Tremaine told the court that for this to have happened so quickly, TMZ had to be satisfied it had reached direct agreement over publication with the copyright holder (or the copyright holder's representatives). As the video was shot by Amber Heard, she was the copyright holder when the footage was created – believed (but never confirmed) to be in February that year.

During her cross-examination, Heard had been directly challenged on whether she had sold the footage to TMZ. She told Depp's attorney:

'I absolutely had nothing to do with that. I wouldn't even know how to do something like that.'

Whether the very public DVRO application (May 2016), the People magazine cover (June 2016) and TMZ's publication of the cupboard-smashing video (August 2016) hastened or delayed the conclusion to Depp and Heard's divorce proceedings is unclear. It certainly kept them in the news. The final settlement was signed on 15 August 2016. In a joint statement released to the media, the couple told the world:

'Our relationship was intensely passionate and at times volatile, but always bound by love. Neither party has made false accusations for financial gain. There was never any intent of physical or emotional harm.'

The truce lasted less than a week.

---

[2] Described in the *What's That Coming Over The Hill?* chapter.

WERE HEARD'S PHOTOS DOCTORED?

In the middle of Depp v NGN, in 2020, a new kite took flight. Team Depp decided some of the photos of Amber Heard's alleged injuries might have been doctored. They wrote to NGN's legal team saying:

'We do not accept that the May 2016 images have not been edited or otherwise manipulated.'

The photos had been studied by both parties for several months. In the run up to the trial, a spreadsheet listing the metadata for each photo had been prepared, which somehow managed to reset the timings on some of the photos to 00:00. It seemed that when the issue was discussed in open court, the correct metadata had been found and agreed, but now Depp's team were claiming the *titles* of the pictures had been altered and the visual representations of the images themselves had possibly been 'saturated or photoshopped'.

Depp went into the UK proceedings convinced he was the victim of a long con. He wasn't the only one. During the trial, Depp's house manager Kevin Murphy told the High Court he was convinced that photos taken by Heard in the aftermath of the headbutt fight on 15 December 2015 were a 'set-up' and a 'fraud'. Now, somewhat out of the blue, Depp's legal team were saying they believed Heard had doctored the photographic evidence of her alleged injuries.

On day nine of the trial, one of NGN's barristers, Adam Wolanski, told the judge:

'That is the first we have ever heard of it. It was not in the opening statement, it has never been pleaded and it is not in any witness statement or correspondence.'

Wolanski told the court that images of Heard's alleged injuries 'are at the very heart of this case', adding it was 'obvious' what Depp was up to[1]. Wolanski proposed both sides instruct expert witnesses to examine the photos and come to some kind of conclusion about the extent to which, if any, they had been manipulated.

The trial clock was ticking. If expert witnesses were going to test this new theory, the judge was going to have to set tight deadlines. Oddly, although it was Depp's team who were claiming there were problems with Heard's photographs, Depp's barrister, David Sherborne, didn't seem keen to call on expert evidence.

---

[1] Though he didn't make clear exactly *what* was obvious.

In a submission made eight days before the trial ended Sherborne told the judge that his side no longer believed the images taken of Heard's alleged injuries were 'photoshopped'. They were instead claiming that:

'Ms Heard altered her appearance in a number of possible ways before taking photographs in an attempt to show some sort of marks.'

Sherborne said this could be through 'the selection of filters or subsequent editing' which 'may have been an attempt' to make her 'face redder'.

The barrister concluded that 'an analysis of all the digital images will not yield much more, if anything, than what the court can see from the images and decide from them and the surrounding evidence of eyewitnesses.'

Claiming in court that evidence has been doctored, then resisting a suggestion it might be professionally examined, is an unusual approach. In the end the judge took up Sherborne's invitation to draw his own conclusions about the photos without the need for experts. Outside court, the speculation was beginning to have an effect.

By the time I found myself speaking to Depp fans on the ground in Virginia in 2022, it had become an article of faith that photos of Heard's injuries had been faked in some unspecified way.

It's understandable as to why Depp supporters would take that view. Entertaining anything else would mean recognizing an unsavory possibility. The judge in the UK was invited to take the photos of Heard's alleged injuries as they were presented to the court. He did, and he used them to aid his decision that calling Johnny Depp a wife-beater was justified.

By the time Depp v Heard began, millions of Depp fans had spent thousands of hours poring over all the photographs they could get their hands on. YouTubers egged them on. 'Johnny Depp Can PROVE Amber Heard Photos Are FAKE But She's BLOCKING HIM!?' yelled Popcorned Planet. SEC went for: 'THE PICTURES DON'T ADD UP – Amber Heard – The Metadata doesn't lie.'

Juries only have to make a few, very simple, collective decisions about an overall case. They do not have to give reasons, or explain themselves to anyone but each other. If a legal team has created enough doubt in the minds of jurors as to what value a body of evidence has, they are entitled to dismiss the evidence, and focus on other matters.

On the first day of the US trial, Benjamin Chew, Johnny Depp's most senior lawyer, set out his case.

'Here's what you should keep in mind when you see these photographs,' he told the jury. 'First, the evidence and expert testimony from [a] forensic pathologist, a doctor, will show that the injuries reflected in these photographs are not consistent with the brutal allegations of abuse Ms Heard has alleged. Second, there are multiple, multiple witnesses, including medical professionals and police officers, who will testify that they did not observe the injuries supposedly reflected in these photographs. And you may be wondering, "How can that be?" Well, you will hear expert testimony that none of these photographs are the originals, not one, and many are stored in an editing program. So they could have been manipulated and cannot be confirmed as authentic.'

Let's take each of those points in turn. The first is inconsistency. Amber Heard's graphic descriptions of abuse, especially as delivered in the US court, were powerful. In *The Bottle Rape* chapter, I quoted Liz James, the Depp supporter who found Heard 'somewhat convincing', yet Liz had the same problem Ben Chew raised with the jury. 'Most of us in the gallery are women', she told me, 'and most of the friends that I've made here are women. And we would look at each other when photos came up on the evidence boards and those screens, going: "Something doesn't look right with these." There's moments where you see these photos of her face, and she says you can see certain things which you're not really seeing.'

In the US I heard multiple assertions that the severity of the beatings Heard described were simply not matched by the photographic evidence. One Depp supporter, Jennifer, showed me the photos of the injuries she said she'd suffered at the hands of her former partner. They were sickening, and markedly worse than anything we saw in court. Other Depp supporters raised the infamous pictures taken of Rihanna after she was beaten up by Chris Brown in 2009. Depp fans wanted to know why, despite describing years of vicious abuse, Heard had not managed to take a single photo which compared to the vivid injuries successfully documented by Rihanna after one assault.

With his second point, Chew was essentially asking the jury to consider whether or not they were looking at faked photographs. There were 'multiple witnesses' lining up to testify 'they did not observe the injuries supposedly reflected in these photographs.'

What Chew says is true, but there are also multiple witnesses, including medical professionals, who did record injuries to Amber Heard. In her testimony in the US trial, Dr Laurel Anderson reported seeing marks around Heard's eyes consistent with those in photos taken on 16

December 2015. Nurse Erin Boerum also saw an injury to Amber Heard in December 2015, which you may remember she recorded in her notes as 'visible bright red blood appearing at center of lower lip.' Melanie Inglessis reported using makeup to artfully conceal injuries around Heard's eyes and a split lip. This testimony tallies with the photographs taken on 16 December of Amber Heard with bruised eyes and a split lip.

Chew finished by saying 'none of these photographs are the originals, not one, and many are stored in an editing program. So they could have been manipulated and cannot be confirmed as authentic.'

Well, up to a point. Unlike the UK, in the US trial digital experts *were* permitted to examine photos. Some photos. On 25 May, on the same day Kate Moss gave evidence and just a week before the verdict, an expert called Norbert Bryan Neumeister testified for Johnny Depp. Mr Neumeister is a helicopter cameraman turned digital forensics specialist. His catchphrase is 'data is data' and his point was data 'doesn't take a side'. Neumeister had been asked to analyze 'groups of photos that were submitted by Ms Heard's legal team.' His purpose was 'to authenticate photos, or to review and see if they were altered in any way.'

The first photograph shown to the jury during Neumeister's evidence was a photograph Amber Heard took of herself in a mirror. In the photograph Heard is wearing a white skirt and top spotted with randomly spaced black dots. She is standing in a room with large black and white tiles on the floor and an oval gold-rimmed mirror behind her. The iPhone she is using to take the photo is in the shot and we can see Heard looking at the iPhone screen as the shot is taken. On her upper arm is a large bruise about the size of a squash ball.

Neumeister then showed the jury that three different versions of these photos had been submitted as evidence by Heard's legal team. He compared them, side-by-side. Each had different file sizes.

Neumeister acknowledged, 'You could say, well, it was sent through email, maybe it's a different size... but there's no way to authenticate any photo that was presented in the way the evidence was collected.'

Asked by one of Depp's attorneys what conclusions he can draw from this, Neumeister said:

'All three of these photos had to go through some type of transformation to change sizes.'

The next photo shown by Neumeister was a picture of Amber Heard taken at 9.24pm on 21 May 2016. Her face is turned square to the camera, and she is looking down. Her right cheek looks as if it has a welt, or swelling, and it is pinker than her left cheek. This was one of the photos taken the night she alleged Johnny had thrown a phone at her, hitting her in the face.

Neumeister said the photo 'had to be rendered, which means composited together in an editing program.'

The data showed the picture was 'a directly photographed image', but Neumeister said: 'That is not gonna be necessarily accurate once it's been through an editor.'

We were taken through several more photos including one of Amber Heard taken on 16 December 2015 which was also shown in evidence in the London trial. Heard is wearing a white top and a black and white checked jacket. This picture had 'Photos 3.0' as the software source. Neumeister said this meant, 'you know it's not anywhere near an original. There's gonna be compression artefacts, because it's a JPEG file.'

Finally, Neumeister compared two versions of the same image of Amber Heard's bruised cheek. In one photo, the data has the software source as 'iOS 9.3.1' and in the other it is 'Photos 3.0'. In one photo Heard's face appears pinker. Neumeister said it was 'the same photo treated two different ways.'

Neumeister was invited to make an observation about the authenticity of the photos he selected for study. He said he could not come to any conclusion about their authenticity, because they have been extracted from an iTunes backup, but he was sticking to 'the fact that photographs were modified.' He finished by telling the court: 'There's no way for any forensic expert to validate any of these photos.'

Under cross-examination, Neumeister agreed he had no evidence that Amber Heard had modified the photos, nor was he able to provide any evidence anybody had 'intentionally modified' any photos. He also conceded that Apple's Photos 3 app was as much a sorting app as an editor. He was taken to a section of his deposition, where he said of one photo:

'Yes, it has changed. Was it intentionally changed? We don't know. In other words, did somebody save it in there and just save the photo? We don't know.'

Neumeister also pointed out that it was very easy to manually change the data of any photo, and there was no way to know if this had or hadn't been done with the images he had been given to examine.

The following day Team Heard put up their own forensic expert, Julian Ackert. Ackert reported to the court that he had looked at all the photos which Bryan Neumeister had examined, and by looking at Amber Heard's devices (or digital images of those devices) he had sourced the original photos in all but one instance. Ackert said it was 'not surprising' that he 'found all these on all the devices because that's how the Apple ecosystem works. It replicates your pictures or synchronizes your pictures across your devices when you take them.'

Under cross-examination, Ackert was asked to agree that some of the photos submitted in evidence by Amber Heard 'reflect the use of a photo editing application.'

Ackert disagreed. He said, 'They show the use of the Photos application, which is a sorting and editing application.'

He was asked straight up: 'Are you prepared to swear under oath that each and every photograph provided by Ms Heard and entered into evidence in this court is an authentic original?'

He replied: 'Based on the metadata that I have reviewed of the specific photographs I have reviewed, I can confirm that those are authentic original photographs. For the ones that Mr Neumeister identified, I identified photos that were authentic originals.'

Depp's attorney pulled up two images of the same three-quarter profile of Amber Heard. Both photos had data attached to them which showed they were both taken at 9.25pm and 12 seconds on the evening of 21 May 2016. Both photos had exactly the same location data embedded into them and the same file name. They are the same image, but the color saturations are different.

'How,' asked Depp's attorney, 'would you have this jury decide which one is real?'

'I think you would need to look at the software metadata field,' replied Ackert.

'But we have two photographs entered into evidence in this court that have the same identifying information, but in your view, look visually different, correct?'

'I don't agree that they have the same identifying information,' said Ackert. 'I don't see a software metadata field here.'

Johnny Depp's attorney highlighted the fact that the visible metadata showed each photo was taken at the same time, down to the exact second. Ackert acknowledged that this information was identical.

For Team Depp, it was a useful exercise. The jury had been shown identical images of Amber Heard's alleged injuries with different color saturation, and they were told there are different types of metadata attached to a photo file, all of which can easily be altered. There was not a shred of evidence that anyone on Heard's side had deliberately manipulated her photos in an attempt to emphasize her injuries. That didn't matter. The message had cut through: *Do not believe what you think you might be seeing. This is not reliable evidence.*

WAPO AND THE ACLU

Whilst Dan Wootton's non-defamatory article in the Sun newspaper may have read as if it was knocked off in an afternoon, Amber Heard's highly defamatory piece for the Washington Post took far longer, and seemed to involve dozens of people, many of whom were lawyers. Within weeks of it being published, Johnny Depp had sued Heard for defamation, leading to 2022's trial in Virginia.

The idea for the WaPo piece came from the American Civil Liberties Union. In 2016 Heard donated a sizeable sum from her divorce settlement to the ACLU. She promised them much more.

We know from court documents that shortly after Johnny Depp and Amber Heard settled their divorce in August 2016, the ACLU received a direct payment of $350,000 from Heard[1]. Heard's payment was made shortly after an introduction email from Elon Musk, an established ACLU donor. The email, dated 18 August 2016, was addressed to the ACLU's executive director, Anthony Romero, and cc'd to Amber Heard. In it, Musk wrote:

'Amber, I described your plan to donate $3.5 million to the ACLU over the next 10 years as you very much believe in what they are doing.'

When a billionaire donor introduces a Hollywood actor to your organization, with a suggestion they're about to start throwing big money at you, you don't just sit around cashing their checks. You get to work.

On 9 September, Anthony Romero wrote to Amber Heard, thanking her for the $350,000 donation and telling her that he was 'honored' by her 'vote of confidence in our work, especially our efforts on behalf of domestic violence victims.' Romero told Heard he was 'incredibly grateful that you have spoken out publicly on this critical issue... With you by our side, we will continue to work with fierce determination to advance civil liberties, today and for years to come.'

Like most high profile charitable institutions, the ACLU maintains a crack unit of celebrity 'ambassadors' who advocate for ACLU causes. These can be artists, musicians, actors or influencers who must have, in the words of the ACLU's chief operating officer, Terence Dougherty,

---

[1] Shortly after a $100,000 payment from Johnny Depp in Amber Heard's name. We'll deal with how this all happened in the *Pledge v Donate* chapter.

'prior expertize in that policy area.' They also need to be able to speak about their cause 'in detail' and have a 'significant following'.

Asked in a deposition for the US court case how the ACLU came to appoint Amber Heard as an ambassador, Mr Dougherty replied that Heard had attended a meeting with representatives of the ACLU's Women's Rights Project and their Reproductive Freedom Project. This was organized by the ACLU's Director of Artist Engagement, Jessica Weitz. According to Dougherty, Heard 'spoke with such clarity and expertize on issues of gender-based violence' that Weitz decided Heard 'would be an appropriate person to ask to become an ACLU ambassador.'

Amber Heard was delighted to accept the invitation and was formally appointed an ACLU ambassador for Women's Rights in October 2018. This was a big deal for the ACLU, especially as Heard was preparing to publicize her role as the female lead in the forthcoming movie blockbuster *Aquaman*. The ACLU's bright minds got to work.

On 6 November 2018, Gerry Johnson from the organization's comms department wrote to Jodi Gottlieb, Amber Heard's publicist. He asked for 'Amber's thoughts on doing an op-ed in which she discusses the ways in which survivors of gender-based violence have been made less safe under the Trump administration and how people can take action.'

An 'op-ed' is newspaper and PR-speak for an opinion piece, usually by a guest writer. Op-eds tend to sit *opp*osite the pages in a newspaper given over to *ed*itorial comment, hence: op-ed.

Mr Johnson continued: 'If she feels comfortable, she can interweave her personal story saying how painful it is as a GBV survivor to witness these setbacks.' GBV stands for gender-based violence.

Amber Heard *was* keen to do an op-ed for the ACLU, weaving elements of her personal story into the article. All the ACLU had to do was draft it, and find a newspaper in which to place it.

On 29 November a first pass of the article was sent to Amber Heard. It was written by an ACLU staffer called Robin Shulman. Shulman told Heard: 'I tried to gather your fire and rage, and really interesting analysis, and shape that into an op-ed form.'

She added: 'Your lawyers should review this for the way I skirted around talking about your marriage.'

Shulman was referencing the elephant in the room. Amber Heard had petitioned for divorce and publicly accused her husband Johnny Depp of domestic violence. Three months later she had signed an NDA, settled the divorce and issued a joint statement with Depp stating their relationship 'was intensely passionate and at times volatile, but... there was never any intent of physical or emotional harm.'

Having signed an NDA, talking about, or even skirting around Heard's marriage was sailing into legally dangerous waters. Yet Heard had set herself up as a campaigner on issues relating to gender-based violence, having demonstrated her 'clarity and expertize' on the matter. What was she to do when she wanted to communicate her expertize in public?

In the event, no fewer than four ACLU lawyers were involved in the drafting and reviewing of the op-ed, with each draft being passed to Heard's PRs and her lawyer Eric George for further review. The ACLU comms team drew up a list of ideal publications to aim for, citing the Washington Post, New York Times, Teen Vogue or USA Today as possibilities. To make the article interesting and relevant, the ACLU was keen to make Heard's personal testimony as strong as possible. This meant writing about her relationship with Johnny Depp. But the more she wrote about her relationship with Johnny Depp, the more likely she was to break the terms of her NDA.

The drafts began going back and forth between the ACLU and Heard's representatives. During this period, ACLU staffer Stacy Sullivan contacted the Washington Post, asking if they might be interested in an op-ed piece written by Amber Heard 'who as you may recall', she wrote 'was beaten up during her brief marriage to Johnny Depp.'

The Post took the bait, but on 11 December the ACLU's Jessica Weitz wrote an internal email to Robin Shulman saying: 'Amber sent back the op-ed with final edits from her legal team which specifically neutered much of the copy regarding her marriage and the domestic violence.'

Both the ACLU and Heard wanted the op-ed published to coincide with the big pre-Christmas promotional push around the release of *Aquaman*, which Terence Dougherty acknowledged would see Heard 'receive an incredible amount of press and be in the public eye.' The ACLU could therefore piggy-back on the buzz around Heard and the movie to generate what Dougherty called 'significant readership about our issues.'

But there were still major problems with the actual text. One of them was a sentence which began: 'Two years ago, I sought a temporary restraining order from my then husband...' Heard's lawyers rejected this *and* a weaker replacement, which read: 'Two years ago, after successfully acquiring a temporary restraining order...'

Concerns were growing within the ACLU that Heard's piece was becoming so diluted it may no longer be of interest to a 'top tier' publication like the Post. For her part, Heard was still keen to make the article as strong as possible. She asked the ACLU if they could attempt an 'artful' way of getting a reference to the restraining order 'put back in' to the op-ed.

It went down to the wire. *Aquaman*'s release date in the US was 21 December. Eventually a draft was signed off by all the lawyers and was submitted to the Washington Post. The article was published online on 18 December with the headline: *Amber Heard: I spoke up against sexual violence and faced our culture's wrath. That has to change.* The piece was accompanied by a red-carpet picture of Amber Heard posing for the paparazzi.

In the op-ed, Amber Heard declared she had been 'exposed to abuse' at a 'very young age' and sexually assaulted at 'college age'. Then she turned to more recent events:

'Two years ago,' she wrote, 'I became a public figure representing domestic abuse, and I felt the full force of our culture's wrath for women who speak out.'

Heard told the Post's readers that by speaking out she had lost a part in a movie and was dropped by a global fashion brand. She reported friends and advisors telling her she would never work in Hollywood again.

'I had the rare vantage point of seeing, in real time,' she continued, 'how institutions protect men accused of abuse.'

In the rest of the op-ed[2], Heard addressed the #MeToo movement and 'female-led opposition' to Donald Trump's statements and behavior. She advocated for the strengthening of the Violence Against Women Act and alerted readers to proposed changes governing the way schools dealt with sexual harassment complaints. Heard finished by alerting readers to 'death threats' she'd been sent for taking a stand, and wrote that she hoped to be part of a movement which will 'ensure that women who come forward to talk about violence receive more support.'

Although the piece did not mention Johnny Depp by name, it took less than 24 hours for other publications to start linking Depp to Heard's words.

---

[2]   Which is still online on the WaPo website.

An article called *Amber Heard speaks out again about domestic abuse* appeared in USA Today, with the same 18 December date stamp. The first paragraph reads:

'Amber Heard, the ex-wife of Johnny Depp who accused him of beating her up, posted a column in the Washington Post late Tuesday lamenting the consequences she paid for speaking out.'

The article mentions Depp eight times and uses two pictures which feature him. One of the other pictures shows the mark on Heard's cheek outside the LA Municipal Courthouse.

New York magazine The Cut called their WaPo follow-up *What Happened After Amber Heard Spoke Out About Johnny Depp*. Elle magazine's was titled *Amber Heard Claims Accusing Johnny Depp Of Domestic Abuse Lost Her Jobs*.

The ACLU's attempts to avoid a situation where everyone would interpret the article as Heard indirectly re-accusing Johnny Depp of domestic abuse had failed. Miserably. 'So much for not mentioning JD,' wrote Jessica Weitz in an internal email, referencing the USA Today piece.

Although the online title to Heard's op-ed was the Washington Post's confection, neither Heard nor the ACLU sought to get it corrected or toned down. The next day, when the op-ed had appeared in the WaPo print edition (with the far less salacious title *A transformative moment for women*), Heard sent a tweet linking to the online version, republishing the Post's online headline.

Johnny Depp, at that point already suing NGN and Dan Wootton for calling him a wife-beater, felt Amber Heard's piece was also defamatory. Eschewing an opportunity to go after the Washington Post[3], Depp trained both barrels on his former wife. The Post's online servers are based in the State of Virginia, which was therefore (according to Depp's lawyers) where Heard had published her op-ed. And this is why, in 2022, the sleepy town of Fairfax in Northern Virginia became the focus of Depp v Heard, celebrity trial of the century.

---

[3] A difficult case to win, given the high bar for libel in the United States. Depp's lawyers would have to prove the Washington Post acted with *actual malice* when it came to a piece WaPo would (likely successfully) argue was published in good faith.

THE DECISION TO TELEVISE

Fairfax, Virginia, February 2022

Once the dust had settled on Depp v NGN I put my thoughts about Amber Heard and Johnny Depp to one side and devoted the remainder of the year to writing a book on a completely different subject[1].

Occasionally I would get messages from Twitter followers asking if I would consider covering Depp v Heard in Virginia. The trial was originally scheduled to take place in the Circuit Court of Fairfax County in September 2020, but had been kicked into May 2021 due to coronavirus. Even then, the logistical challenge of getting to the US was still pretty severe. Between November 2020 and January 2021 the UK was stuck in a lockdown hokey-cokey and visas to the US were hard to come by. Thankfully (for me, anyway) Depp v Heard was delayed again, this time until April 2022. Things had calmed down to the extent I was able to pick up a US visa and I was lucky enough to be able to crowdfund a flight.

Depp v Heard was looking interesting. Shortly after the UK trial finished back in 2020, Amber Heard had jacked up the stakes in Virginia by adding a counter-suit to Depp's defamation claim. This was prompted by three statements[2] Adam Waldman had given to the Daily Mail calling Amber Heard's claims of abuse a 'hoax'. Heard contended Waldman was acting as a proxy for Depp, and by claiming – through Waldman – that her allegations were a hoax, Depp had defamed her. Heard sought $100m in damages. With a swingeing UK trial judgment in her favor, Heard's counter-claim had teeth.

On 25 February 2022 there was a pre-trial hearing at Fairfax Circuit Court. Depp's lawyers wanted to let cameras into the courtroom. Heard's team, led by Elaine Bredehoft, were set against this. No transcript of the hearing has been released, but there were reporters present, including the redoubtable Joan Hennessy from Courthouse News, who I later got to know through working alongside her in Virginia. Joan reported the explosive allegation – made in open court for the first time that day – that Amber Heard was the victim of sexual assault – 'including rape' – before and during her marriage to Johnny Depp. Bredehoft

---

[1] The book is called *The Great Post Office Scandal* and is still very much available from all good outlets.

[2] Discussed in detail in the *One Little Lie* and *Waldman's Defamatory Statement* chapters.

argued that Heard's status as an alleged victim of sexual violence meant cameras should be excluded from proceedings. Giving her reasons, Bredehoft drew attention to the existence of what she called a number of influential anti-Heard online 'networks'.

Presciently, Bredehoft warned these 'networks' would 'take anything that's unfavorable – a look... [an] out of context statement, and play it over and over and over and over again.'

Depp's lawyer, Ben Chew, dismissed Bredehoft's concerns on the grounds that Amber Heard was 'a liar' who had already 'trashed' Depp's reputation publicly. The upcoming trial was an opportunity for the public to hear and see the truth. 'Mr Depp believes in transparency,' he told the court.

The judge noted that banning cameras when dealing with cases of sexual assault was only mandated in criminal trials. As this was a civil trial, the court had jurisdiction. In one of the most consequential decisions of her career, the newly-promoted Chief Judge Penney Azcarate ruled that cameras should be allowed in the courtroom to cover Depp v Heard, apparently on grounds of safety. According to Variety magazine, the judge told the court she was 'getting a lot of media requests, and she had a responsibility to keep the proceedings open to observers.' The judge apparently 'worried' that if cameras were not allowed, 'reporters would come to the courthouse, potentially creating a hazardous condition there.'

The decision to allow cameras was therefore not taken in the interests of open justice. It was taken because the judge felt having a lot of journalists at her courthouse was somehow hazardous. As to whether it was fair that a woman should be forced to recount the detail of her alleged abuse in front of a live, worldwide audience, the judge shrugged: 'I don't see any good cause not to do it.'

Azcarate made an order allowing Court TV to broadcast and stream live footage on a pool basis – which meant it had to be made available to other broadcasters. What happened to it after that seemed to be of no interest to her. If Azcarate had ordered that the footage should not be edited or re-shared by unaccredited sites, it is likely that responsible social media platforms would have at least attempted to police this. The world could still see the trial being streamed live on Court TV or the Law and Crime TV network, or watch edited reports on the broadcast news channels, but no – she decided to empty the live footage straight out of the courtroom window and wash her hands of it.

The judge's lack of awareness about what would happen as a consequence of her ruling was betrayed by a comment she made in the final week of the trial. During legal argument about witness contamination, she said with a bewildered shrug: 'The problem is the courtroom, in this particular case, appears to be the world.' The naivety behind her failure to consider trying to control the lens through which the trial would be viewed (and re-edited, and manipulated) was breathtaking. What did she *think* was going to happen?

WELCOME TO AMERICA

Two weeks before the trial started, Azcarate issued a ruling making it clear just how unwelcome journalists were in her court. All electronic items were banned, which put paid to live-tweeting. Accreditation by a recognized body counted for zilch. Anyone who wanted a place in the gallery (beyond the parties' nominated associates) would have to join a daily queue for wristbands. These would be issued on a first-come, first-served basis from 7am every morning outside the court building. There were 100 places available in the 200-seat courtroom (to allow for social distancing) and a further 50 available in an overflow court on the same floor. The first row on each side of the main court was reserved for each party's legal team.

At 4am on Monday 11 April 2022 – jet-lagged and sleep-deprived – I stumbled out of an Uber onto a service road which separates the Fairfax County Court building from the large grassy square it overlooks. It was dark. And cold.

Gathering my kit, I gazed up at the imposing five-floor building and wondered what the next few weeks might bring. I was the first reporter on the scene, but not the first person. Standing near a solid-looking tripod, in warm outdoor clothing, was a TV news cameraman, staking out the court building's front entrance. I introduced myself. Paul from Fox News was friendly and helpful, even if he didn't know much more about what was going on than I did. At least I was in the right place. Within half an hour, another figure shuffled into focus out of the gloom. She was wearing a racoon tail hat, a big coat, lots of rattly jewellery and warm boots.

'Excuse me,' I said, rather awkwardly. 'Are you here for the Johnny Depp trial?'

'Yes,' she replied.

'Are you… a fan?' I asked, chancing my arm. She didn't look like a reporter.

'Yes,' she said decidedly. 'I am.'

I introduced myself. Her name was Natasha.

'Pleased to meet you,' I said, unsure as to whether I should try to shake her hand. 'You're the first one here.'

For lack of anything better to do, I set up my tripod in the dark and interviewed Natasha for my YouTube channel. She told me she was 40 years old and had driven 2,500 miles in her truck from Reno to support

Johnny Depp. Natasha felt Depp had 'got a really bad rep in the beginning... people were quick just to believe everything that was said, and then more and more came out and... people just want to see what happens, and they want to see him be okay.'

I warmed to Natasha. She was funny, open and friendly. As dawn broke, I had a chance to better orient myself. Fairfax seemed a quiet little place with a village feel, despite being at the intersection of two fairly major roads. The grassy square outside the main court building was the site of an early civil war skirmish, and beyond it was the town's original courthouse, built in 1800, now a historic records center and museum. Fairfax Town contrasted neatly with the grandeur of nearby Washington DC. It appeared supremely unbothered by the impending sprinkling of Hollywood stardust.

After 6am Natasha and I went to find the queue for wristbands. Five or six more fans had turned up, including the irrepressible 58-year old Yvonne ('Same age as Johnny!') who declared herself Depp's number one fan, and spent the morning loudly proclaiming his innocence to anyone in earshot. The queue started at the bottom of a colonnade which stretched along the western wing of the court building. I would spend many hours of the next six weeks under that colonnade, sheltering from the elements, watching one dawn break after another. As we waited in line, more TV crews turned up and put their tripods down opposite the courthouse. At 9am (my day one wristband secured) I caught my first glimpse of Johnny Depp's legal team walking into the courthouse. They smiled at the small group of people gathered outside. It was still cold, but the sky was a beautiful shade of blue. My nerves were settling. Everything was going to be okay.

As it got closer to 9.30am the number of people waiting outside court swelled to a couple of dozen. I introduced myself to another group of Depp fans, and I spotted a lone Amber Heard supporter who arrived bearing a placard which said: 'Save a Life – Amber Heard'.

There was a sense of anticipation. Were Depp and Heard actually coming? If so, would we see them arrive? As the crowd grew the Deputy Sheriffs took control. We were ordered back from the service road onto the grass by the courthouse. We waited there a little longer, until it became apparent neither Depp nor Heard were going to be making a grand entrance.

I joined the queue for security and took my first look inside the court building. It was open and functional and carried that almost compulsory slightly stale public building smell. We quickly found the enormous canteen on the lower-ground floor. Here I was introduced to the delights of American cuisine, including half-and-half, blondies and pork fritters. A video of Judge Penney Azcarate telling visitors it was an offense to take photographs or film anywhere in the building ran on an endless loop by the lift.

The biggest court – 5J, up on the fifth floor – had been allocated to the trial. The first day of proceedings involved jury selection, which meant none of us who queued for wristbands could sit in the main court as it was needed for all the potential jurors. This seemed a bit unnecessary – could we not get in at the back? I tested the water. Arguing the toss with the Deputy Sheriffs was a non-starter. They were polite, but unyielding.

Reporters and spectators were directed to the overflow court, also on the fifth floor. We observed as the judge and both sides' attorneys began the process of selecting the jurors, who sat off camera. Those with legitimate reasons not to serve, and those deemed unsuitable for the task were dismissed. Johnny Depp's fame meant that no one was expected to not know who he was, but those who had seen more than three of his movies were questioned closely. Anyone who had seen more than one Amber Heard film was also asked supplementary questions before being kept in the pool or dismissed. General queries including 'Do you have a strong or negative opinion of anyone who uses cruel or foul language?' and 'Do you tape record or film yourself or friends on social media?' were also asked. By 2pm a pool of sixty had been whittled down to twenty-one.

The judge had previously ruled that jurors should not be made aware of the outcome of the UK trial at any stage of proceedings. This was to avoid prejudicing the evidence they would hear and see in Depp v Heard. To deal with this point at jury selection, potential jurors were asked by the judge if they knew anything at all about the wider dispute between Depp and Heard. Those who did were questioned over how much they knew privately. This was to prevent them revealing anything significant in front of the other potential jurors. By mid-afternoon, the final eleven jurors had been selected. Sources close to the legal teams of both parties have told me they are not aware that any juror who made the final eleven volunteered any specific prior knowledge of the UK case before being sworn in. The stage was finally set – time for the players.

THE VIPS ARRIVE

We soon found out how Depp and Heard were getting into court. Round the back of the main judicial building was a long courtyard, protected by two automatic gates and ten foot high brick walls. The VIP entrance. Each day, at around 9.15am, a black SUV containing Depp and his entourage would turn off Judicial Drive and swing through the courthouse gates under the watchful eye of the armed and vigilant Deputy Sheriffs. Around the same time (but never at *exactly* the same time), a dark grey pick-up truck carrying Heard and her team would do the same.

The small number of Depp fans present at the start of the trial developed their own routines. Some would pick up their wristbands at 7am, then head round the back of the courthouse to wave their man into the car park. Job done, they would return to the main entrance to go through security and get inside the building. Once inside, some would grab breakfast. Others would head straight to the fifth floor to queue up outside Court 5J. For them, it wasn't just about being in the same room as Johnny Depp, it was about securing the best seat in the house. This was generally agreed to be directly behind Depp's team on the left-hand side of the court, allowing fans to catch Depp's eye as he walked to his seat.

To ensure Depp and Heard could avoid rubbing shoulders with spectators or journalists (or each other), both were given separate entrances to the courtroom. Depp came in via a door just behind the witness box to take his place on the judge's right, closest to the jury. Heard entered from a door on the opposite side of the court, and remained on the judge's left, distant from the jury. Court TV placed two discreet remote cameras on the left-hand side of the courtroom facing away from the jury. The camera at the back of court could either provide a wide shot of the spectators' gallery and the legal teams, or close-ups of the protagonists. The second camera faced forward to capture the witness box and the judge's bench. The sound was controlled by the judge, who could cut all mics when a 'sidebar' discussion was requested. Sidebars are a regular feature of US trials (so much so that the Law and Crime TV network has its own daily analytical podcast called 'Sidebar'). During sidebars, attorneys for both sides can approach the judge's bench, usually to discuss a legal point. In Virginia, during the sidebars, the courtroom speakers would play white noise to ensure neither we nor the jury could hear what was being said. The live stream would broadcast silence. One person who could hear everything, including sidebar discussions, was Judy, the Court Reporter. Judy sat wearing headphones in a pose of intense concentration throughout the trial, transcribing proceedings onto her laptop.

Each session began the same way. Spectators and supporters with designated use of the reserved gallery benches would file into court from the main double door entrance at the back of the courtroom. Depp and Heard would enter with their frontline legal teams from their separate entrances either side of the judge's bench. We would be required to rise for the judge, under instruction of the court bailiff (a senior Deputy Sheriff). Once the judge had dealt with any legal matters (some in open court, some as sidebars), the jury would be called. The spectators were not required to stand for the jury, but Depp, Heard, their legal teams and everyone on the reserved benches shot to attention as another Deputy Sheriff led the jurors to their places on the judge's right, a few feet away from the witness box and Depp himself. New witnesses were called from the back of the court.

Jury trials in the UK usually start with twelve people. Long trials might see one or two drop out for various reasons. Judges can accept verdicts from as few as nine jurors. In Fairfax, we started with eleven, but only seven jurors would be required to make the final decisions. Each juror had a number, and at the beginning of the trial, the numbers of four jurors were put into an envelope. If there were no dropouts over the course of the trial, at the end of proceedings, the four jurors whose numbers were in the envelope would be excluded from final deliberations. As it happened, two jurors dropped out quite early on, leaving a core of nine to sit through the whole thing. This meant at the end of the trial two jurors who had sat through the entire trial were excluded from the final deliberations. The burden fell on the remaining seven jurors (two women, five men) to come to a unanimous decision on Depp's claim and Heard's counter-claim.

On 12 April, Elaine Bredehoft confirmed that sexual assault allegations against Johnny Depp were going to be front and center in this trial, as she faced the jury to give her opening statement. Bredehoft took them swiftly to Australia, using the present tense to give her words more urgency:

'He rips off her nightgown. He has her jammed up against a bar... He tells her he's going to fucking kill her. He fucking hates her... And then he penetrates her with a liquor bottle. That's the Johnny Depp that you're going to hear about in this case.'

Bredehoft's opening was not as fluid as I had expected, and the sudden switch from polite courtroom formalities into graphic language jarred. . She leapt around the chronology of the alleged violence at breakneck speed, giving details of multiple events the jury could have no knowledge of. Camille Vasquez for Johnny Depp was better, telling the jury that Amber Heard had 'painted herself before the world as a representative of abuse victims', and had been 'living and breathing this lie for years.' Vasquez told the jurors that for Heard, this trial would be the 'performance of her life.'

Both sides had a lot to say about the pictures of Amber Heard with various bruises and a cut lip. This was by far the most dangerous evidence for Depp. If the jury believed the images and the injuries were genuine, it would be a short step to wondering what or who caused them.

I was just happy we were underway. The proxy war was over and I was once more back in a world of contradictory sworn narratives and inexplicable alternate realities. Already we were being asked to doubt the evidence of our eyes and ears. The lawyers were giving jurors a relentless message: *You can't trust the other lot. You can't trust what you think you are seeing or hearing. You **can** trust me, though. Let me tell you a story...*

EARLY SKIRMISHES

Fairfax, Virginia, April 2022

Depp's first witness was Christi Dembrowski, his older sister and personal manager. Dembrowski seemed unenthusiastic about giving evidence, to the point of being wooden. But her pragmatic ordinariness helped the jury connect Johnny Depp the movie star to the mundanity of family life and the tedious logistics of his schedule. Dembrowski anchored him in reality, to some degree, whilst also painting Heard as a cliquey nightmare.

Under cross-examination Dembrowski became shifty. There was absolutely no way she was going to say anything bad about her brother or his drug consumption. When shown some texts from 2014 in which she told Depp: 'Stop drinking', 'Stop pills' and 'Stop coke', Dembrowski refused to accept she might be telling him to stop doing anything, and only reluctantly accepted coke referred to cocaine.

Depp's long-time friend, Isaac Baruch, followed Dembrowski, injecting some welcome charisma into proceedings. He is a big man with a big personality, and you could understand why Depp wanted to keep him around. Watching him in the witness box, you couldn't imagine not enjoying his company. Baruch clearly adored Heard, and told the court:

'I fell in love with her just like Johnny fell in love with her. I fell in love with her. She's totally respectful... gracious to me, she's got great teeth!... she treated me with complete respect.' The teeth comment and the way he delivered it provoked laughter in the gallery. Depp smiled at his friend throughout. Baruch became emotional about the way the relationship had ended, but maintained he saw no injuries on Amber Heard even as, on 22 May 2016, she was inviting him to inspect the supposed bruise on her cheek.

Baruch had been an entertaining witness in the UK trial and pressed exactly the same buttons in Virginia, but this time to a national TV audience. His performance sparked a brief flurry of Baruch-mania, as the man who described Depp to a High Court judge as an "ubermensch" got a brief taste of the limelight.

The next big moment came courtesy of Kate James, Amber Heard's personal assistant, who had made such a vivid contribution to the London trial.

The issue of Heard allegedly stealing James' experience of being raped was not put into evidence, but her recorded deposition was nonetheless enthralling. James maintained a steely, stone-cold demeanor throughout and was *dripping* with contempt for her former client. James claimed to have been on the end of serious verbal abuse from Heard on multiple occasions, telling attorneys 'it was so random and ongoing. You would never know when it was gonna come left of center.'

James recalled one specific occasion when she was moving from part-time to full-time working. During their negotiations over pay, James said Heard 'leapt up out of her chair, put her face approximately 4 inches from my face, and began spitting in my face, telling me how dare I ask for the salary I was asking for... she felt that gave her the right to spit in my face.'

During the three years they worked together, James said she received 'barrages' of abusive text messages from Heard 'day and night'. James also said Heard had a 'kick the dog' relationship with her 'poor sister' Whitney, and that Paige was 'terrified' of Amber. When it came to substance abuse, James described seeing Heard intoxicated 'often', adding that when Heard was intoxicated, she would become more 'belligerent and abusive' towards her.

In terms of any alleged violence, James says she saw nothing of the kind between Depp and Heard and no evidence it happened – no bruises, cuts or swelling on Heard's face or body. Asked if she was privy to observing much of Heard's body, James said she would regularly see her boss in states of undress, adding that when she was at home, Heard 'had no issue with walking around naked quite often.'

Whilst the evidence we heard over the first three days was absorbing and eminently reportable, I kept getting distracted by the way witnesses are dealt with in American courts. In the UK, unless a barrister states something which is factually untrue, or asks a blatantly leading question, their opposite number tends to let them get on with it. Witnesses are given some leeway to ramble on a bit. The US system is very different. It seemed no attorney was able to ask a question without their opposite number leaping up to object. Grounds for objection deployed on the first day alone included lack of foundation (failure to establish the witness had knowledge of the matter being asked about), hearsay (something the witness only heard about rather than witnessed), 404 (a reference to rule 404 – prohibiting an attorney from establishing the idea that someone's general character might suggest they would act according to their character in a given situation) and leading (suggesting the answer to a question within that question).

Over the course of the trial I learned about many, many more objections: argumentative, non-responsive, relevance, asked-and-answered, calls for speculation, compound (two questions asked of a witness at the same time), beyond the scope (not what a witness is there to answer questions about). Every objection required a judge's instant ruling. Azcarate could overrule (allow the question or answer), sustain (stop a line of questioning), strike out the testimony or just see where the questions were going before making a decision. Attorneys could also respond to an objection, either at the invitation of the judge or before the judge had made her decision. The most frustrating objection was (lack of) foundation. A perfectly reasonable question, such as: 'Did you drive to the supermarket?' could prompt an objection on the basis that the attorney asking the question had not yet established whether the witness had a car, could drive, knew where the supermarket was and needed to buy something.

It wasn't like that all the time – several minutes of testimony could go by without an objection, but in the first few days it was a frustrating experience, and not just for me. Bewildered witnesses were regularly interrupted by what seemed like impenetrable legal argument, only to forget what they were talking about, requiring the attorney who first asked them a question to do so again[1]. Worse, some started to second guess the objections before they came (Depp got particularly good at this), making the whole process so artificial it became hard to see how the jury were meant to be making any sense of what was going on.

Outside court hours, I was expending a prodigious amount of mental energy trying to assimilate the logistics of the trial. Journalists who showed up to cover the story were essentially left to their own devices. The Deputy Sheriffs were friendly, but unforthcoming. I didn't see the court's Information Officer (whose job included media liaison) on the fifth floor once, and she seemed to take pride in providing the bare minimum of information on email. To try to counter this, I fell in with a few British hacks. We quickly formed a transatlantic alliance with some of the American reporters, and between us worked out what we needed to know.

Despite Johnny Depp's presence in the courtroom, the number of people queuing for wristbands during week one was tiny. It was possible to bowl up to the deputies staffing the registration desk well after 7am and collect a wristband without even having to queue. YouTube's myriad trial watchers were primed and streaming, and the sexual

---

[1] Even the attorneys got confused. One of Amber Heard's famously managed to object to his own question, causing much merriment online.

assault allegations referenced by Bredehoft in her opening statement made for interesting copy, but the wider world didn't seem that interested in Depp v Heard. Yet.

On the ground there was plenty to report. During week one, two Johnny Depp supporters were expelled from court for allegedly sending threatening tweets about Amber Heard. It transpired at least one of those tweets was several years old. Someone on Team Heard was surveilling the Depp fans and correlating their identities with their online activities. This seemed a little unnecessary – court attendees went through metal detectors before coming into the building and were well-policed by the deputies. Many Depp fans were perfectly happy to spit venom online (one offending tweet read: 'I can't wait for the day I kill Amber Heard'), but in person most spectators were polite, co-operative and well-behaved. It was interesting to observe the fuss the expulsions caused amongst the Depp supporters at court. Judging by the reactions it was the first time some of them realized there might be personal consequences to what they post on social media. Not that it caused much in the way of self-reflection – one of the ejected tweeters was quoted in the New York Post, defiantly telling Elizabeth Rosner 'we aren't fans, we are abuse survivors who are supporting another survivor... this kind of thing does not belong in newspapers. This isn't entertainment, this is a domestic violence trial where a man was almost killed, and we are private citizens.'

The thing I wanted more than anything else was access to the official daily transcripts. I asked Depp and Heard's PR teams if they would release them to me, and received little more than polite acknowledgments. I asked the lawyers directly via email and got no response until I approached Camille Vasquez outside Court 5J to see if she was even aware of my request. Vasquez told me it was unlikely the parties would want to release the transcripts, given they contained all the sidebar discussions. I approached Planet Depos, who employed Judy the Court Reporter and asked if I might be able to buy the transcripts directly. I was told they could not be passed on to me without the written agreement of both parties, or a court order.

I parked that thought whilst I focused on what was happening around me. As soon as proceedings finished each day, I had to try to make editorial sense of them for various outlets. The large grassy square outside the court building became an outdoor YouTube studio, during which I conducted a series of instant-reaction 'park bench' interviews with various people who had been in the public gallery that day. Some were fellow journalists, many were partisans, and the vast majority were pro-Depp. Occasionally I would prepare an as-live TV report for 5 News back in the UK, or do a live report into the Australian Channel 9 breakfast show, or guest on programmes broadcast around the trial by Court TV or the Law and Crime TV network.

Once I had completed my duties on site I would head back to my apartment in DC. There I would finish editing and uploading my YouTube stuff whilst formatting and sending a newsletter to the subscribers who had crowdfunded my passage to America. The last thing I would do before turning in was send an audio file back to London to my colleagues at TBI Media. They reversioned it into a daily podcast, leaving me instructions to record and file any extra commentary lines before breakfast the next day. When court was in session, if you include queueing time, my working days were usually between 15 and 19 hours long. It was gruelling, but rewarding, particularly towards the end of the first week, when the drama in and around court ramped up once more.

MUTUAL ABUSE

Dr Laurel Anderson is a clinical psychologist who has been practising in Los Angeles for more than forty years. She provides psychotherapy for individuals and couples, dealing with – in her words – the 'evaluation' of a couple's problems, the 'conceptualization' of what is really going on in their relationship and the 'intervention' needed to make some kind of positive change. In October 2015 Anderson began treating Johnny Depp and Amber Heard. Her pre-recorded deposition was shown to the court on 14 April 2022.

Anderson noted that during counselling, Amber Heard spoke over Depp a lot, with a 'jackhammer style of talking.' This made it difficult for Depp to get his point across: 'He didn't have a voice,' Anderson told the attorneys. 'He couldn't keep up with her rapid-fire way of conversation.'

Anderson was candid about the violence reported to her in the relationship. When asked:

'Is it your testimony that while Mr Depp may have said he wasn't violent with any of his other partners, there was violence from Mr Depp toward Amber, correct?'

The psychologist replied: 'Yes, you're right. He had been well controlled, I think for almost, I don't know, 20, 30 years... And then with Ms Heard, he was triggered. And they engaged in what I saw as mutual abuse sometimes. I know she led on more than one occasion, and started it to keep him with her because abandonment and having him leave was her worst nightmare. And I think he may have initiated it on occasions too, that I'm less sure on.'

This was, to my knowledge, the first time any authoritative neutral party had said Depp may have admitted to initiating violence, or responding to an attack with violence. And it was the first time I had heard the term 'mutual abuse'.

Anderson was taken through her notes, which seemed to record both Depp and Heard candidly acknowledging their violence towards each other. In one solo session, Depp spoke to Anderson about the argument after Heard's birthday in the early hours of 22 April 2016. Her notes record: 'chaotic, violence, but gave as good as she got.'

Asked what that might mean, Anderson said: 'I think he talked about how chaotic it was, how violent it was, and she gave as good as she got.' Pressed further, Anderson replied: 'She initiated fights. She started violence. She rose to the challenge if he started first... she fought as hard as he did. And he tried to de-escalate far more than, I think, she did.'

Anderson also reported seeing bruises on Heard's face on 17 December 2015, which Heard said had been caused by Depp. The bruises 'around her eyes' tallied with the accidental or non-accidental headbutt on 15 December, the night before the James Corden show. Amber Heard claims not to remember how the fight started. A 'treatment summary' written by Anderson from her 'jumbly' notes states that Heard's bruises came about as a result of an argument which Heard admitted starting by 'slapping' Depp 'when she was offended by what he said.' Later in the deposition, Anderson says that when Heard came in to show her her bruises, they (bizarrely) didn't discuss the reason for them. Anderson told the attorneys she recalled 'nothing about physical abuse, nothing.' The conversation instead revolved around the planned Christmas trip to the Bahamas.

Anderson was reasonably sure both Depp and Heard were hitting each other. Once more, the word 'mutual' came up in a near contemporaneous treatment summary, written by Anderson, in which she states: 'The physical violence that occurred between them appeared to me to be mutual.'

The next witness was a posh and slightly dippy Englishwoman, Gina Deuters, who was married to Stephen Deuters, Depp's assistant. Mrs Deuters is currently a 'freelance creator', but between 2002 and 2016 she worked as a 'visual effects coordinator' on movies including Depp's *Charlie and the Chocolate Factory* and *Pirates 4*. Deuters met Depp in 2005 through her husband, and was soon part of his inner circle. She told the court she had seen Depp drink alcohol throughout her friendship with him, but she had never seen him drunk. Deuters also said she had seen him smoke weed and had joined him in taking cocaine. In fact, she'd seen him take cocaine around twenty times, but it was Amber Heard and her gang who first introduced Deuters to MDMA. Deuters was just about to start reminiscing about what happened in Australia when there was an abrupt halt to proceedings. The jury was sent out. A sidebar conference between the attorneys took place at the judge's bench. After a short while, Judge Azcarate turned to Deuters.

'Ms Deuters,' she said. 'A question for you. Have you been watching the trial this past week?'

There is a rule in the US known as the witness rule. If invoked, non-expert witnesses were not allowed to watch other witness testimony before testifying themselves.

'I've seen clips of it online. Yeah,' replied Deuters.

'Okay,' said the judge. 'And witness testimonies?'

'Yeah, I've seen clips,' said Deuters.

'You've seen them... All right, you're excused ma'am. You're excused,' said the judge, making it clear Deuters was to leave the witness box. Turning to the court, Azcarate announced she would instruct the jury to strike Deuters testimony.

After watching Deuters' dismissal and Anderson's deposition I wrote a newsletter and put together a YouTube video, both of which I called *Mutual Abuse*. They hit a nerve. I received *a lot* of feedback through various social media platforms, and the YouTube post remains the most watched of the videos I put together in Virginia.

Mutual abuse, I was led to understand by many respondents, 'cannot' exist. There is an abuser and a victim, and any violence on the part of the victim is 'reactive abuse' – possibly a physical response borne out of fear for their lives, or an explosion of pent-up anger after being on the receiving end of relentless abuse.

If you search for *mutual abuse* online, you get articles headlined *The Myth of Mutual Abuse* and *There Is No Such Thing As Mutual Abuse*. Many articles are written with reference to Anderson's evidence in Depp v Heard, but you can find plenty more which precede it. The American National Domestic Violence Hotline states any idea abuse can be mutual 'allows the abusive partner to shift blame.' It calls this a 'common tactic' and advises:

'If your abusive partner is claiming that you're equally or more responsible for an incident, or that you too were abusive, this is their way of manipulating you into believing you did something to deserve this treatment.'

Many of my respondents felt that by simply reporting (and, admittedly, highlighting) the term I was giving credence to it, opening the door to the idea that Amber Heard was not the sole abuser in the Depp/Heard relationship.

I thought Anderson's evidence was newsworthy. Depp and Heard's own psychologist had reported that Heard 'initiated fights' and 'started violence', and she also believed Depp had acknowledged he was violent towards Heard and may even, on occasion, have initiated violence himself.

And that was that for the first week of Depp v Heard. Or so we thought.

EVE BARLOW

Although court did not initially sit on Fridays during the trial, the judge did hold untelevised hearings without the jury for attorneys from both parties. This was largely to resolve run-of-the-mill legal arguments. On the morning of Friday 15 April I did not go to court, instead sleeping late into the day. When I eventually opened my laptop, it was all kicking off. One of Amber Heard's most vocal online supporters, Eve Barlow, had been banned from court, by order of the judge, for the rest of the trial. The order, which was posted on the Fairfax Circuit Court website, had been screenshotted and tweeted by an influential Depp supporter, Laura Bockov. The next day, Bockov tweeted screenshots of the Friday hearing *transcript*.

It transpired that Eve Barlow, described by Ben Chew as 'a journalist and Ms Heard's current girlfriend', had been misbehaving. Only 'attorneys of record' were allowed to use electronic devices in court. Barlow, sitting on Heard's bench of supporters, had sent a (subsequently deleted) tweet from court at 4.31pm on Thursday 14 April, in direct contravention of this court order. More troublingly, she was also directly responsible for Gina Deuters' dismissal as a witness. Whilst Deuters was giving evidence, Barlow had passed a screenshot of an Instagram post made by Deuters to Amber Heard's attorney, Ben Rottenborn. Deuters' post stated that her 'dear friend' Johnny Depp had 'got a few wins in court this week and yet some press continue to belittle him.'

Rottenborn took the phone carrying this screenshot to the judge and, as we know, the judge asked Deuters if she had been watching the trial online. When Deuters confirmed she had, she was dismissed. By Friday morning, Depp's team had discovered that Deuters' Instagram message referencing Depp's 'few wins in court this week' had been posted on 8 January 2021. Chew told the judge that Barlow's actions essentially represented a 'fraud upon the Court'. He chastised Rottenborn ('as an officer of the Court') for failing to properly check what he was handing to the judge, especially as 'it was handed to him by someone improperly sitting in the first row, a reporter and Ms Heard's girlfriend.'

Chew accepted that Deuters had impeached herself by admitting to watching clips of the US trial online, but the matter would not have been raised had Barlow not found Deuters' post from 2021 and passed it off as being contemporary.

Invited to give a response, Amber Heard's attorney, Elaine Bredehoft, began by telling the court, 'Eve Barlow is not a journalist. Second of all, she's not Ms Heard's...'

The judge cut across her, telling Bredehoft, 'I really don't care all about that. She was live-tweeting in my courtroom.'

Bredehoft had no comeback. Barlow was banned from court for the duration of the trial.

The thing that exercised me about this episode, aside from Barlow's extraordinary behavior, was how Laura Bockov had got access to the transcript of Friday's hearing.

Depp's PR during the US trial was run by Hiltzik Strategies, brought on board in spring 2021. One Hiltzik staffer on the ground in Fairfax was Carolina Hurley, who worked for Donald Trump during his tenure at the White House. Hurley and her colleague Colleen were helpful to journalists, supplying them with access to evidence once it had been brought up in open court. When I asked if Hiltzik had anything to do with supplying the Friday hearing transcript to Laura Bockov, Hiltzik would not comment, but a reliable source who knows the organization well told me they had nothing to do with it. I have no reason to disbelieve them.

By making enquiries over the weekend I was able to verify what Bockov had tweeted was genuine, and I was able to prise a copy of the same transcript out of a reliable source on the grounds it was already in the public domain, but something felt off. If the parties were not going to allow transcripts to be released to anyone, that was their prerogative. If someone close to the parties or the court was going to be selectively leaking partial transcripts into the pro-Depp twittersphere, that was something else.

That evening I wrote an application to the court. I asked Chief Judge Azcarate to order the parties to supply journalists with daily transcripts, or order Planet Depos to start making them available on request. Given proceedings were being transmitted on live TV anyway, it didn't seem too much to ask.

To give further context to my request, I mentioned that a transcript of Friday's hearing had made its way into the public domain, after being published by a Depp influencer. This, I said, suggested that transcripts might be leaked selectively over the course of the trial. Hopefully the judge would see this was not really in the interests of open justice. I offered to make further oral submissions, if required, before proceedings began at the start of the week.

On Monday 18 April I got to the wristband queue at around 6am. Laura Bockov was already there. I congratulated her on her weekend scoop. At 9am, having secured my wristband, I visited the third floor of the judicial complex building to see if I could speak to Judge Azcarate's clerk. The clerk did not want to speak to me, but one of the administrators I'd been dealing with in the run up to the trial came out to say hello. I persuaded her to take a copy of my application to the clerk. Within fifteen minutes the administrator returned to tell me that the clerk had received my application and put it before the judge, who decided she was not going to address it. And that was that.

As word about the trial spread and fans began to stake places in the wristband queue from 1am, it became impossible for journalists to get into court without their employer paying a substitute to queue up overnight on their behalf. The Court TV crew got a small number of passes as part of their deal with the judge to provide pool pictures. This ensured they could put a reporter into the courtroom, but that reporter was not working as a pool reporter – she was serving the interests of her channel. When she was absent from court there were occasions when there were no journalists in the courtroom covering the trial at all. I would find myself sitting in the corridor outside Court 5J with my fellow reporters, watching and listening to what was happening a few yards away on our laptops. It was not satisfactory. Representations were made by at least one other news organization during the trial to see if provision could be made for credentialed reporters to get access to the court, but Chief Judge Azcarate did not seem interested.

There are many reasons Depp v Heard got completely out of hand on social media, and I think Azcarate bears some responsibility. Allowing the trial to go out unmediated on TV whilst refusing to give sensible access to journalists cleared the way for YouTubers and TikTok influencers to shape the public discourse. Azcarate did not seem to recognize (or maybe care) how journalism can play a role in responsibly communicating court proceedings to a worldwide audience. Shutting reporters out of court and refusing to address their concerns suggested, at the very least, a rather parochial mindset. I am aware there is more than a hint of special pleading in this argument, but it doesn't stop it being true.

SHOWTIME

Despite the terrible internal CCTV connection we had to live with during the London trial in 2020, it was still possible to witness Johnny Depp's presence enveloping the courtroom whilst he gave evidence. His voice modulated to fill the space, and despite being given a kicking during his cross-examination, Depp radiated studious charm throughout. He was on point answering questions and did what he could to make his case. In terms of audience figures, it was possibly the smallest performance of his career. No one outside the Royal Courts of Justice saw it.

Amber Heard was no slouch either. In London, Heard was poised, articulate and ultimately successful. Mr Justice Nicol read thousands of pages of evidence, witnessed the cross-examinations, re-read the transcripts and after three months of careful study, decided to accept Heard's testimony over Depp's.

When it comes to live evidence, judges are expected to minimize the performance aspect of any testimony and assess a case on the available facts. In the US, the oral evidence and how it was presented was essential. The jury had no access to transcripts of the proceedings and only a fraction of the documents Nicol reviewed were submitted into evidence. The fact-finders in Virginia decided who they wanted to believe mainly by listening to and watching the protagonists testify in open court. An undeniable part of that would involve considering who they warmed to most.

In the UK trial, Johnny Depp was the first witness on the stand. In the US, he had to wait a week. The Virginia Johnny Depp seemed markedly older and heavier than the figure who cut a dash bounding up the main steps of the High Court in London in 2020. When I suggested this to a group of supporters outside court, one remarked that quite a few of us had gotten a little bigger during the last two years of on-off lockdowns. It was a fair point.

Throughout the trial, Depp wore impeccably tailored suits, often with a dark shirt. In the first week of the trial, he had chosen to wear his hair down. From week two onwards Depp's highlighted, shoulder-length mop had been swept back into a tight ponytail. Week one gave us the chance to get used to observing Depp sitting quietly in the unusual environment of the courtroom. In week two, the jury and watching world would get the opportunity to hear and see Depp make his case in person. It was showtime.

At 2pm on Tuesday 20 April, Depp was sworn in. Whether there was some kind of agreement between the parties' attorneys, or because everything Depp was asked and responded to was relevant, the objections-per-minute ratio slowed to a level which allowed Depp to give evidence without too much interruption. Depp's attorney, Jessica Meyers, started with perhaps one of the broadest opening questions in legal history, asking her client:

'Can you please tell the jury why you're here today?'

Thankfully Depp didn't get too existential, embarking instead on a history of his legal dispute with Amber Heard, remembering to state unequivocally: 'Never did I myself reach the point of striking Ms Heard in any way, nor have I ever struck any woman in my life.'

Depp described Heard's 2016 domestic violence allegations as 'heinous and disturbing' and told the court it was his responsibility to clear his name, not just for himself, but for his two children, who found themselves having to deal with 'this horrid thing'.

'My goal is the truth...' Depp told the jurors. 'Truth is the only thing I'm interested in. Lies will get you nowhere... I'm obsessed with the truth. And so, today is actually the first opportunity that I've been able to speak about this case in full.'

And speak about his case, in full, is what Depp did for the rest of the week.

It's easy to be sniffy about actors, to dismiss them as ciphers, capable only of channeling other peoples' wit and intelligence through their perfect diction and natural-born good looks. Having met a few A-listers down the years, I would suggest anyone making that assumption is chronically underestimating what it takes to reach the very top. You don't get anywhere in Hollywood just by being a pretty face. Of course, looks *help*. To get off the mark you need to be the most photogenic person in a very large room full of photogenic people. That might get you a meeting. To get a part, you need humility, ability, a gargantuan work ethic and the social skills to make connections and build relationships which matter. To get beyond the mediocre stuff you need to be interesting, sharp, funny, self-deprecating, entertaining, self-aware and present in the moment. The people riding along the top of any industry tend be super-bright, and actors are no different. The best are high-functioning, driven and intelligent. I'm sure they can also use their super-powers to be world-class assholes too, but when they are presenting you with the best possible version of themselves, they can be irresistible.

To have a chance of persuading the Virginia jury that he was an unlikely wife-beater, Johnny Depp did not need to give the performance of his life. His entire life is a performance. He just needed to answer the questions he was asked, tell his truth and be himself. Of *course* the evidence in the case was going to be essential, but Depp still had to walk out into the spotlight and deliver, or he would get burned.

And Depp did deliver. He was slow, at first, feeling his way into his new environment. When he was groping for an idea Depp could disappear off into circuitous tangents, but when he hit a groove, his language was compelling. Taking drugs was an attempt to numb himself of 'the ghosts, the wraiths' which plagued him. Dealing with fame was a situation where 'your arms are too short to box with God.' Depp was also quick to exploit the artificiality of his environment with humor. Objections and arcane procedural interruptions were met with gracious amusement. Depp particularly delighted in the surname of Amber Heard's attorney, pronouncing *Rottenborn* with a slow-rolling relish. He wasn't so stupid as to be obviously taking the mickey, and was never admonished by the judge, but he found quick glimpses of the ridiculous in a way which communicated a bemused awareness of the madness swirling around the trial, the court and his life.

Depp told us that, at first, Heard was 'too good to be true... attentive... loving... smart... kind... funny' and 'understanding'. The first warning sign allegedly came when Depp upset a little ritual the couple had got into. At the end of each day, Heard would remove Depp's boots and pour him a glass of wine. One day he returned home to find Heard on the phone, so he removed his own boots. Depp claimed Heard was not happy at all. Her angry reaction caused Depp to 'take pause'. He didn't see why she should become so 'visibly shaken or upset that I had broken her rules of routine.' Depp said that after this episode, he began to 'notice other little tidbits' and claimed that 'within a year, a year and a half,' Heard had become 'another person, almost.'

This other person was, according to Depp, a vicious nag, variously haranguing him for drinking, being a bad parent and belittling or ignoring his attempts to help with career advice. Depp experienced a not uncommon realization that 'you are in a relationship with your mother, in a sense.'

Everyday disagreements allegedly escalated into blazing rows. Depp did not know why, but speculated they might come from a place of 'jealousy' or 'hatred'. He told the court that Heard's behavior 'was meant to feed her need for conflict. She has a need for conflict. She has a need for violence. It erupts out of nowhere.'

Asked why he didn't leave the relationship, Depp mused aloud: 'Why did I stay? I stayed, I suppose, because my father stayed. I suppose because I had been in that relationship with Vanessa [Paradis], and that was lost. And I didn't want to fail. I wanted to try to make it work. I thought maybe I could help her. I thought maybe I could bring her around. Because the Amber Heard that I knew for the first year, year and a half, was not this... opponent.'

Depp was adamant he had never once raised his hands to Heard, summarizing what he saw as the futility of such an approach with a rhetorical question: 'Why would you hit someone to make them agree with you? I don't think it works.'

By day two, Depp had got the hang of the inevitable objections. He started by launching into the story about Heard's 30th birthday party:

'We'd set up a dinner,' Depp told the court, 'with all her friends and Josh Drew, Rocky's boyfriend who was some sort of chef. So, he asked her what she would like for him to cook...'

There was a pause as Depp checked himself.

'That's hearsay, I guess...' said Depp, looking for guidance from the attorneys.

There was laughter in the gallery. The judge floundered a little. 'Yes...' she said 'I'm not sure it's offered for the truth of the matter, so...'

'He got it,' volunteered Rottenborn, to more laughter.

The judge continued to flounder. 'Okay. All right. Well, then...'

Depp deadpanned: 'I'm learning.'

When it came to his cross-examination, Depp was more trenchant than he appeared in 2020. He repeatedly challenged Ben Rottenborn, and some of what he was saying hit home. Rottenborn found himself either ignoring or dismissing Depp's challenges in order to try to get a yes or no answer to the question list he was trying to get through. I can imagine a jury might have thought it sounded like hectoring, with Rottenborn unable or unwilling to listen to what Depp was trying to say.

On the third day of giving evidence, Depp began to enjoy himself. He relaxed into his combative role, turning what could have been a straightforward legal process into a jousting competition. Depp was playing to the gallery, the cameras, and the world.

After one protracted set of questions, Rottenborn told him: 'We're gonna fast forward in time a little bit, Mr Depp.'

'Yes,' agreed Depp, pausing a beat to marvel at the possibility of courtroom time-travel. 'I can feel it.'

Depp had either learned from his experience in London, or just found himself more comfortable in front of Heard's attorneys who certainly seemed like they had a lot of ground to cover in a limited amount of time. Depp was in no hurry at all. He knew no one was in court to hear Rottenborn's questions – the jury, the judge, attorneys, spectators were there to hear Depp's answers. When Depp launched into a story about Elton John, Rottenborn cut him short with:

'My only question was just to confirm that you had sent that message to Elton John, nothing else.'

Bemused, Depp replied: 'So, I'll just go... okay, I'll just stop talking then.'

Rottenborn responded with appreciation, but Depp didn't hear what he said.

A little impatiently, Rottenborn repeated: 'I just said I want to be respectful of the court's time and the jury's time and I trust that you do too.'

With a knowing drawl, Depp replied: 'I don't feel like I'm wasting *anyone's* time.'

During the three days Depp gave evidence in the second week it was still possible to join the wristband queue well after dawn and get into the main court. By week three it was a different matter. Depp's testimony was box office, and clips of it were being cut and rebroadcast across America. Many Virginians who realized what was happening on their doorsteps decided they would head to Fairfax and take a look for themselves. On Monday 25 April the queue for wristbands stretched the length of the judicial complex colonnade. Hardcore fans and journalists were now outnumbered by day-trippers smiling and waving for my camera in the cold morning sunshine. It's not every day a globally-recognized movie icon comes to town – why not go and breathe some of the same air in your local court for a while?

On Depp's fourth day of evidence he was asked again about Amber Heard's 2018 Washington Post article – the matter on which his legal action in Virginia hinged. He described the op-ed as 'a blinding hurt. It was like somebody hit me in the back of the head with a two by four.' He very carefully linked the article to an indication from Disney that he would not feature in any more *Pirates* movies. Depp told the court he felt 'betrayed by the people... I had worked hard for.'

Online, the Depp meme machine was firing up. A video called *Johnny Depp Being Hilarious in Court!* was posted the day after he finished giving evidence. Hilarious might be pushing it, but the video fished out many of Depp's moments of sarcasm and rebarbative humor, slapped on some (deliberately inaccurate) transcription, added the imagined thoughts of those in shot and ran the Nintendo Mii Channel Plaza Theme underneath it. Every time Amber Heard appeared in frame it was alongside an animated turd, and when the judge said anything to Depp, it was accompanied by a swooning hearts emoji. The video caught a wave – eventually picking up more than 25m views.

The bandwagon was beginning to roll.

PSYCH OUT

Before Amber Heard got her chance to testify we had the trial's first expert witnesses. In Virginia more than a dozen were brought in to 'opine' on various aspects of the case. In the UK there were none. By far and away the most significant expert witnesses in the US were Dr Shannon Curry and Dr Dawn Hughes, both clinical and forensic psychologists. Curry was hired by Depp and Hughes was hired by Heard. Both were instructed to carry out a thorough psychological evaluation of Amber Heard and explain their conclusions.

Heard was forced by the court to undertake these examinations because, as part of her counter-suit, she claimed her experiences with Depp had given her Post-Traumatic Stress Disorder (PTSD). Despite the efforts of Heard's team, Depp was not required to undergo a similar evaluation as he was not claiming Heard's actions had done anything to his mental health, just his reputation.

Dr Curry went first. In order to be accepted by a US court as an expert witness, you first need to have your bona fides paraded in front of the jury. Covering Dr Curry's took ten minutes. She has a bachelor's degree in psychology and social behavior, a master's degree in psychology and a doctoral degree in clinical psychology. She was one of two civilians accepted annually into Tripler Army Medical Center in Hawaii to complete her year-long doctoral internship where she specialised in PTSD. She then completed two years of post-doctoral training at Hawaii State Hospital, a locked forensic psychology facility, dealing with criminals who have severe mental illness. Here, she specialised in working with trauma populations whilst conducting forensic psychological assessments, either for the courts or 'doing assessments for the military to determine whether somebody has sustained a mental disability after combat.' She set up her own 'multi-specialty mental health center', the Curry Psychology Group. Most of her clients are military personnel, veterans and their families. At the time of giving evidence she was a certified forensic evaluator for the state of Hawaii and several courts in Southern California, occasionally contracted by the US Department of Defense 'for evaluations of PTSD from service members.' Although Curry had produced plenty of reports for civil and criminal cases before, this was, she told the court, the first time she had ever testified in a civil case.

And she was dazzling. Poised, relaxed and informed with a level of fluency and surety I don't think I've seen from anyone in a court, before or since. She just... breezed it. Even when her conclusions came under sustained cross-examination, Dr Curry was completely unfazed. She delivered her answers with aplomb, turning to the jury with a smile when explaining any jargon or technical concepts. She simply could not have been better cast.

Curry undertook her evaluation of Amber Heard in late 2021. To do this, she reviewed case documents (including the audio recordings, photographs, witness statements, testimony and declarations). She also looked at Heard's 'prior mental health treatment records', plus the notes of Drs Kipper, Banks, Jacobs, Cowan and Nurse Erin Boerum. Curry also assessed Heard face-to-face over twelve hours on 10 and 17 December 2021.

Before explaining her diagnoses, Curry told the jury what she meant by the terms 'personality' and 'personality disorder'. For her, our personalities 'are the traits, the characteristics, the way we think, we feel, and we act that make us who we are.' These traits 'are pretty stable over time and across situations... overall, if somebody were to describe us or if we were to describe ourselves, we have a pretty good sense of who we are.'

A personality disorder is distinct from other sorts of mental illness: 'When you think about something like depression, that's episodic. It comes and it goes. And when it's treated with medication, it can pretty much be completely mitigated or minimized in a person's life.' A personality disorder was something different; it means 'there's gonna be disturbances in several different areas that are visible in almost all different facets of their lives.'

After considering the evidence and the results of her evaluation, Curry concluded Amber Heard had Borderline Personality Disorder and Histrionic Personality Disorder.

'One of the hallmark characteristics of Histrionic Personality Disorder,' she told jurors, 'is an overly dramatic presentation. We call this impressionistic speech. It tends to be very flowery. It uses a lot of descriptive words like magical, wonderful, and it can go on for quite some time, and yet it really lacks any substance.'

According to Curry, Heard did this quite a bit. 'She would suddenly be one way, and then she would become very animated or very sad. And when people are displaying these emotions with this personality disorder, there's a sense of shallowness to it.'

As for Borderline Personality Disorder: 'It's instability. And it's instability in personal relationships, it's instability in their emotions, it's instability in their behavior, and it's instability in their sense of self and their identity.'

The instability is apparently 'driven by this underlying terror of abandonment... when somebody is afraid of being abandoned by their partner or by anybody else in their environment and they have this disorder, they'll make desperate attempts to prevent that from happening. And those desperate attempts could be physical aggression, it could be threatening, it could be harming themselves.'

Curry explained how playing out that growing fear of abandonment can become a driver. 'The thing these people fear most is being abandoned but, over time, the anger, the explosive anger that they show when somebody is needing space or when somebody is really not doing anything wrong... they'll react in this heightened manner that is just exhausting for their partners. Oftentimes, their partners will try to make them happy at first and really allow themselves to be a punching bag, thinking that they can somehow solve this problem, that somehow, they can make this better. And eventually, it just overwhelms them.'

Curry went into specifics. She administered what is known as the Minnesota Multiphasic Personality Inventory test (MMPI-2) on Heard to see if she had PTSD. On concluding the test, Curry wrote up a 25-page report, which she summarized to the court. Heard, she said, 'had a very sophisticated way of minimizing any personal problems.' She also had scores correlating toward 'externalization of blame' and a 'tendency to be very self-righteous.'

Someone with Heard's scores, said Curry, would essentially claim to be 'very non-judgmental and accepting' whilst actually being 'full of rage, really.'

With bright, smiling, matter-of-factness, Curry kept plunging in the knife. She told the court Heard's MMPI-2 scores were similar to the sort of people who 'tend to be very passive-aggressive. They may be self-indulgent, very self-centered. They could use manipulation tactics to try to get their needs met. They are very needy of attention, acceptance, approval... Initially, they may seem very charming... they can present as very fair and balanced but, in actuality, they really might be very judgmental of others and unaware of problems in their behavior and their thinking.'

The MMPI-2 test assigns scores or 'codes' according to how the questions in the test are answered. Heard came out as a 3-6 code type.

Curry told the court this was typified by 'cruelty – usually [towards] people who are less powerful.' A 3-6 code type is apparently 'very concerned with their image, very attention-seeking, very prone to externalizing blame to a point where it's unclear whether they can even admit to themselves that they do have responsibility in certain areas.'

Depp's attorney wondered about people with BPD and HPD and their capacity for violence.

'They can react violently,' replied Curry, 'they can react aggressively. They will often physically prevent their partner from trying to leave if their partner wants to get space from all of this intense emotion. And oftentimes, they will be abusive to their partners in these situations. Sometimes they'll physically restrain them from leaving and become injured that way.'

Then came Curry's *coup de grâce*. Borderline Personality Disorder, she volunteered, 'seems to be a predictive factor for women who implement violence against their partner. And one of the most common tactics that they'll use is actually physically assaulting, and then getting harmed themselves.'

This, said Curry, was known in her profession as 'administrative violence... essentially... they'll make threats using the legal system. So, they might say that they are going to file a restraining order or claim abuse, or they might do these things to essentially try to keep their partner from leaving.'

As well as administering the MMPI-2 test, Curry used the Clinician Administered PTSD Scale, known as the CAPS-5 assessment, on Amber Heard. Curry described this as the 'gold standard' PTSD test 'accurate for use not just with service members but also with civilians, men, women, all genders, and also all ethnicities.' It was, she said, also shown to be valid 'specifically for use in a courtroom setting.'

Curry explained that the CAPS-5 test was so useful, 'you're actually taking something that would typically be kind of subjective – an interview... and you're making it more objective.' CAPS-5 gives 'a scoring protocol' so the likelihood of PTSD can be effectively scored.

Depp's attorney asked: 'As a result of applying those protocols, what did you conclude?'

'Ms Heard did not have PTSD,' she replied. 'And there were also pretty significant indications that she was grossly exaggerating symptoms of PTSD when asked about them.'

Dr Curry spent the next ten minutes telling the court how and why she was absolutely certain that Heard did not have PTSD, and why she thought Heard was trying to kid the CAPS-5 test.

From the moment Dr Curry began her testimony, the Virginia trial stopped being about the veracity of the documentary or witness evidence behind each of Heard's allegations. Instead we, and the jury, had to ask ourselves if Heard's accusations were the fantasies of a potentially dangerous, high-functioning, mentally unstable liar.

Johnny Depp must have been delighted. He could not have written an assessment more aligned with his own personal opinion of Heard if he tried. In fact, you may remember the audio recording (which was played to the Virginia court on a separate date), in which Depp personally diagnoses Heard with Borderline Personality Disorder[1]. It turns out Dr Depp was right. Ain't that a thing?

Elaine Bredehoft took on the task of cross-examining Dr Curry. Bredehoft noted it was an amazing coincidence that Curry had come up with exactly the same diagnosis as Johnny Depp, Curry's client. Bredehoft also made much of the fact that Curry was retained by Team Depp after a four-hour 'dinner and drinks' session at Depp's house, attended by Depp and members of his legal team. She noted more than once that Curry was not board-certified – a national accreditation awarded after a process of examination and peer-review.

Bredehoft also asked Dr Curry about what was excluded from her expert report. Curry agreed she had, as Bredehoft put it, 'never arrived at the opinion that Ms Heard exhibits patterns of behavior that suggest her allegations of abuse against Mr Depp are false.' She also agreed that she had 'never been asked to testify on whether an individual is being truthful in saying that they are a survivor of IPV [intimate partner violence].'

Curry noted that it was outside the task of a psychologist to determine whether an event occurred. 'We assess behavior,' she said. 'We assess mental status. We don't detect crimes.'

To the lay people in the courtroom, it seemed like every negative description of Amber Heard's behavior described in the witness statements and testimony of her enemies had been medically diagnosed and explained in terms which made sense of what poor Johnny was having to deal with. We knew an alternative expert opinion was coming down the pipe, but I cannot overstate Dr Curry's impact. Her natural authority and charisma made sure her points landed, and her points explained why Heard might be making everything up: *because she was nuts.* It felt like an important piece of Team Depp's jigsaw had fallen into place.

---

[1] See the *Cruel Invective* chapter.

Dr Curry appeared part way through Johnny Depp's thirty-nine eventual witnesses. Her effect was such that when the time came for Amber Heard's witnesses to take the stand, the very first person to be sworn in was Team Heard's clinical and forensic psychologist, Dr Dawn Hughes.

If Dr Curry was all West Coast sunshine, Dr Hughes brought some East Coast grit to the proceedings. Eventually. Firstly, Elaine Bredehoft spent twenty minutes asking Dr Hughes to take the court through her CV. It was impressive. After obtaining her degree in New York, Hughes completed a masters and PhD at Nova Southeastern University in Florida before heading to Yale, where she began to specialise in substance abuse treatment, traumatic stress and interpersonal violence. Hughes had a decade's more experience than Dr Curry and *is* board-certified. She told the court she had treated 'hundreds upon hundreds' of patients, including victims of childhood sexual trauma, heroin addicts and US military veterans. She currently has her own private practice in Manhattan and is president-elect of the trauma division of the American Psychological Association. Hughes was also involved in training New York State Supreme Court justices on issues of intimate partner violence and traumatic stress, including the use of 'female force' in these situations. As Hughes put it, 'if both people are fighting, how do we know that this is intimate partner violence?'

Once Hughes was accepted as an expert witness, Bredehoft spent a further 45 minutes asking about intimate partner violence and domestic abuse in all its forms, including physical violence, sexual violence, coercive control, psychological aggression, emotional abuse and economic abuse. Whilst it made for a fascinating primer, none of it answered the question – was it more likely than not that Johnny Depp had, in Dr Hughes' opinion, physically abused Amber Heard?

We were getting there. After more than an hour listing her achievements, giving us an explanation of what abuse was, and describing the assessments she made of Heard, we got to the crunch. Hughes told those of us still awake that Amber Heard's reports of domestic abuse were 'consistent' with 'genuine' reports of 'physical violence, psychological aggression, sexual violence, coercive control, and surveillance behaviors.' Furthermore, Hughes had diagnosed Heard with PTSD, the cause being 'intimate partner violence by Mr Depp.'

Of the assessments undertaken by Dr Hughes, her results showed 'there was a high degree of serious violence perpetrated by Mr Depp toward Ms Heard' and 'there was violence more on the mild level perpetrated by Ms Heard toward Mr Depp.' Hughes says she administered four tests for PTSD and concluded Heard 'has experienced a moderate degree of post traumatic stress disorder.' When Bredehoft asked if this PTSD might be a result of childhood trauma, Hughes said the 'triggers' for PTSD 'were all specific to Ms Heard's relationship with Mr Depp.'

Hughes came to this conclusion after conducting twelve assessments with Amber Heard over 21 hours of face-to-face sessions in New York plus two lengthy Zoom calls. Hughes also reviewed Heard's deposition, her UK trial testimony and the medical records of Drs Jacobs, Cowan, Anderson and Banks, plus 'nursing notes'. Hughes said she also conducted further interviews with Drs Jacobs and Cowan and Paige Heard, and she, like Dr Curry, reviewed the texts, emails and audio recordings that formed part of the evidence in both trials. 'And I also saw the video in the kitchen,' she added.

Dr Curry felt that Heard was 'grossly exaggerating' the extent of her symptoms almost to the point of feigning them. Bredehoft asked Dr Hughes if this was the case. Hughes replied that it was not, and claimed Dr Curry's interpretation of the test data was 'inaccurate'. Hughes told the court that, in contrast, she had 'really robust data' to show Heard was neither 'malingering or faking her psychological symptomatology.'

Amazing. Amber Heard's forensic psychologist had come up with a conclusion which just so happened to exactly match that of her client! Just like Dr Curry with Johnny Depp.

Hughes' performance in the witness box was not as fluent as Curry's. She kept referring to her notes, and kept being pulled up on it by Depp's attorney, who was concerned Hughes might be reading from them, which is not allowed. Dr Curry's accomplished performance loomed over proceedings to the extent Elaine Bredehoft managed to call Dr Hughes 'Dr Curry' twice, to Hughes' evident annoyance.

I found Hughes' testimony, when laid next to Dr Curry's, difficult to fathom. How could two eminently qualified, experienced clinicians study the same person, using objectively measured scientific techniques, and come up with *diametrically* opposing conclusions? Imagine either Curry or Hughes being appointed by a court to determine everything about *your* future on a single diagnosis. Heads you're a mentally ill liar, tails you're a legit abuse survivor. Most ordinary citizens don't get a second opinion. The authority with which these people wield their expertize would mean their diagnoses are taken seriously, and it's no exaggeration to say their conclusions as to the state of someone's mental health could be badly wrong, yet life-changing, for the person they diagnose.

Is it possible that Hughes or Curry tailored their diagnoses to the wishes of their clients for financial gain, reputational benefit or even ideological reasons? The day Dr Curry gave evidence, Michelle (who you met in the *Cruel Invective* chapter) accosted me in the Red Hot and Blue[2] restaurant parking lot behind the Fairfax County Courthouse. This was before she decided Amber Heard was lying. Michelle told me she thought the whole 'dinner and drinks' thing at Depp's house rendered Dr Curry's evidence 'shady'. I guess if that cross-examination tactic undermined Curry's independence for Michelle, it might work on a jury, but an expert witness's first responsibility is to the court. No credible clinical professional is going to risk their reputation and career by saying something on oath which they can't stand up, or don't personally believe. The conclusion I drew from watching Drs Curry and Hughes in the witness box is that forensic psychology's 'scientific' conclusions should be treated with extreme caution, particularly when expressed anywhere near a courtroom.

---

[2] Not blue in the British sense of saucy or explicit (although it did look from the outside like it could be a strip joint). Red Hot and Blue is named for its Southern BBQ food served with 'blues music in the background & memorabilia on the walls'. The Fairfax branch never seemed to be open when I went round.

MEME-IFICATION

Fairfax, Virginia, May 2022

As the trial progressed, dozens of YouTubers, TikTokers and tweeters started doing serious business. The appetite for pro-Depp analysis and humor was almost limitless, and the content kept on coming.

Whilst the 2022 proceedings in Virginia were still in full swing, Vice magazine published two brilliant and bleak long reads. In a piece called *YouTubers Are Rushing to Get In On the Johnny Depp Trial Coverage*, Anna Merlan noted that previously little-watched gaming and tutorial channels had racked up millions of views and thousands of new subscribers by reversioning trial content. The magic formula required posting footage appended with 'unflattering captions imagining especially stupid or venal thoughts from Heard', multiple times a day.

Merlan found a 15-year old kid making wildly popular videos. He told her: 'Johnny Depp is innocent. Because he's cool.' As for Amber Heard, she was 'a turd... I always thought that. She looks like one.'

In Vice's *The Meme-ification of the Johnny Depp and Amber Heard Trial*, Charlotte Colombo tracked down some of the TikTokers re-purposing TV pictures of the trial into 'hilarious' online snippets. 'I believe the edits or videos are all in good intention,' said one. 'Nobody is here to make light of such a serious topic like domestic abuse... Johnny Depp makes jokes and laughs [in court] so we should be allowed to laugh too!'

A third Vice article revealed that an influential Trump-supporting media site The Daily Wire spent at least $35,000 promoting pro-Depp, anti-Heard content on Facebook and Instagram.

As videos, TikToks and tweets dropped by powerful influencers seemed to be flooding the internet, the suspicion arose that individual content creators and sharers may have had assistance. In trying to prove this *before* the trial Team Heard hired a company called Bot Sentinel[1] to look at online activity around anti-Heard content. Bot Sentinel's first (unpublished) report for Amber Heard's lawyers found a 'significant portion' of online activity against Amber Heard 'wasn't organic'.

A subsequent report produced by Bot Sentinel *after* the trial found that nearly a quarter of anti-Amber Heard accounts were less than

---

[1] Bot Sentinel and its founder, Christopher Bouzy, have come under sustained attack online since working for Amber Heard. Whatever the merits of the organization and/or the individual running it, their findings – with specific regard to non-organic pro-Depp/anti-Heard content – are not, to the best of my knowledge, credibly disputed.

seven months old, and hundreds were involved in what the company called 'platform manipulation' – using hashtag spamming and copy-and-pasted tweets to spread the pro-Depp, anti-Heard message. Bot Sentinel's report also had a look at the trolling activity against Amber Heard. It published examples of post-verdict mean tweets such as: 'the bitch... got what she deserved, cant wait to hear her dying in overdose after her life falls apart' and 'Her parents should be ashamed of the scum whore they produced and created.'

Eve Barlow, as a prominent Heard supporter, was told she was a 'turd licker' (a reference to the Amber Turd meme) and a 'rusty slut' who 'would look good nailed to a cross.' Barlow is a Jewish rights campaigner.

So where did this 'non-organic' traffic and content come from? Was money changing hands to generate or propagate it?

Social media has given anyone with a bit of nous the ability to reach large audiences before anyone can properly scrutinize the quality of the information provided or present it in a way that gives balanced context. Bot Sentinel found demonstrable examples of non-organic pro-Depp content. We don't know who commissioned it. A right-wing website spent thousands of dollars promoting pro-Depp content on social media. We don't know why. The wider question is: are these things poisoning the public discourse, or helping re-balance it?

In 2016, Johnny Depp was accused of serious criminal offenses – repeated domestic violence. Heard was filmed outside a courthouse with a supposed bruise on her face. The accusations went worldwide, yet Depp was never charged with any offense. After their divorce, Heard became a spokesperson for gender-based violence, drawing on what she claimed were her experiences of being in a relationship with Depp. Depp tried to defend himself in the mainstream media, and said all he got for his pains was 'hit-pieces'.

You can say, and I have said, that Amber Heard does not deserve the rivers of online vitriol that made her one of the most hated celebrities in America. Amongst several people I got to know around the trial in the US, this is a minority view. They feel Amber Heard lied about a good man, and feminists, progressives and the mainstream media were all too ready to believe her, despite inconclusive evidence. And for some people, supporting Depp as he succeeded in turning the online tide was part of an important battle in a wider war.

AMBER ON THE STAND

Fairfax, Virginia, 4–16 May 2022

Amber Heard's testimony started well. Asked by Elaine Bredehoft who she was, Heard replied:

'I'm an actor, er... mostly.' The 'mostly' was delivered with an unselfconscious smile. It was the '*mostly*', her activism, which had landed her in court. The unspoken acknowledgment was disarming. Unfortunately this moment of connection and naturalness evaporated within seconds. Heard had decided to answer her attorney's questions by staring straight at the jury.

It was really odd to watch. I'm not sure why, given it was precisely the same technique used to such effect by Dr Shannon Curry when she was explaining her conclusions as an expert witness. Perhaps the difference was the subject matter. Curry was explaining technical concepts in the same way a teacher might address a class. Heard was talking about deeply traumatic personal experiences, opening up her soul. Most Brits I know would have recoiled in horror if a stranger had started on them in this way. I wondered if there was an expectation that American jurors would lap it up, but I doubted it. If I were a juror, I'd want to watch what was going on, not made to feel part of the action, or worse, somehow complicit. I just could not understand why anyone would sign this strategy off. Anyway, it happened.

In her testimony Heard was taken chronologically through her upbringing, early career and initial contact with Depp. She described being blown away by a charismatic movie star who would 'lavish gifts and lavish expressions of love' on her.

It didn't take long before we got to the alleged violence, starting with the tattoo incident. We were told that a few days after it allegedly happened, a bewildered Heard began to get texts and calls from Depp 'apologizing profusely' saying he'd rather 'cut off his hand' than lay it on her. Heard referenced Depp's powerful turn of phrase, saying 'it felt like poetry.' She was seduced into going back. 'We talk and he tells me that he had put this thing away, that I could trust him, that it would never happen again... he said to me, over and over again. "I've put that fucker away, I killed that monster. I'll kill it again, it's done. And I'll never lay a hand on you again." And I wanted to believe him, so I chose to.'

Heard described Depp's drinking, jealousy and violence escalating in equal measure. He accused her of having affairs. He would punch walls and smash things. Bredehoft took Heard through the specifics. It took two full days, separated by the trial's week-long break. The dynamics of Heard's evidence was disorientating. She was being forced to go into extreme and graphic detail about events Depp claimed she was just making up. He had put her on the stand to do this, but only because she had decided to try to carve out a career as a spokesperson for domestic abuse based (largely) on her experience of his alleged violence. What if she was lying? What if she was telling the truth? She certainly seemed to believe what she was saying with every fibre of her being, but then, she's an actor, like Depp.

Heard was emotional on occasion, particularly when it came to describing the violence. This was grist to the mill for the online meme army, who found endlessly artful ways to repurpose Heard's testimony into a vicious form of comedy. Heard's apparent inability to produce tears whilst sobbing became a rallying cry for amateur body language experts, who declared this to be proof her evidence was fake.

Heard wasn't done any favors by her former acting coach, Kristina Sexton, who appeared as a witness the day after Heard finished her evidence. Sexton testified to seeing Depp drunk, abusive, trying to control Heard's career and on one occasion launching himself at her. She also testified to seeing Heard with injuries, but her evidence stuck in the mind for one throwaway comment she made whilst describing the last year Depp and Heard were together. Sexton said most of their coaching sessions would begin with Heard 'sobbing' so much, she would have to build in 'cushion time' around their appointments so she could stop crying, calm down and try to get something accomplished. 'Ironically,' said Sexton, Heard 'has a little difficulty crying, acting-wise.'

You could almost hear the jury's brains putting two and two together. I don't know why Amber Heard didn't produce many tears in the witness box, despite displaying extreme emotion. I don't know what the correct sobbing-to-tears ratio is for witnesses in defamation trials accused of lying about being beaten up.

Amber Heard's cross-examination was handled by Camille Vasquez. Vasquez was ferocious, skilfully deploying choice excerpts from the couple's audio tapes to emphasize the idea that Heard was the abuser in the relationship. Having played some of the recordings and invited the jury to recognize this as the real Amber Heard, Vasquez switched to the apparent lack of hard evidence when it came to documenting the injuries Heard says she sustained at Depp's hands. Vasquez took her back to 22 March 2013, a beating during which Vasquez reminded her she told the court Depp hit her 'in the face so many times that you don't remember.'

'That's correct,' replied Heard.

Heard was shown the picture she took in the mirror after the incident, showing the squash ball sized bruise on her arm.

'There's no injuries to your face in this picture, are there?' said Vasquez.

'Not that this picture shows,' replied Heard.

Vasquez took her to a photo taken in Russia in 2013 around the time Depp was with Heard promoting *The Lone Ranger*.

'You have no visible injuries to your face, do you?' asked Vasquez.

'None that you can see,' replied Heard.

'Even though Mr Depp whacked you in the face so hard that your nose bled?'

'He did.'

'While wearing chunky big rings, right?'

'That's correct.'

Despite the aggressive questioning, in which Heard was repeatedly invited to agree she was an abuser, a liar and, essentially an evil vicious bitch, there was only one flash of anger, which came when Vasquez asserted that Depp had got Heard her role in *Aquaman*.

'Excuse me?!' responded Heard.

'Mr Depp got you that role in *Aquaman*, didn't he?' repeated Vasquez.

'No, Ms Vasquez,' said Heard, regaining her composure. 'I got myself that role by auditioning. That's how that works.'

Vasquez quickly moved on.

On the final day, the chronology of what happened on the night Heard claimed Depp raped her with a bottle was discussed at length. Heard didn't seem quite able to explain whether or not Depp had sliced his finger before he raped her (as she initially suggested), or indeed whether he had picked up the bottle before he held her down by the neck or vice versa. When challenged on the details, Heard was unable to offer anything close to a satisfactory explanation. She told Vasquez: 'I have never claimed that I can remember the exact sequence of these things. This was a multi-day assault that took place over three horrible days... It was the worst thing that ever happened to me.'

Depp's team targeted Heard's evidential weak spots and went after them relentlessly. It was an uncomfortable piece of performance theatre in which Heard was essentially invited to play the role of punchbag. Vasquez landed blow after blow. By the end I didn't feel much wiser. If the violence Heard was describing *did* happen, then we were watching the American legal system and several highly paid lawyers re-abuse and very possibly re-traumatise a victim for the satisfaction of the rich man sitting directly in her eye line. If Heard had invented everything, and then managed to persuade herself that her imagined abusive universe was real, she needed help. There was also the slim possibility that she was coolly lying. If that was the case, then Amber Heard is a very dangerous woman.

PLEDGE V DONATE

Fairfax, Virginia, 17 May 2022

Amber Heard's biggest mistake of the trial had nothing to do with domestic violence, and everything to do with the proposed donation of her $7m divorce settlement to two charities – the American Civil Liberties Union (ACLU) and the Children's Hospital of Los Angeles (CHLA).

In 2016, Heard's attorneys felt she could have secured a far more significant sum from Depp when they split. An email dated 8 August from her divorce lawyer, Samantha Spector, sets this out. Spector told Heard that information received from Depp's financial manager, Ed White, showed her husband had earned $21,000,000 in 'back-end' earnings (typically percentages from box office and occasionally merchandise on top of the initial filming fee) from *Pirates 1* alone. Depp had also earned $33,000,000 on the back-end of *Pirates 4*. *Pirates 5* was made whilst the pair were married. Spector told Heard the film was therefore 'a community property asset and... you are entitled to half of the income from this asset.'

Spector acknowledged that Heard intended to waive this, but warned she was potentially kissing goodbye to 'tens of millions of dollars.' The email asked Heard to sign an agreement stating that she fully understood she was acting against the advice of her own attorneys.

'Candidly,' Spector wrote, 'you are being amazingly true to your word that this is not about the money.'

The settlement agreement signed by Depp and Heard on 15 August 2016 was actually worth more than $7m. Depp made a $500,000 contribution to Heard's legal fees, gave her a black Land Rover and agreed to take on the joint (mainly tax) liabilities[1] incurred by the couple during their marriage. Ed White said these amounted to $13.25m. According to White, Heard's lawyers also demanded she receive her $7m settlement net of tax, which saw Depp handing over a total of $14.25m.

In a statement made three days after the divorce was finalised, Heard announced that the full (net) amount of her divorce settlement – the headline figure of seven million dollars – 'is being donated' to

[1] One of the *non*-tax joint liabilities was an outstanding $160,000 bill from their local off-licence. In the US trial the court was told (by Depp) that Heard had developed a taste for Vega Sicilia red wine, which Ed White said retailed at $500 a bottle!

charity. She added: 'The donation will be divided equally between the ACLU, with a particular focus to stop violence against women, and the Children's Hospital of Los Angeles, where I have worked as a volunteer for the past 10 years.'

Depp immediately smelt a rat. In their Depp v NGN appeal application ruling, the UK judges wrote: 'It is clear that Mr Depp believed from the moment that Ms Heard made her public announcement that she did not intend to give the $7m to charity.'

As soon as Heard made her post-divorce donation announcement Depp instructed Ed White to write two checks, each for $100,000 and send them to the ACLU and the Los Angeles Children's Hospital. Depp's representatives released a statement saying: 'Johnny Depp has sent the first of multiple instalments of those monies to each charity in the name of Amber Heard, which, when completed, will honor the full amount of Ms Heard's pledge. Ms Heard's generosity in giving to these wonderful causes is deeply respected.'

Team Heard cried foul. The pledge was her business, not Depp's. As Ed White had spelled out, though the headline fee for the divorce was $7m, Depp was committed to handing over $14m to cover Heard's tax liabilities and legal fees. Heard's publicists suggested Depp's intercession might be an attempt to avoid his signed undertakings.

'If Johnny wishes to change the settlement agreement,' said Heard's spokeswoman 'we must insist that he honor the full amount by donating $14m to charity... Anything less would be a transparent attempt by Johnny's counsel, to reduce their client's true payment by half under the guise of newfound concern for charities that he has never previously supported.'

The idea that Depp has never previously supported the CHLA doesn't quite square with him being honored by them in 2006. He was given their 'Courage to Care' award for his 'longtime private advocacy of children and children's charities.'[2]

Depp did not rise to the bait. Heard received her $7m, starting with a $1m payment on 1 November 2016. The payments continued throughout 2017 and the final payment of $2.3m was made on schedule on 1 February 2018.

---

[2] In his rebuttal evidence Depp also told the US court he had 'a relationship with the CHLA for probably 20 years or so' through the Make-a-Wish foundation.

Within two weeks of Depp's $100,000 payment, Heard had given the ACLU $350,000. But she waited a while before giving the LA Children's Hospital any money.

Heard's donation to the ACLU was accompanied by an *intimation* (made via Elon Musk) that she would be donating a similar amount every year for the next ten years, by which stage she would have fulfilled her public commitment. This is an unremarkable way to fulfil a large pledge. There are tax efficiencies to be gained by the donor and the recipient can budget for the recurring donation. The ACLU even sent Heard a standard pledge form listing payment schedules for her to fill out and sign. This gives a charity some comfort that a prospective donor is committed to honoring their pledge. Heard never signed it.

What did happen was that in July 2017 a donor fund, possibly controlled by Elon Musk, made a $500,000 donation in Amber Heard's name to the ACLU. In December 2018, just before Amber Heard was revealed as an ACLU ambassador, the ACLU received another $350,000 from a different donor fund in Amber Heard's name. With Depp's $100,000 donation, this amounted to $1.3m worth of donations, either made by Amber Heard or in her name, over the space of two years. As Heard had indicated she intended to make annual payments of $350,000, she was, in effect, ahead of her planned donation schedule. The fact the cash didn't come directly from Amber Heard didn't matter to the ACLU. It was in her name. Heard was fulfilling her pledge.

In January 2018, Heard made her first post-divorce direct donation to the Children's Hospital of Los Angeles – a sum of $250,000.

Between 2016 and the end of 2017 most media reports qualified Heard's donations by stating she had 'pledged to donate' or 'is donating' or 'will be donating' her divorce settlement to charity. By late 2017 some outlets were describing the settlement-to-donation process as being complete. In December 2017, Business Insider magazine reported Heard had 'donated her $7 million settlement to charities with "a particular focus to stop violence against women".' The same month, in a piece criticizing JK Rowling for hiring Depp for *Fantastic Beasts*, Vox magazine wrote that: 'Heard, incidentally, donated her divorce settlement to charity.'

People were starting to make assumptions, and Heard did not dispel them.

In a studio interview on a Dutch TV channel in October 2018, Amber Heard told her host:

'$7m in total was donated to... I mean, I split it between the ACLU and Children's Hospital of Los Angeles.'

After clarifying for his audience what the ACLU is, the host praised her:

'Well, more power to you because that's something that I've never heard of.'

'I wanted nothing,' replied Heard.

From February 2019, Heard had an excuse for not making any more donations to the ACLU or the CHLA. She was being sued by a very rich man and needed cash reserves to pay for her lawyers. Sizeable donations to both charities totalling $1.65m had been chalked against her name. She had neither publicly nor privately *committed* to any schedule of payments. Being sued gave her the perfect opportunity to publicize her donations to date, and explain apologetically that, whilst she still intended to fulfil her pledges, she couldn't make any more payments as she was being hounded through the courts by her former husband.

Instead, as you will remember, in a sworn witness statement to the UK courts made in February 2020, Amber Heard wrote: 'The entire amount of my divorce settlement was donated to charity.'

This statement is patently untrue. But it was never withdrawn. And, as we know, it was referred to in Mr Justice Nicol's finding against Johnny Depp when he said Heard's 'donation of the $7 million to charity is hardly the act one would expect of a gold-digger.'

It is perhaps no wonder that Depp felt the issue should be an important part of his application to appeal the UK judgment. That application failed, but by the time the US trial came round, Depp had what he needed – documents and depositions from the ACLU and the CHLA which proved the sum total of Heard's donations. Heard was on a sticky wicket.

Mystifyingly, Heard and her legal team attempted to play this by trying to suggest the words pledge and donate meant the same thing. They don't. If you have pledged money, you have committed to handing it over. If you have donated money, you have already handed it over. During Heard's cross-examination, she was skewered. Camille Vasquez began by raising the Dutch TV interview:

CV: You said that you had 'donated' your entire divorce settlement to charity, right?

AH: That's correct.

CV: And in fact, your exact words were, '7 million in total was donated to... I split it between the ACLU and the Children's Hospital of

Los Angeles.'

AH: That's correct, I made that statement as soon as I got a divorce and we reached the settlement. That's when I pledged it, right then.

[...]

CV: Sitting here today, Ms Heard, you still haven't donated the $7m divorce settlement to charity, isn't that right?

AH: Incorrect, I pledged the entirety of the $7m to charity and I intend to fulfil those obligations.

CV: Ms Heard, that's not my question. Please, try to answer the question. Sitting here today, you have not donated the $7m... donated, not pledged, *donated* the $7 million divorce settlement to charity?

AH: I use pledge and donation synonymous with one another... They're the same thing.

CV: But I don't. Ms Heard, I don't use it synonymously.

The attempt to equate a donation with a pledge came unstuck as Vasquez drilled down:

CV: You've testified under oath, 'The entirety of your divorce settlement was donated to charity?'

AH: That is correct, I pledge the entirety.

[...]

CV: You testified under oath, 'The entirety of my divorce settlement was donated to charity.' That statement wasn't true.

AH: It is true. I pledged the entirety to charity.

CV: The statement...

AH: When you say you buy a house, you don't pay for the entire house at one time, you pay it over time.

Vasquez went in again.

CV: You didn't donate it, it's a yes or no.

AH: I haven't been able to... I mean, to fulfil those obligations.

CV: So, that's a no right, Ms Heard?

AH: I made the pledge. I want to be very clear, I pledge the entirety. I haven't been able to fulfil those pledges because I've been sued.

Heard had just admitted in court that her claims – made on TV and in a sworn witness statement – to have donated the entirety of her divorce settlement to charity were untrue, as Depp anticipated they would be from day one. The jury took note.

ONE LITTLE LIE

Fairfax, Virginia, 23–27 May 2022

By the final week of the trial the circus really had come to town, even the animals. During a pre-trial deposition which had not been shown to the jury, Johnny Depp stated he would never work for Disney again – not for '$300 million and a million alpacas.' This phrase was repeated in court by Ben Rottenborn.

With an eye for a bit of free publicity, a pair of Virginian alpaca keepers brought along two of their charges to join the growing throng outside court. Dolce and Inti were impeccably groomed and exceptionally telegenic. Their images went global. In the final week, the owners had them dressed in pirate costume. Depp's lawyers were photographed petting them.

The crowds waiting to see Johnny Depp's SUV sweep into court had been growing daily. In week one, the number of fans waiting round the back of court could be counted on the fingers of one hand. By the final week Deputy Sheriffs were having to stop traffic and provide Depp with a motorbike escort as he approached the building, waving to the crowds and blasting music through the open windows of his vehicle. Amber Heard arrived to massed chants of 'Amber Turd! Amber Turd!' Both stars were filmed by a Court TV roving camera operator from the moment they got inside the courthouse gates. Sleepy old Fairfax had gone a little bit La-la Land.

Depp supporters who'd been around since the start of the trial were relating stories of fights in the overnight queue for wristbands and the offers they'd received to sell their precious loops of paper. Some had reportedly changed hands for ridiculous sums, and the Deputy Sheriffs were now physically pulling and checking each band before allowing spectators into court.

The final week's testimony was spectacular. Depp's attorneys produced four surprise rebuttal witnesses. Three of them – Kate Moss, Morgan Tremaine and Morgan Night – we have already met. The fourth was Beverly Leonard, live via video-link from Arizona. Leonard worked at Sea-Tac International Airport in 2009. She witnessed Amber Heard allegedly assaulting her then partner Tasya van Ree. What the jury were not told, by agreement between the attorneys and the judge, was that Beverly Leonard was a cop, and the arresting officer.

Leonard informed the court that in 2009 Heard 'grabbed her traveling companion and pulled something from her neck.' Leonard and a colleague intervened 'to try to break up what appeared to be a fight.' Leonard described Heard as 'aggressive', noting 'she seemed to be not very steady on her feet. Her eyes were blurry and watery, and I could smell alcohol.'

Conversely, van Ree 'was pretty stoic'. Leonard said she sustained an 'abrasion on the side of her neck where the necklace was, like a rope burn from the chain as it was removed.'

Asked why she had come forward, Leonard said she was motivated to do so by an anonymous email. She had been watching the trial and 'waited for a call and wondered why I hadn't been contacted.' Once she took the initiative, Depp's attorneys were super-keen to get her on the stand.

Another final week drama came via the two opposing psych docs, Curry and Hughes. They were recalled to tear strips out of each others' methodology and conclusions. Curry alleged Hughes 'misrepresented the tests and the results that she utilized in her evaluation. She also apparently misrepresented my testing and the results that I obtained in my evaluation. And she provided testimony in a manner that presented essentially her own opinions and the self-report of Ms Heard as facts.'

The gimlet-eyed Hughes was not impressed. On returning to the witness box, she described Dr Curry as 'confused'. Defending her own work on the case, Hughes reminded the court she had examined Heard over 29 hours using twelve different psychological tests, reviewing therapy records and interviews 'and then I made my conclusions based on my clinical education, knowledge, and training to come up with a professional expert opinion.'

'That,' she told the court, 'is what a solid forensic methodological exam looks like.'

In English courts, experts from opposing sides are often required to work together, producing a paper detailing areas on which they agree. This document is often incredibly useful to the court, for obvious reasons. I do wonder what Hughes and Curry would have been able to come up with if they were required to go through a similar exercise for Depp v Heard. Instead, the jury was being asked to follow highly technical arguments about test papers they would never see by two people in vehement disagreement about each others' methodology and conclusions.

The super-double bonus rebuttal witnesses were Depp and Heard themselves, giving the world an opportunity to pore over their testimony once more. Depp gave evidence on the same morning as Dr Curry and Kate Moss. He spoke like a man who felt the wind at his back, summarizing the trial by telling the court:

'No matter what happens, I did get here, and I did tell the truth. And I have spoken up for what I've been carrying on my back reluctantly for six years.'

Depp zeroed in on Heard's 2016 allegations of domestic violence and how it affected the people close to him: 'You've got your family, you've got your kids, you've got your... my mom, thankfully, didn't get to read any of this, because that would kill her. But my father, my family, everyone that I've met, the people that supported me, suddenly I'm scum. And why? Never had to happen. One little lie.'

The way Depp ruminatively said 'One little lie' brought me up. I was taken by how his perspective had changed since Depp v NGN. In 2020 Depp believed he was the victim of a long-term, multi-faceted hoax, prepared, perpetrated and maintained by Heard and her friends over a period of years. The hoax idea was dropped before the 2022 trial, but I couldn't quite see what had replaced it until that final day. Depp's One Little Lie theory seemed to explain Heard's decision to accuse him of domestic violence. Quite simply, the DVRO, the One Little Lie, gave Heard leverage in the divorce negotiations. The resultant negative publicity would encourage Depp to settle quickly. But having publicly claimed to be a victim of domestic violence, Heard was now caught in a trap. When her claims were scrutinized, Heard had to keep digging, turning the One Little Lie on her DVRO into multiple Big Lies, paraded in court on both sides of the Atlantic.

Depp's theory (if that *is* what he was trying to articulate) doesn't quite hold up. Heard was self-reporting abuse to her doctors, parents, sister and friends a long time before the relationship began to collapse. Nonetheless, the idea of One Little Lie felt potent.

Heard was the very last witness on the stand. She said that as a result of going public, she had been 'harassed, humiliated [and] threatened every single day... People want to put my baby in the microwave and they tell me that. Johnny threatened... promised, promised me if I ever left him, he'd made me think of him every single day that I lived.'

Heard said Depp had succeeded in this aim via 'the campaign against me that's echoed every single day on social media and now, in front of cameras in this room. Every single day, I have to relive the trauma. My hands shake, I wake up screaming, I have to live with the trauma and the damage done to me.'

Heard referenced Depp's relaxed demeanor in court: 'I'm not sitting in this courtroom snickering, I'm not sitting in this courtroom laughing, smiling, and making snide jokes. I'm not. This is horrible, this is painful, and this is humiliating for any human being to go through. And perhaps it's easy to forget that, but I'm a human being. And even though Johnny promised that I deserve this and promised he'd do this, I don't deserve this. I want to move on.'

Heard summarized her perspective on the previous six years:

'I receive hundreds of death threats regularly, if not daily,' she said. 'Thousands since this trial has started. People mocking my testimony about being assaulted... It's been agonizing... I hope no one ever has to go through something like this. I just want Johnny to leave me alone... Protecting the secret that I did for as long as I did has taken enough of my voice. Johnny has taken enough of my voice. I have the right to tell my story. I have the right to say what happened to me. I have the right to my voice and my name. He took it long enough. I have a right as an American to talk about what happened to me, to own my story and my truth. I have that right.'

It was a good speech, but there was no feeling of any following wind.

After listening to days and days of evidence and hearing hundreds of thousands of words spoken in testimony we came to the final moments of the trial. The jury had to agree whether three specific sentences – just 62 words in total – taken from the 2018 Washington Post article by Amber Heard were defamatory to Johnny Depp. They were:

– *Amber Heard: I spoke up against sexual violence – and faced our culture's wrath. That has to change.*
– *Then two years ago, I became a public figure representing domestic abuse, and I felt the full force of our culture's wrath for women who speak out.*
– *I had the rare vantage point of seeing, in real time, how institutions protect men accused of abuse.*

If the jury unanimously agreed the statements were made with malice, they could award damages. If the jury unanimously agreed that three statements given by Adam Waldman to the Daily Mail were made under Depp's direction and made with malice, they could award damages to Amber Heard. Waldman's statements were longer, a walloping 139 words. He had told the Daily Mail:

– *Amber Heard and her friends in the media use fake sexual violence allegations as both a sword and shield, depending on their needs. They have selected some of her sexual violence hoax 'facts' as the sword, inflicting them on the public and Mr Depp.*

– Quite simply, this was an ambush, a hoax. They set Mr Depp up by calling the cops, but the first attempt didn't do the trick. The officers came to the penthouses, thoroughly searched and interviewed, and left after seeing no damage to face or property. So, Amber and her friends spilled a little wine and roughed the place up, got their story straight under the direction of a lawyer and publicist, and then placed a second call to 911.

– We have reached the beginning of the end of Ms Heard's abuse hoax against Johnny Depp.

Before they were sent out, the jury heard closing arguments from the parties' attorneys. Camille Vasquez asked the jurors to give Depp 'his life back' and 'hold Ms Heard accountable for her lies.'

'There is an abuser in this courtroom,' she said, theatrically, 'but it is not Mr Depp... The evidence presented at this trial has shown that Ms Heard is in fact the abuser and Mr Depp the abused.'

Vasquez expertly summarized the testimony Depp's witnesses had put into evidence, using the audio tapes to ram home her point. Vasquez also reminded the jury of Heard's failure to cry much, saying: 'You saw it. Ms Heard sobbing without tears while spinning elaborate exaggerated fantastical accounts of abuse. *It was a performance.*'

Ben Chew picked up the baton from Vasquez and reminded the court of one salient fact. 'No woman ever before Amber Heard, ever claimed that Mr Depp raised a hand to her in his 58 years.' Nor, he said, 'has any woman come forward since. This is #MeToo without any #MeToo.'

Ben Rottenborn described Depp's behavior as typical for a domestic abuser:

'If you didn't take pictures, it didn't happen. If you did take pictures, they're fake. If you didn't tell your friends, you're lying. And if you did tell your friends, they're part of the hoax. If you didn't seek medical treatment, you weren't injured. If you did seek medical treatment, you're crazy. If you do everything that you can to help your spouse, the person that you love, rid himself of the crushing drug and alcohol abuse that spins him into an abusive, rage-filled monster, you're a nag. And if you finally decide that enough is enough, you've had enough of the fear, enough of the pain, and you have to leave to save yourself, you're a gold-digger.'

Rottenborn raised the First Amendment as a sticking point in this case, and something which should make it a non-starter. He told the jury:

'You cannot simultaneously protect and uphold the First Amendment and find in favor of Johnny Depp on this claim. You simply cannot.'

Rottenborn showed the jury the cupboard-smashing video and played a tape of Depp calling Heard a 'fucking cunt'. He went to town on the text messages Depp sent, reminding the jury of several, and concluded by widening out the idea of violent abuse to abuse in general, telling the jury: 'It's this simple. If you believe that Depp was abusive to Amber one time ever, in any of the various forms of abuse, not only physical, verbal, emotional, psychological, sexual, any of the ways of abuse, then your job is very easy... We ask, ladies and gentlemen, that you hold Mr Depp accountable for his actions. Stand up for victims of domestic abuse everywhere who suffer in silence. Stand up for the freedom of speech, the freedom to speak about your life that the First Amendment protects. Give Amber Heard her voice back. Give Amber Heard her life back.'

Once the closing arguments were over, the judge revealed the numbers of the two jurors who had been pre-selected as redundant and would not be allowed to deliberate. One of them, a middle-aged woman, smiled at Depp and shrugged. The judge then gave some administrative instructions, ordered all the jurors not to 'consult dictionaries or reference materials, search the internet, visit websites or blogs, or use other tools to obtain information about this case', and sent them out.

Azcarate then turned to Depp, Heard and their attorneys and thanked them for their 'kindness' and 'great demeanor' towards the courthouse staff. She praised the deputies for being 'phenomenal' and called the court reporter, Judy, a 'rock star', which elicited a round of applause.

'Well, that's a first,' said the judge.

As the court rose, the two protagonists hugged their attorneys. Depp shook hands with the court staff and made a special fuss of Judy. As he did so, a number of spectators in the public gallery stood up, and began to shuffle silently towards the front of the spectators' seating area. Some started waving. Unaware of what was happening behind him, Depp started walking towards his exit at the back of court. Before it was too late, someone in the crowd found the courage to yell: 'Johnny!'

Depp turned around, and was visibly taken aback by the sea of faces which had maneuvred their way into position a few feet behind him. He waved and put his hands together. 'We love you Johnny!' said a supporter. 'Good luck, Johnny!' said another. Depp waved again, and made his way out of court.

WHAT THE JUROR SAW

Fairfax, Virginia, 26 May 2022

The main jury room for the entire Fairfax County Court complex was right next to Court 5J on the fifth floor. Jurors and potential jurors for pending cases would wander in and out all day. The Depp v Heard jurors would use the jury room as a relaxation area, occasionally venturing out to the toilets or canteen (where they had a special area to sit). In doing so, they used the same corridor shared by attorneys, spectators and journalists. Because it was right next to a power socket, I would often sit in a corridor seat directly opposite the entrance to the jury room. The number of comings and goings meant the door would often be left open. From my seat it was possible to observe jurors and potential jurors sitting quietly, chatting or scrolling through their phones.

Despite the daily intermingling, everyone observed the rules. We didn't speak to the jurors and the jurors didn't speak to us. We would also tense up and politely lower our voices if a juror walked by so they wouldn't inadvertently hear what we were discussing. Approaching a juror would be A Very Bad Thing, so everyone left them alone. But what the jurors were thinking, or might be up to, was a matter of constant speculation. They were not sequestered, which would involve putting them in a hotel, removing the TVs and restricting access to their phones. At the end of each day, the jurors in Depp v Heard went home to their families and their laptops. They were allowed to keep and use their phones. The judge put them under strict instructions not to look at the news or social media or discuss the case, but the issue of jury contamination was a live one. When one American journalist told me they'd all be reading up about the case online, I was shocked. I mentioned this to a criminal attorney I'd befriended in the courthouse canteen. He looked at me incredulously. 'You think they're not?' he replied.

On the penultimate day of the trial, I was walking back from the canteen along the fifth floor corridor when I was stopped by a young woman called Cali. I'd struck up a friendship with Cali after meeting her in the wristband queue. Cali was a university student in her early twenties, studying international affairs and advocacy. She was being paid to attend court and take notes on the jury by an older student, who was writing a university paper on Depp v Heard.

'Oh hi, Nick,' she said, in her unhurried, southern-tinged accent. 'Could I talk to you for a second?'

She looked concerned.

'Sure,' I replied, and suggested we move back along the corridor, away from Court 5J and potential eavesdroppers.

Cali wanted my advice. A week previously she had been outside court, sitting in the very corridor seat which afforded a direct view into the jury room. The corridor was quiet. A Depp v Heard juror Cali had been observing walked out of the jury room. They were looking at their phone, inadvertently held at an angle which allowed Cali to see the screen. The phone displayed a web page. Part of the large text visible on the phone's screen read 'Amber H'. Cali thought it looked like the juror had a YouTube video up. She told me the juror then took a call. Standing in the corridor, apparently oblivious to Cali's presence, the juror told whoever they were speaking to that the case was 'crazy'. The juror then listened for a few seconds and replied, 'I didn't know people thought that!' As they walked off down the corridor the juror said something indistinct which ended '... both monsters.'

Cali wanted to know what to do. 'I've kinda had sleepless nights about this,' she said. 'I don't know whether to report it or if it's just assumed the jury are following the trial out of court. I keep telling myself to forget about it, but I can't.'

I asked her if she was sure about what she witnessed. 'Yeah,' she replied. 'I took a note straight after it happened so I wouldn't forget the exact words.'

I told Cali referring the incident to someone in authority was the best course of action. If she sat on the information, she might continue to worry. Whilst I didn't know what the implications might be, I warned her it could entail being required to address the judge, possibly in open court. Simply reporting the incident could mean her name might become public knowledge, especially if her intervention led to the dismissal of a juror. Given the worldwide attention now being afforded to the trial, it would be global news.

Cali processed this. She seemed ready to stand by her recollection. I thought Cali's contemporaneous notes would be taken seriously. We both agreed the time available to do anything was running out. The judge would be far less likely to act after the remaining 'redundant' jurors had been dismissed, a process due to happen after closing arguments the following day.

I suggested we both go and speak to a Deputy Sheriff. Deputy Williams had been a friendly presence throughout the trial, and was at that moment on duty outside Court 5J. I approached and politely wondered if I could inform her about a situation. Deputy Williams did not look like she wanted to hear about any situation, but when I gestured to

Cali and said she had witnessed a juror potentially break the rules, the deputy agreed to hear us out. We moved away from court and found a quiet corner.

I introduced Cali properly and told Deputy Williams why she was at court, stressing she was neither a journalist nor a supporter of either party. We explained what Cali had witnessed. Deputy Williams looked less than thrilled. We had just given her a problem, which, if taken seriously by her superiors, could create a mountain of paperwork, some of which would bear her name.

'The jury isn't sequestered,' said the deputy, in a half-hearted attempt to dismiss the matter. 'They're allowed to have their phones.'

I reminded her the judge told the jury on a daily basis they were not allowed to research the case or talk to anyone else about it.

I could see Deputy Williams regretting ever having been friendly towards me.

'Okay, alright,' she said, and addressed Cali. 'You're going to have to write this all down. Stay there.'

The deputy walked off. Cali seemed relieved. I told her she'd done the right thing. Once Deputy Williams had taken Cali's statement, the issue was no longer her responsibility. I suggested Cali make sure she either held on to her original notes or took her own copy.

I caught up with Cali at the end of the day. Deputy Williams had taken her to a senior deputy who told her to write out her details, and surrender her notes. Cali ensured she photographed them beforehand. The deputy later told Cali the judge had been made 'aware' of her concerns.

And that was it.

Taking this at face value – Judge Penney Azcarate had been warned in good time that a juror had potentially been disregarding her daily entreaties (reinforced in stronger, lengthier terms at the end of each week) to ignore anything happening outside court. The juror was, if Cali had accurately understood what she was seeing and hearing, talking to people and reading or watching online material about Amber Heard. Azcarate could, if she wanted to, summon the juror to hear their explanation.

Whatever happened (if anything) behind closed doors, the juror remained in place to deliberate on the verdict. They were not dismissed, nor were they one of the two jurors told at the end of the case their services were no longer required.

There may have been a perfectly innocent explanation for what Cali saw and Cali may be mistaken in her recollection, but it does raise an important question. How can any jury wholly avoid the noise around a trial like this, especially when it is televised? The best we can say is that we do not know if the jury in Depp v Heard were affected by what they encountered outside the courtroom, but given what was happening *everywhere* in the media, the fuss must have been difficult to ignore.

VERDICT DAY

On Wednesday 1 June we assembled in court to be told that the jury in the Depp v Heard case had decided all three of Amber Heard's statements in the Washington Post were defamatory and made with malice. Depp was awarded $10m in compensatory damages and $5m in punitive damages (the latter reduced to $350,000 by a Virginia state cap). Heard failed on two counts, but won on the longer of Waldman's statements, which specifically referred to the phone-throwing incident. That, the jury decided, was defamatory, authorised by Depp and made with malice. Heard was awarded $2m in compensatory damages and nothing in punitive damages.

Despite Heard's single consolation win, this was a comprehensive victory for Johnny Depp. He had successfully persuaded a Virginia jury that he was not an abuser, but a victim of abuse. The graphic and shocking claims made by Amber Heard had been comprehensively disbelieved. In their eyes, she made it all up.

Only Heard was present to witness the verdict. Depp had flown to the UK as soon as the trial finished to guest on Jeff Beck's[1] arena tour. In court, Heard looked down, displaying no emotion as her crushing defeat was confirmed. At one point her head dropped forward, but she quickly composed herself. Once the hearing was over, she vanished.

The only statements made outside court came from Ben Chew and Camille Vasquez, who had been transformed into celebrities by the case. As the attorneys walked out into the sunshine they were cheered by several dozen fans who lined up either side of the courthouse entrance.

Surrounded by the world's media, Vasquez spoke first into the battery of microphones.

'Hi everyone!' she started. 'Today's verdict confirms what we have said from the beginning – that the claims against Johnny Depp are defamatory and unsupported by any evidence. We are grateful, so grateful, to the jury for their careful deliberation, to the judge and the court staff who have devoted an enormous amount of time and resources to this case.'

Chew picked up: 'Our judicial system is predicated on each person's right to have his or her case heard. And we were honored, truly

---

[1] Jeff Beck sadly died in January 2023 after contracting bacterial meningitis.

honored, to assist Mr Depp in ensuring that his case was fairly considered throughout the trial. We are also most pleased that the trial has resonated for so many people and the public who value truth and justice. Now that the jury has reached its conclusive verdict, it's time to turn the page and look to the future. Thank you all so much.'

They did not take questions.

Bekka Fontanilla, a flame-haired Depp supporter I met on the first day of the trial, was there to witness the end. There was an overwhelming sense of relieved vindication washing around the place, but Bekka seemed calm.

'I had no doubts,' she told me, 'but you just never know... maybe I'm in shock a little bit because I've spent two years... two and a half years of my life researching this case... I'm not a follower at all. I make conclusions on my own, based on what I have in front of me, and from the divorce to the UK trial through this... it really made me pay attention to the actual evidence, and not my feelings about someone.'

An attorney I befriended, John Witherspoon, was one of the people who joined the group of silent wavers in court at the end of the trial. He was in a great mood:

'I thought the verdict was a great validation of the jury system,' he said. 'The fact that the jury agreed with what appears to have been the public sentiment was a great reflection on the fact that the jury is made of people from the community. I'm glad that their view was the same as the community... I think it reflects well, quite honestly, on the United States.'

On the evening after the verdict I wandered around the Fairfax County Judicial Complex watching everything wind down. I was due to guest on Court TV's evening broadcast, so I couldn't head back to DC immediately. I wasn't sure I wanted to. I filmed the intro to my final youtube piece and started to write a newsletter whilst perched on one of large grassy square's park benches. It was just a few hours after Chew and Vasquez had given their press statements, but the place was transformed. The crowds had disappeared, the news cameras, fans and deputies had gone. I was pretty much on my own. The courthouse had been my job and my social life for eight weeks. It was my only extended experience of America. Now it was just another building, and I no longer had a place there.

As I sat on the park bench with dusk falling, I could feel those visceral experiences of the trial falling away from my understanding of what I had witnessed. I realized, as it was happening, that everything I knew about the case before the verdict would from now on be filtered through a psychological trap-door. A singular, dominant narrative was descending on this story via the fact of the outcome. I discovered, with some concern, that I couldn't reach back into the unreality any more. Recent psychologically intense memories were turning to dust.

I didn't say any of that on Court TV. I told my host, Vinnie Politan, that the jury's verdict had clearly aligned with public sentiment against Amber Heard, and that I suspected doctoral theses would be written about the case, especially given how sharply it contrasted with the UK judgment. And then I went home.

WALDMAN'S DEFAMATORY STATEMENT

Despite Depp's victory, there was that fly in the ointment. How was it that, after listening to six weeks of evidence, a jury of five men and two women could unanimously reject Amber Heard's multiple and graphic allegations of sexual and physical abuse over a four-year period, dismiss two of her attempts to counter-sue Depp for claiming she was making her allegations up and then unanimously agree that one of the allegations made against her by a Depp proxy was malicious and defamatory?

The two *non*-defamatory statements made by Adam Waldman on behalf of Johnny Depp to the Daily Mail between April and June 2020 were:

'Amber Heard and her friends in the media use fake sexual-violence allegations as both a sword and shield depending on their needs. They have selected some of her sexual-violence hoax "facts" as the sword, inflicting them on the public and Mr Depp.'

And:

'We have reached the beginning of the end of Ms Heard's abuse hoax against Johnny Depp.'

The single defamatory statement was:

'Quite simply this was an ambush, a hoax. They set Mr Depp up by calling the cops, but the first attempt didn't do the trick. The officers came to the penthouses, thoroughly searched and interviewed, and left after seeing no damage to face or property. So Amber and her friends spilled a little wine and roughed the place up, got their stories straight under the direction of a lawyer and publicist, and then placed a second call to 911.'

The common word linking all three of Waldman's statements is 'hoax'. In 2020, Depp told NGN's barrister that hoax was 'probably the best word one could use. Because the allegations, all of the allegations, are patently untrue.'

The three statements by Waldman containing the word 'hoax' weren't chosen for the counter-claim by accident. Heard's alleged hoax would have to be proved by Depp, if the words weren't to be defamatory.

After many hours of legal argument, Judge Azcarate accepted it was feasible that Adam Waldman was acting on Depp's orders and was essentially a spokesperson for him. Heard's legal team invited the jury to entertain this, and Depp's lawyers made no real attempt to persuade them otherwise.

But what about the hoax idea itself? Did that run?

In 2020, Depp's theory was that by using her evil feminine wiles, Amber Heard had plotted to ensnare him in a relationship. Once embroiled, Heard used her power over Depp to enrich herself, improve her social standing and advance her career. To achieve her wicked goal, Heard recruited her acting coach, her makeup artist, her sister Whitney, iO Tillett-Wright, her best friend Raquel Pennington and Pennington's boyfriend, Josh Drew, as co-conspirators. Having inveigled her way into his affections, Heard then did her utmost to provoke Depp into violence whilst secretly filming and recording him. When the relationship had served Heard's purpose, she took her evidence, her co-conspirators' testimony, added a load of unevidenced stuff she had just made up and then cried domestic violence, exiting the relationship and trashing Depp's reputation in the process. This left Heard's way free to become a wildly successful movie star, a darling of the feminist movement and a heroine survivor.

Depp, in 2020, saw it all. Heard had been waiting for a dumb mark, and found one on the set of *The Rum Diary*. She mimicked his interests, and pretended to find him attractive. Depp believed he had met a kindred spirit. He thought an angel had come into his life. In fact, he had been seduced by a pathologically ambitious nut-job who played him like a violin, making her move with the DVRO in 2016. Seven years after they first met, the long con was in.

Civil courts deal in probabilities. Depp's hoax scenario was certainly *possible*. He was also entitled to believe it and put it forward in court, but even in 2020 his own barrister subtly distanced himself from Depp, telling the judge:

'He says it was a hoax... it was insurance... you can understand why Mr Depp... started to piece it together in that way.'

By the time 2022 swung round, the suggestion Depp believed Amber Heard had engaged in a hoax (or at least, anything too elaborate and pre-planned) had been dropped. It was not mentioned by Depp or any of his lawyers. But Adam Waldman's 2020 statements to the Daily Mail were on the record, and now had a $100m lawsuit riding on them. The jury was required to make a decision.

The shortest of Waldman's three statements is the least difficult to understand: 'We have reached the beginning of the end of Ms Heard's abuse hoax against Johnny Depp,' he said.

This, the jury decided, was *not* defamatory, presumably because they thought it was true. This meant on the specific issue of abuse, alleged only by Amber Heard, there *was* a hoax, and a long-running one at that. She *was* making it up.

The other non-defamatory statement is more complicated to unpack. The first sentence was: 'Amber Heard and her friends in the media use fake sexual-violence allegations as both a sword and shield depending on their needs.'

This goes a lot wider than suggesting there was a self-contained conspiracy to destroy Johnny Depp involving Amber Heard and her immediate circle of friends. It channels the language of culture war.

Who are Amber Heard's unnamed friends in the media – journalists? PRs? Activists? Feminists? The ACLU? Some, or all, of these people were (according to Waldman) using 'fake sexual-violence allegations' as both 'a sword and shield depending on their needs.'

After setting up the sword and shield metaphor, Waldman went on to say that Heard 'selected some of her sexual-violence hoax "facts" as the sword, inflicting them on the public and Mr Depp.'

Waldman's second statement is running several ideas in parallel. The first appears to be that there is a conspiracy by feminists and their allies to weaponize fake stories of violent sexual abuse to gain power and influence in the political sphere. The second is that Amber is part of this movement, and she is quite happy using her fake stories of sexual violence to help her and her political friends gain power and influence. The third is that either because they are fake, or because these political ideas are dangerous (or both) they are inflicting general harm on the public and specific harm on Johnny Depp.

Well, okay. Pulling it apart, the political element to Waldman's statement cannot be defamatory. You might think he is wrong to claim that there are people going round in the media weaponizing false abuse allegations to gain political capital. You might think it is *exactly* what is happening, but Waldman's opinion on that matter is squarely protected under the first amendment.

The defamation question therefore turns on the issue of what Waldman calls Heard's 'sexual-violence hoax "facts".' His statement can only be defamatory if the jury believes calling Heard's allegations of sexual violence and domestic abuse 'hoax "facts"' is false. The jury did not find the statement defamatory on that basis, which means they believe Heard's allegations are false. A hoax.

So where does that leave the one statement which the jury did find defamatory? Let's read it again:

'Quite simply this was an ambush, a hoax. They set Mr Depp up by calling the cops, but the first attempt didn't do the trick. The officers came to the penthouses, thoroughly searched and interviewed, and left after seeing no damage to face or property. So Amber and her friends spilled a little wine and roughed the place up, got their stories straight under the direction of a lawyer and publicist, and then placed a second call to 911.'

Although Waldman is casting aspersions about the activities of a group of people, Heard is a member of that group, so she is, by implication, alleged to have either taken part in, or conspired to effect the events he describes. Next, the core allegation is *not* that Amber Heard faked a violent or sexual attack. The core allegation is that she set up an 'ambush', called 911, and when the police decided no crime had taken place, fraudulently caused damage to the ECB apartments. She then enlisted the help of her publicist and lawyer to conspire to produce fraudulent statements, before again placing a fraudulent call to the emergency services.

This is different to a hoax accusation of domestic abuse. It is therefore possible to understand how the jury could find this allegation different from the other two 'hoax' statements and draw a clear distinction between them. On this occasion, with this statement, the jury was not being asked to make a decision about violent abuse. Although domestic violence was central to the alleged incident, it was not directly addressed in this specific statement.

Having decided that with this statement Waldman was referring to a very different 'hoax', the jury were able to separate it from his other two statements. They looked at the evidence and concluded the statement *was* defamatory. The central thesis to his specific allegation – that Heard and her friends took part in a conspiracy to defraud the LAPD and frame Depp – was determined both malicious and false.

THE AFTERMATH

Depp remained in the UK after the verdict. He appeared on stage the following day with Jeff Beck in the north east of England and received a rapturous welcome. On the day of the verdict itself he was pictured in a Gateshead pub with local star Sam Fender. Fender called Beck and Depp 'serious heroes', but within three days had posted an apology on Instagram, saying: 'Using the word "heroes" was meant in reference to their careers, but in the context of the trial was severely misinformed... it was ill judged and I was ignorant with regards to the trials as a whole, and thoughtless on what my post could imply.'

This reference to the 'trials as a whole' was a recognition that, in Britain at least, the US verdict only meant so much.

Heard posted a note on social media saying: 'The disappointment I feel today is beyond words. I'm heartbroken that the mountain of evidence still was not enough to stand up to the disproportionate power, influence, and sway of my ex-husband.'

Heard went on to state that the verdict 'sets back the idea that violence against women is to be taken seriously. I believe Johnny's attorneys succeeded in getting the jury to overlook the key issue of Freedom of Speech and ignore evidence that was so conclusive that we won in the UK.'

Within two days, Heard's lead attorney, Elaine Bredehoft, gave a TV interview bemoaning the fact she hadn't been able to tell the jury about the UK judgment. 'We had an enormous amount of evidence which was suppressed in this case,' said Bredehoft, who felt Depp's legal team had done everything they could to 'demonize' Heard. Bredehoft, like the attorney I spoke to in the Fairfax courthouse canteen, was convinced the jury had been swayed by social media. 'There's no way they couldn't have been influenced by it,' she said. 'It made it a zoo.' The attorney also stated there were 'excellent grounds' for appeal and revealed Heard could not afford to pay the damages awarded to Depp in the trial.

Ben Chew and Camille Vasquez began touring the TV studios. They gave their first interview to Good Morning America, telling their host the key to victory was 'focusing on the facts and the evidence.' Vasquez praised Depp's ability to 'connect with the jury' and Chew described speaking to an 'over the moon' Depp after the verdict. 'It was like the weight of the world had been taken off his shoulders,' he said.

Amber Heard did a big set-piece interview with NBC. She told viewers she would stand by her testimony and accusations against

Johnny Depp to her 'dying day'. Heard was asked if Depp's denial about hitting her was a lie. Heard replied: 'Yes it is.'

In the UK this would be known as repeating a libel, and therefore actionable, but in the US things are different. Having been successfully sued for alluding to a temporary restraining order she took out against Depp, Heard was now apparently allowed to go on television and tell the world that everything she said about Johnny Depp being a violent, jealous, controlling rapist was true. Go figure.

ABC News found and interviewed one of the male jurors who told the network Heard's testimony was 'not realistic.' Heard's tactic of 'staring at the jury' apparently made all of the jurors feel 'very uncomfortable.' The juror said Heard 'would answer one question and she would be crying and two seconds later she would turn ice cold.' The term 'crocodile tears' was apparently used by more than one person in the jury room. Depp was 'more believable' and 'a little more real in terms of how he was responding to questions.' It sounds like a lot turned on who was a better actor, and Depp, as I think most people would agree, is a better actor.

The juror described the pledge/donate fiasco, as, well, a 'fiasco', and he made a point of saying that they weren't influenced by social media:

'We followed the evidence,' he told ABC. 'Myself and at least two other jurors don't use Twitter or Facebook. Others who had it made a point not to talk about it.'

The juror felt that Depp and Heard were 'abusive to each other', which made neither of them 'right or wrong' but 'to rise to the level of what she was claiming, there wasn't enough or any evidence that really supported what she was saying.' The juror added that he believed Depp did *not* hit Heard.

Johnny Depp, meanwhile, was having the time of his life. He spent the rest of the summer touring Europe with Jeff Beck, released a single and album with him, and was mobbed whenever he went out in public. Depp was also pictured in costume as Louis XV, filming a new movie in France. He then announced he would be directing and co-producing (with Al Pacino) his first feature film in 25 years. An image of Depp was beamed into millions of homes from the Glastonbury Festival Pyramid Stage when Paul McCartney screened a few seconds of Depp's appearance in the 2012 video to his song *My Valentine*. One of the biggest living cultural icons was giving Depp a public and powerful message of endorsement. Depp also made a pre-recorded cameo as the Moonperson at the MTV Video Music Awards – his face was projected into the helmet of an astronaut floating in space. 'You know what?' he told the screaming audience, '... I needed the work.'

Heard's attempt to appeal the verdict swung into action with a surprise. Elaine Bredehoft was jettisoned, and a new law firm was brought on board. The notice of appeal argued that Depp's case 'proceeded solely on a defamation by implication theory, abandoning any claims that Ms Heard's statements were actually false.' It also stated the verdict against Heard was incompatible with the partial finding for her. On the issue of malice, which triggered the compensatory damages payments to Depp, the appeal papers claim Depp's team 'presented no evidence that Ms Heard did not believe she was abused.' Instead, they said, the evidence overwhelmingly supported Heard's belief that she was the victim of abuse at the hands of Mr Depp. 'Therefore, Mr Depp did not meet the legal requirements for actual malice.'

Team Heard wanted the verdict set aside, and a re-trial. Depp followed suit, appealing Heard's partial win against him and the $2m damages award.

In the autumn of 2022, Depp and Beck took their arena tour to the US, selling out everywhere they went. Ben Chew was pictured at the Washington DC gig sporting a studded leather jacket and Johnny Depp t-shirt. Three of the Deputy Sheriffs who monitored our activities in Fairfax were also spotted at the same gig. Amber Heard, by contrast, temporarily withdrew from public life. She sold her home in Yucca Valley, California, deleted her Twitter account and flew to Europe. She was pictured in Majorca, where she is said to be renting a luxury property in the village of Costitx.

Depp's victory, on the face of it, was total, and Heard's humiliation complete, but the single counter-claim win gave her legal leverage. It would have been a tough battle to get the Virginia verdict set aside (let alone the whole case re-tried), but Heard had a shot. Whether she had the funds to pursue it is another matter. Perhaps inevitably, a compromise was reached. On 19 December 2022 Heard announced she was dropping her appeal. Shortly afterwards Depp confirmed he was dropping his counter-appeal, agreeing as part of the settlement to reduce the sum he was owed by Heard from $8.35m to $1m.

Chew and Vasquez released a statement saying: 'We are pleased to formally close the door on this painful chapter for Mr Depp, who made clear throughout this process that his priority was about bringing the truth to light. The jury's unanimous decision and the resulting judgement in Mr Depp's favor against Ms Heard remain fully in place.'

With a knowing wink, the attorneys added: 'The payment of $1m – which Mr Depp is pledging and will donate to charities – reinforces Ms Heard's acknowledgement of the conclusion of the legal system's rigorous pursuit for justice.' Cute.

Heard's statement to mark the end of legal hostilities took the form of a long Instagram post in which she said she had 'lost faith' in the American legal system where her 'unprotected' testimony 'served as entertainment and social media fodder.'

She was not alone in holding this view. More than a hundred leading feminists and women's groups (including Gloria Steinem, the National Organization for Women and Military Rape Crisis Center) signed an open letter to 'condemn the public shaming of Amber Heard and join in support of her.' The letter suggested that the Virginia verdict indicated 'a fundamental misunderstanding of intimate partner and sexual violence and how survivors respond to it.' The signatories decried the 'harassment' suffered by Heard, which they say was 'fuelled by disinformation, misogyny, biphobia, and a monetized social media environment where a woman's allegations of domestic violence and sexual assault were mocked for entertainment.'

Whitney called the letter 'a much needed breath of fresh air' and felt moved to suggest that 'finally, the tides are shifting.'

I'm not so sure. Prominent women are starting to endorse Depp. Rihanna made a point of inserting him into a video for her Savage X Fenty fashion line and Helena Bonham-Carter made worldwide headlines in November 2022 when she told The Times newspaper her old friend had been 'completely vindicated', and was now in the clear.

With the MTV and Rihanna shows, the Glastonbury appearance, the French movie and the Al Pacino collaboration, Depp has begun working his way back into mainstream public acceptance. A starring role in *Pirates* 6 (indeed, any kind of on-screen involvement in the next *Pirates* instalment) would crown his return. Jerry Bruckheimer, who produces the franchise, told journalists at the 2023 Oscars there is a *Pirates* 6 screenplay in development and he would 'love' to see Depp return. Disney will have the last word on that.

Despite the WaPo op-ed disaster, Amber Heard has hinted she might continue telling 'her' truth in public once more. Heard's statement dropping the appeal included the line: 'I have made no admission. This is not an act of concession. There are no restrictions or gags with respect to my voice moving forward.'

Quite what she can say without getting sued again is unclear. Unless she decides to campaign in the UK.

Heard's prospects as an actor hinge to some degree on whether or not *Aquaman 2* will be re-edited or re-shot to erase or replace her. *Aquaman* made more than a billion dollars at the box office and she was the female lead. If Heard stays in the sequel it will be a de facto endorsement, and a sign that some execs at Warner Bros are willing to bet their careers on the adage that all publicity is good publicity. If Warners drop Heard, there may be unintended consequences, but it is a far less risky option. Emilia Clarke's name was in the frame to re-shoot Heard's part as Mera, but that no longer seems to be on the cards.

However Depp and Heard try to pursue their careers, they will carry the baggage of their relationship and legal battles to their graves. Their psychodrama got caught up in the culture war, and the (checks Twitter) endless ongoing bunfight between antagonistic factions who will continue to target, abuse and harangue each other until the earth crashes into the sun.

The arc of Johnny Depp and Amber Heard's relationship wasn't just a toxic self-indulgent mess; it was about money, power, memory, allegiance, culture, society, taboo, identity, hero-worship, celebrity, violence, control, jealousy, anger and love. The multiple strands to this narrative have been atomized and reassembled in a way that rips our perceptions and preconceptions of truth and reality apart. It's not entertainment. I've tried to keep foremost in my mind that at the center of this story are two human beings, and I hope, one day, they both find peace.

WHO'S WHO

Ackert, Julian	Forensic expert for Amber Heard in Depp v Heard.
Allison, Lori Anne	Johnny Depp's first wife.
Anderson, Dr Laurel	Clinical psychologist who testified in the US trial. Provided counselling to Johnny Depp and Amber Heard.
Ashford, Ben	British journalist. Reporter at the Daily Mail.
Azcarate, Judge Penney	Chief Judge, Circuit Court, Fairfax County.
Barlow, Eve	Supporter of Amber Heard. Banned from court during Depp v Heard.
Baruch, Isaac	Friend of Johnny Depp. Witness in both trials.
Beck, Jeff	Guitarist and friend of Johnny Depp (died January 2023).
Bett, Sean	Member of Johnny Depp's security team. Witness in both trials.
Bettany, Paul	Actor and friend of Johnny Depp.
Bloom, Jake	Johnny Depp's former lawyer – sued by Depp in 2017.
Bockov, Laura	Online influencer and supporter of Johnny Depp.
Boerum, Nurse Erin	Addiction and mental health nurse. Witness in Depp v Heard. Married name Erin Falati.
Bonham-Carter, Helena	Actor. Friend of Johnny Depp.
Bredehoft, Elaine	Amber Heard's lead attorney in Depp v Heard.
Bruckheimer, Jerry	Producer of *Pirates* franchise.
Bush, Kate	UK pop superstar.
Cage, Nicolas	Actor and friend of Johnny Depp. Dated Lori Anne Allison after her split with Depp.
Caldecott, Andrew	Barrister who led Johnny Depp's application to appeal judgment in Depp v NGN.
Cali	University student who reported a juror during Depp v Heard.
Callaghan, Bernadette	Magistrate in Southport, Queensland.
Carino, Christian	Johnny Depp and Amber Heard's former agent. Witness in Depp v Heard.
Chew, Ben	Johnny Depp's lead attorney in Depp v Heard.
Connolly, Malcolm	Member of Johnny Depp's security team. Witness in both trials.
Cowan, Dr Connell	Psychologist Dr David Kipper assigned to Amber Heard.
Curry, Dr Shannon	Clinical and forensic psychologist. Johnny Depp's expert witness in Depp v Heard.

de Cadenet, Amanda	Former confidant of Amber Heard.
Dembrowski, Christi	Johnny Depp's older sister. Witness in Depp v Heard.
Depp, Jack	Son of Johnny Depp and Vanessa Paradis.
Depp, John Christopher	Johnny Depp's father.
Depp, Johnny	Actor, producer, director and musician. Full name John Christopher Depp II.
Depp, Lily-Rose	Daughter of Johnny Depp and Vanessa Paradis.
Deuters, Gina	Content creator and visual effects coordinator on some of Johnny Depp's movies. Dismissed as a witness in Depp v Heard. Married to Stephen Deuters.
Deuters, Stephen	One of Johnny Depp's assistants. Witness in Depp v NGN. Married to Gina Deuters.
Diener, Officer Christopher	LAPD police officer who visited the ECB penthouses with Officer William Gatlin on the evening of 21 May 2016 after the visit by Officers Saenz and Hadden.
Divenere, Laura	Interior designer who worked for Amber Heard, Johnny Depp and Elon Musk. Witness in Depp v NGN.
Doohan, Mick	Australian motorcycle racer. Five time 500cc Grand Prix world champion. Former owner of the Diamond Head compound on Australia's Gold Coast.
Dougherty, Terence	Chief Operating Officer, ACLU. Witness in Depp v Heard.
Drew, Josh	Former chef. Lived at the ECB with Raquel Pennington. Witness in both trials.
Fender, Sam	English musician.
Franco, James	Actor who played alongside Amber Heard in *The Adderall Diaries* and *Pineapple Express*.
Gatlin, William	LAPD police officer who visited the ECB penthouses with Officer Christopher Diener on the evening of 21 May 2016 after the visit by Officers Saenz and Hadden. Witness in Depp v Heard.
George, Eric	Lawyer. Cleared the text of the Washington Post op-ed. Witness in Depp v Heard.
Gottlieb, Jodi	Amber Heard's publicist.
Hadden, Officer Tyler	LAPD police officer who visited the ECB penthouses with Officer Melissa Saenz on the evening of 21 May 2016. Witness in Depp v Heard.
Hathaway, Rochelle	Woman with whom Amber Heard accused Johnny Depp of having an affair.
Heard, Amber Laura	Actor and activist.
Heard, David	Amber and Whitney Heard's father.

Heard, Paige	Amber and Whitney Heard's mother (deceased).
Heard, Whitney	Amber Heard's sister. Married name Whitney Henriquez. Witness in both trials.
Hennessy, Joan	Reporter at the US trial.
Holmes, Nathan	One of Johnny Depp's assistants.
Howell, Jennifer	Founder of The Art of Elysium charity. Witness in Depp v Heard.
Hughes, Dr Dawn	Clinical and forensic psychologist. Amber Heard's expert witness in Depp v Heard. Diagnosed Heard with PTSD.
Inglessis, Melanie	Amber Heard's makeup artist and friend. Witness in both trials.
James, Kate	Amber Heard's former personal assistant. Witness in both trials.
Jenkins, Starling	Member of Johnny Depp's security team. Witness in both trials.
Johnson, Gerry	Staff member in the ACLU's comms department.
Joyce, Barnaby	Australia's former Minister of Agriculture and Deputy Prime Minister.
Judge, Jerry	Johnny Depp's head of security (deceased).
Kelly, Megyn	News anchor on SiriusXM.
Kelly Sue	Friend of Amber Heard.
King, Ben	House manager. Worked for Johnny Depp in UK and Australia. Witness in both trials.
Kipper, Dr David	Johnny Depp's addiction doctor. Witness in Depp v Heard.
Laws, Eleanor	One of Johnny Depp's barristers in Depp v NGN.
Leonard, Beverly	Arrested Amber Heard in 2009 at Sea-Tac International Airport. Witness in Depp v Heard.
Levy, Angenette	Reporter, Law and Crime TV network.
Lloyd, Nurse Debbie	Addiction and mental health nurse. Witness in Depp v Heard.
Mandel, Joel	Depp's former business partner.
Marz, Elizabeth	Raquel Pennington's childhood friend. Witness in Depp v Heard.
McGivern, Travis	Member of Johnny Depp's security team. Witness in both trials.
McMillan, Savannah	Amber Heard's friend and sometime assistant.
McMillen, Samantha	Johnny Depp and Amber Heard's stylist.
Meyers, Jessica	One of Johnny Depp's attorneys in Depp v Heard.
Moss, Kate	Supermodel. Former partner of Johnny Depp.

Mulrooney, Michele	Domestic relations attorney hired by Amber Heard.
Murphy, Kevin	Johnny Depp's house manager.
Musk, Elon	Billionaire business magnate. Dated Amber Heard.
Neumeister, Norbert Bryan	Forensic expert for Johnny Depp in Depp v Heard.
Nicol, Mr Justice	UK trial judge.
Night, Morgan	Trailer park resort owner. Witness in Depp v Heard.
Palmer, Robert	Mr Justice Nicol's son.
Paradis, Vanessa	Singer, model and former partner of Johnny Depp. Mother of Lily-Rose and Jack Depp.
Pennington, Raquel 'Rocky'	Former friend of Amber Heard.
Politan, Vinnie	Court TV anchor.
Richards, Keith	A Rolling Stone.
Roberts, Tara	Johnny Depp's island manager in the Bahamas.
Robinson, Bruce	Writer and director of *The Rum Diary* movie.
Robinson, Jennifer	Amber Heard's former lawyer.
Romero, Anthony	Executive Director, ACLU.
Rottenborn, Ben	One of Amber Heard's attorneys in Depp v Heard.
Rowling, JK	Harry Potter creator. Cast Johnny Depp in *Fantastic Beasts*.
Ryder, Winona	Former partner of Johnny Depp.
Saenz, Officer Melissa	LAPD police officer who visited the ECB penthouses with Officer Tyler Hadden on the evening of 21 May 2016. Witness in both trials.
Sexton, Kristina	Amber Heard's former acting coach.
Shapiro, Lauren	iO Tillett-Wright's friend.
Sherborne, David	Johnny Depp's lead barrister in Depp v NGN.
Shulman, Robin	ACLU staffer.
Spector, Samantha	Amber Heard's divorce attorney.
Stanhope, Doug	Comedian and friend of Johnny Depp.
Steinem, Gloria	Feminist.
Sullivan, Stacy	ACLU staffer.
Thompson, Hunter S	Deceased gonzo journalist. Friend of Johnny Depp.
Tillett-Wright, iO	Amber Heard and Johnny Depp's former friend.
Tobin, Sam	Journalist at PA Media.
Tremaine, Morgan	Former TMZ staffer.
Underhill, Lord Justice	One of the judges who dismissed Johnny Depp's application to appeal Depp v NGN.

van Ree, Tasya	Former partner of Amber Heard.
Vargas, Hilda	Johnny Depp's housekeeper. Found The Grumpy.
Vasquez, Camille	One of Johnny Depp's attorneys in Depp v Heard.
Waldman, Adam	Johnny Depp's lawyer. Witness in Depp v Heard.
Wass, Sasha	NGN barrister in Depp v NGN.
Wasser, Laura	Johnny Depp's divorce attorney.
Weitz, Jessica	Director of Artist Engagement, ACLU.
Wells, Betty Sue	Johnny Depp's mother (deceased).
White, Judge Bruce	Former Chief Judge, Circuit Court, Fairfax County.
White, Ed	Johnny Depp's financial manager.
Witkin, Bruce	Lori Anne Allison's brother-in-law and former friend of Johnny Depp.
Wolanski, Adam	One of NGN's barristers in Depp v NGN.
Wootton, Dan	Former executive editor of The Sun. Sued by Johnny Depp for libel.
Wyatt, Keenan	Sound tech and friend of Johnny Depp.

TIMELINE

1963	9 June	Johnny Depp is born.
1983	December	Depp marries Lori Anne Allison.
1984	November	*A Nightmare on Elm Street* is released.
1985		Depp and Allison divorce.
1986	22 April	Amber Heard is born.
1989	June	Depp meets Winona Ryder; they start a relationship and become engaged.
1990	December	*Edward Scissorhands* is released.
1993	May	Depp's relationship with Winona Ryder ends.
1994	February	Depp and Kate Moss begin dating.
1998		Moss and Depp split up.
1998	June	Depp meets Vanessa Paradis. They start a relationship.
1999	27 May	Lily-Rose Depp is born.
2002	9 April	Jack Depp is born.
2003	July	First *Pirates of the Caribbean* movie is released.
2008	March	Amber Heard enters 'domestic partnership' with Tasya van Ree.
Late 2008/ Early 2009		Johnny Depp and Amber Heard meet.
	March	Depp and Heard begin filming *The Rum Diary*.
2009	14 September	Amber Heard is arrested after allegedly assaulting Tasya van Ree at an airport. Charges are dropped.
2011	October	Depp and Heard hook up on *The Rum Diary* press tour.
2012	June	Heard's split from van Ree reported.
	June	Depp and Paradis announce their separation.
2013	March	Disco Bloodbath.
	June	Hicksville.
2014	May	The Plane Kick.
2015	3 February	Depp and Heard marry.
	March	Heard flies out to join Depp in Australia. Depp loses part of his finger. Heard says she was raped.
	23 March	The Closed Fist Punch at the ECB.
	21 April	Depp and Heard fly back to Australia with their dogs Pistol and Boo.
	15 December	The Headbutt.

2016	18 April	Depp and Heard appear on video apologizing for illegally bringing Pistol and Boo into Australia.
	21 April	Amber Heard's 30th birthday party.
	22 April	The Grumpy.
	20 May	Johnny Depp's mother, Betty Sue, dies.
	21 May	The Phone Incident.
	23 May	Amber Heard files for divorce.
	27 May	Heard successfully applies for a Domestic Violence Restraining Order.
	8 August	Cupboard-smashing video published by TMZ.
	15 August	Depp and Heard settle their divorce.
2018	27 April	The Sun newspaper publishes the article: *How can JK Rowling be 'genuinely happy casting Johnny Depp in the new Fantastic Beasts film after assault claim?'* Depp sues the author of the piece and The Sun's owners, NGN.
	18 December	The Washington Post publishes the opinion piece (op-ed) by Amber Heard: *Amber Heard: I spoke up against sexual violence – and faced our culture's wrath. That has to change.* Depp sues Amber Heard.
2020	July	The Depp v NGN libel trial takes place at the High Court in London.
2020	10 August	Amber Heard counter-sues Johnny Depp over three statements made by Adam Waldman, which assert that Heard's claims are a hoax.
	2 November	Depp v NGN judgment handed down. Depp loses.
2021	25 March	Court of Appeal declines to allow Depp to appeal Depp v NGN.
2022	April/May	The Depp v Heard defamation trial takes place in Fairfax, Va.
	June	Jury find for Johnny Depp on all three counts of his claim awarding him more than $10m in damages. Jury find for Amber Heard on one count of her counter-claim awarding her $2m. Both parties appeal the verdicts.
	19 December	Depp and Heard drop their appeal claims. Heard agrees to pay Depp $1m to settle the case.

SPEECH AND SPELLING

Speech is messy. It is rarely 100% fluent or coherent. What people say verbatim does not often read at all well on the page. To give you a comfortable reading experience, I have excised repeated words from many passages of direct speech, and I have removed many (but not all) filler words including 'so', 'like', 'kind of', 'you know' from verbatim transcripts. Where I have shortened verbatim speech to remove phrases, half-completed thoughts or digressions irrelevant to the main point of the sentence being spoken, I have either used ellipses or broken up the text, separating (or connecting) the words spoken with my own narration. On rare occasions I have inserted a word or two [in square brackets] where I think it might aid clarity.

I have been careful to ensure that in 'tidying-up' some of the idiosyncrasies of verbatim speech, I have only reduced the clutter around pertinent quotes and only done so in a way that does not change the general or specific meaning of what was being said. You can check this against the daily transcripts of both court cases and other source documents published on my website reportingdeppvheard.net.

When it comes to audio or video recordings, transcribers listening to them being played in court can get words or phrases wrong, particularly if the audio is quiet or captured in poor quality. Where I have transcribed audio or video for the purposes of this book, I have not relied on official or unofficial transcriptions, but done them myself by listening repeatedly until I am sure I have faithfully transcribed the exact words. If a word or section of speech is inaudible to my ears, I mark it in square brackets as [inaudible] or [indistinct].

When quoting *written* sources (e.g. text messages, emails, witness statements) I have tried to render short sentences as closely as possible to the way they were originally presented, with their original grammar, spelling, punctuation and capitalisation. With longer texts and emails it has sometimes been necessary to re-punctuate them to improve clarity. Again, *very* occasionally, I have added a word or two to a quote to clarify a meaning, but these words are made obvious by placing them in [square brackets]. In all cases I have kept the meaning being expressed.

After a lot of discussion with my publisher we have decided to Anglicise most American spellings for the UK/Australian version of this book and Americanise most English spellings for the US version. This, again, is purely to aid readability.

Every possible care has been taken to ensure the factual accuracy of this text. All errors are my responsibility.

SOURCES

The main sources for this book are the volumes of formal documents generated by Depp v NGN and Depp v Heard and various other legal filings, notably the DVRO claim and the divorce proceedings. In the UK trial I received the transcripts from both parties after my application to the court. Many documents from the trial bundle were supplied on request. These either came from the parties' representatives or via PA Media, the independent wires service, who distributed them to journalists.

Transcripts were not supplied by the parties in Depp v Heard. Thanks to a timely donation to my crowdfunding pot, I was able to have the YouTube recordings (on Court TV, the Law and Crime TV network and E! News) of the trial professionally transcribed. They are unofficial transcripts and therefore not a formal record of what was said, but they helped me locate important testimony, which I could then check against the YouTube recordings.

Documentary evidence arising from Depp v Heard came via a number of routes – the parties supplied journalists with some information during the trial, and a lot of information was posted to the Fairfax District Court website (have a look for Depp v Heard in their High Profile Cases section). It was also possible to see (and screenshot) documentary evidence shown to the court during the trial broadcasts. Material relating to all the legal cases involving Johnny Depp and Amber Heard has been published by a number of official and unofficial sources. Any documents I have retrieved from unofficial sources have either been cross-referenced with other sources and verified or I have indicated the source and its reliability.

I have posted a lot of source documentation used in this book on the website reportingdeppvheard.net. It is not a complete archive, but it should be a good starting point for anyone wanting to do further research. There are many more public archives on Depp and Heard online, some more reliable than others. All of the academic articles, journalism and judgments cited are also available online.

Finally, I drew inspiration from, was diverted by and/or pulled information out of several longer texts over the course of the last twelve months. Some are directly relevant, some are tangential. They are:

The Rum Diary – Hunter S Thompson
The KLF: chaos, magic and the band who burned a million pounds – John Higgs

Johnny Depp: A modern rebel – Brian J Robb

Rape: from Lucrezia to #MeToo – Mithu M Sanyal

Anatomy of a Moment – Javier Cercas

A Companion to Chivalry – edited by Robert W Jones and Peter Coss

The Coming Storm (podcast) – written and presented by Gabriel Gatehouse for BBC Sounds

Smoke 'Em If You Got 'Em (podcast) – Sarah Hepola and Nancy Rommelman

The Respondent – Greg Ellis

Feminism for Women: the real route to liberation – Julie Bindel

The Red Pill (documentary film) – Cassie Jaye

Flow My Tears, the Policeman Said – Philip K Dick

For Honour and Fame: Chivalry in England 1066–1500 – Nigel Saul

DOMESTIC ABUSE HELPLINES

If you live in the US and you are experiencing domestic abuse, you can reach out to the National Domestic Violence Helpline (https://www.thehotline.org), which operates a confidential 24/7 helpline and text service.

Text the NDVH at: 88788

Call the NDVH on:

1-800-799-SAFE(7233) or

TTY 1-800-787-3224 or

(206) 518-9361 (Video Phone Only for Deaf Callers)

The NDVH service is provided without regard to race, color, national origin, religion, gender, age, or disability (including deaf and hard of hearing). Assistance is available in English and Spanish with access to more than 170 languages through telephonic interpreter services.

Remember it is difficult to erase all trace of internet usage. Be careful about where and how you access websites.

ACKNOWLEDGMENTS

Profound thanks to everyone who kindly crowdfunded my reporting of this story. Without your contributions, I would not have been able to cover either trial in the way that I did. Thank you.

An army of people helped me get this book over the line. Some are close to the events described and cannot be named. They have my particular gratitude. Others provided more visible assistance. Thanks to David, Helen and Hannah for their editing and publishing brilliance, Clare and David for the legals, Mark for the stunning cover, Tom for the ECB floorplan, Stephen for the proofing, Katie, Claire and Julia for their work on publicity and Andrew's wizarding skills with the Reporting Depp v Heard website.

Folded hands emojis to the early readers – Alex, Ellie, Gwen, Krissie, Max, Natasha, Sarah, Simon, Monica and Tom – whose comments and suggestions made this book immeasurably better. Stuart, your support of this and my wider work has been something special, I am grateful.

Thanks to all at Channel 5 News – especially Cait, Jess and Emma. Without you, this book would not have happened. Wes and Val, I am forever in your debt. Thanks also to everyone in Fairfax and DC who welcomed me and treated me so well – Depp supporters, Heard supporters, neutral spectators, journalists, TV crews, local attorneys, Deputy Sheriffs and court staff. We'll always have Virginia in the spring. Special regards to Natasha, my breakfast buddy, who kept me sane and made me laugh.

I write mainly at home, which creates its own stresses. My thanks to Nic, Amy, Abi and James for putting up with me. I love you all very much.

Finally, a heartfelt thank you to Bekka, Ed, Lina and Lessa. Your generosity, hospitality and basic human kindness is something I will never forget. Your friendship means the world.

INDEX

ABOUT THE AUTHOR

Nick was trained up by the BBC and has worked as a broadcast journalist for most of his career. He has won national and international awards for his work on the Post Office Horizon IT scandal, which saw more than 600 people wrongly given criminal convictions due to faulty IT evidence. This became the subject of his first book – *The Great Post Office Scandal: The fight to expose a multimillion pound IT disaster which put innocent people in jail*. Nick's interest in Johnny Depp's legal travails began when he was sent to cover the first day of Depp v NGN at the High Court in London during in 2020. He has followed the story ever since. This is his second book.

The Great Post Office Scandal: the fight to expose a multimillion pound IT disaster which put innocent people in jail is Nick Wallis' first book for Bath Publishing. It describes the most widespread miscarriage of justice in UK legal history, perpetrated by a government-owned agency. Weaving personal stories and Nick's own reportage into a compelling factual thriller, *The Great Post Office Scandal* is the story of how innocent people had their lives ruined by a once-loved national institution and how, against overwhelming odds, they fought back to clear their names.

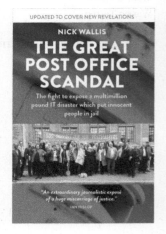

Ingram Content Group UK Ltd.
Milton Keynes UK
UKHW040324250523
422306UK00001B/1